New Directions in Islam

Series Editors
Joshua M. Roose
Faculty of Arts and Education
Deakin University
Melbourne, VIC, Australia

Bryan S. Turner
Australian Catholic University and The Graduate Centre
City University of New York
New York, NY, USA

The *New Directions in Islam* series will promote creative ways of conceptualizing the practice of Islam in new, challenging contexts and present innovative and provocative interdisciplinary studies examining intellectual, political, legal, economic, and demographic trajectories within Islam. Although recognised as the world's fastest growing religion, many Muslims now live in secular societies where Islam is a minority religion and where there is considerable social conflict between Muslim communities and the wider society. Therefore it is vital to engage with the multitude of ways by which Muslims are adapting and evolving as social and cultural minorities.

How are they developing their faith in line with local and national customs? How are converts and subsequent generations adapting in these challenging contexts? These series moves beyond dichotomies about radicalism, citizenship, and loyalty evident in the proliferation of descriptive and repetitive studies of Islamophobia and Orientalism, which have become both negative and predictable. Rather, contrary to the perception of Muslims as victims of secular modernity, we are interested in 'success stories' of Muslims adapting in and contributing to society at local, national and even transnational levels, such as the case of Muslim middle classes in Canada, the United States, South Africa, and Argentina.

These series will go beyond the geographic boundaries of the Middle East to examine Islam from a global perspective in vastly different contexts from Brazil to Vietnam and Austria to Papua New Guinea.

Rano Turaeva • Michael Brose
Editors

Religious Economies in Secular Context

Halal Markets, Practices and Landscapes

palgrave
macmillan

Editors
Rano Turaeva
Ludwig Maximilian University of Munich
Munich, Germany

Michael Brose
East Asian Studies Center
Indiana University
Bloomington, IN, USA

New Directions in Islam
ISBN 978-3-031-18602-8   ISBN 978-3-031-18603-5 (eBook)
https://doi.org/10.1007/978-3-031-18603-5

© The Editor(s) (if applicable) and The Author(s), under exclusive licence to Springer Nature Switzerland AG 2023

This work is subject to copyright. All rights are solely and exclusively licensed by the Publisher, whether the whole or part of the material is concerned, specifically the rights of translation, reprinting, reuse of illustrations, recitation, broadcasting, reproduction on microfilms or in any other physical way, and transmission or information storage and retrieval, electronic adaptation, computer software, or by similar or dissimilar methodology now known or hereafter developed.

The use of general descriptive names, registered names, trademarks, service marks, etc. in this publication does not imply, even in the absence of a specific statement, that such names are exempt from the relevant protective laws and regulations and therefore free for general use.

The publisher, the authors, and the editors are safe to assume that the advice and information in this book are believed to be true and accurate at the date of publication. Neither the publisher nor the authors or the editors give a warranty, expressed or implied, with respect to the material contained herein or for any errors or omissions that may have been made. The publisher remains neutral with regard to jurisdictional claims in published maps and institutional affiliations.

This Palgrave Macmillan imprint is published by the registered company Springer Nature Switzerland AG. The registered company address is: Gewerbestrasse 11, 6330 Cham, Switzerland

Acknowledgements

Our sincere appreciation goes to the editorial and content editing work performed by our colleague and friend Jennifer Cash without whose critical comments and language improvement of all the texts, this book would not have made it to seeing publishing lights. We wish to acknowledge the substantial support from several sources that have made the publication of this book possible. The coeditors received substantial institutional support from the Max Planck Institute for Social Anthropology in Halle Saale in Germany, generous financial support from the Fritz Thyssen Foundation in Germany for organizing the event on which the book is based as well as other costs related to the publication of the book. We also would like to thank the Office of the Vice President for International Affairs at the Indiana University Bloomington for their support at the initial stage of the publication project. The generous support of these institutions allowed us to hold our initial international workshop at Indiana University's Berlin Gateway office, expertly staffed by Andrea Adam Moore and Annabelle Turk.

Contents

**1 Introduction: Religious Economies in Secular Contexts—
Halal Markets, Practices, and Landscapes**   1
Rano Turaeva and Michael Brose

Part I   Halal Certification   19

**2 Halal Certification in the United States and the Expansion
of Halal Markets**   21
Nurcan Atalan-Helicke

3 Building Halal in Italy: The Case of Halal Italia   57
Lauren Crossland-Marr

**4 Halal Business in Russia: Standards of State and Non-state
Certification**   71
Izzat Amon

vii

viii Contents

Part II Halal Market Growth 83

5 **Between Religion and Ethnicity: The Politics of Halal in China** 85
Guangtian Ha

6 **Bacon or Beef? 'Fake' Halal Scandals in the Russian Federation: Consolidating Halal Norms Through Secular Courts** 121
Silvia Serrano

7 **Halal in Contemporary Ukraine: Markets and Administration** 147
Denis Brylov

Part III Moral Economy of Halal 169

8 **Sufism and Islamic Market in Central Asia: From Kolkhoz to Halal Economy in Kazakhstan?** 171
Yana Pak

9 **Sustainable Halal? The Intersection of Halal, Organic, and Genetically Engineered Food in Turkey** 193
Nurcan Atalan-Helicke

10 **Sustainability and Halal? Global Trade, Molecular Halal, and Exclusionary Politics** 219
Shaheed Tayob

Index 239

Notes on Contributors

Rano Turaeva is a lecturer at the Ludwig Maximillian University of Munich, in Germany. She finished her second single-authored monograph on Migration and Islam in Russia and her first book was published in 2016 with the title *Migration and Identity: the Uzbek Experience*. She edited a book with Rustamjon Urinboyev titled: *Labour, Mobility and Informal practices in Russia: Power, Institutions and Mobile Actors in Transnational Space* published in 2021. She has been writing on the topics of debt relations, informal economies, informality and urban transformations in post-Soviet cities, migration, entrepreneurship, gender, border studies, identity and inter-ethnic relations among many other topics which she published in such journals as Cities, Nationalities Papers, Inner Asia, Asian Ethnicity, Communist and post-Communist studies, Extreme Anthropology among other journals.

Michael Brose is a Professor of Practice in the Department of Central Eurasian Studies at Indiana University Bloomington. He researches the Mongol conquest of China and history and contemporary status of Islam in China.

Nurcan Atalan-Helicke is an associate professor, Skidmore College Environmental Studies and Sciences Program. She studies the sustainability of food systems, both the conservation of agricultural biodiversity and farmer livelihoods and consumers' access to clean and healthy food.

Notes on Contributors

Her research about conservation of wheat landraces in Turkey and genetically engineered food and Islam was published in peer review academic journals and edited volumes, including *Gastronomica, Agriculture and Human Values,* and *Journal of Environmental Studies and Sciences.* She teaches a variety of courses, including Politics of Food, Global Environmental Governance, and Human Rights and Development.

Lauren Crossland-Marr is a post-doctoral researcher on an EU-funded project that explores public awareness and acceptance of new biotechnology use in agriculture. In May 2020, she received her PhD in cultural anthropology from Washington University in St. Louis. From 2017 to 2018, she conducted participant observation on the halal certification industry in Milan, Italy, to determine the impact of local cultural foodways on certification schemes meant for global markets. In 2014, Lauren received an MA in Anthropology from the Catholic University of America. In 2007, she received her bachelor's degree from the University of Maryland, College Park.

Izzat Amon a prisoner of conscience, independent researcher, and human rights activist, was based in Moscow, Russia, and is now in prison in Tajikistan. He has been actively defending the rights of migrants from Central Asia in Russia. He provided them with legal services and continuously collected funding to do charity work to support migrants. He also conducted extremely important work to support migrants in COVID-19 pandemic in Russia. Izzat Amon openly criticized the Tajik authorities' lack of support to Tajik migrants living in Russia which led to his eventual imprisonment.

Guangtian Ha is an Assistant Professor of Religion at Haverford College (USA). He is the author of *The Sound of Salvation: Voice, Gender, and the Sufi Mediascape in China* (2022).

Silvia Serrano is Professor of Post-Soviet Studies, Eur'Orbem, Sorbonne University and Sorbonne University Abu Dhabi. She is an author and an editor of numerous books and academic articles on the Caucasus, such as *Development in Central Centra Asia and the Caucasus. Migration, Democratisation, and Inequality in the Post-Soviet Era* (2014), Londres,

I.B. Tauris [with Hohmann Sophie, Mouradian Claire, Thorez Julien]; *Ordres et Désordres au Caucase* (2010), Bruxelles: Editions de l'Université libre de Bruxelles, 232 pages [with Aude Merlin]; and *Géorgie. Sortie d'empire,* 2007 Paris: CNRS éditions, 342 pages.

Denis Brylov is a senior researcher of the A. Krymskiy Institute of Oriental Studies of the National Academy of Sciences of Ukraine (Kyiv) and a visiting research fellow at Leibnitz ZMO (Center of Modern Orient). He is a psychologist and anthropologist of religion and Doctor of Philosophical Sciences (DSc) in Religious Studies and Theology. His main academic interests are Islam, political activism in Islam and transnational Islamic movements, religious factors in conflicts, and religion and nationalism.

Yana Pak is a PhD candidate at l'Ecole des Hautes Etudes en Sciences Sociales (School of Advanced Studies in Social Sciences) Paris, France. Her thesis "Network of Sufi Entrepreneurs in Central Asia" aims to analyze the emergence and confessionalization of new forms of solidarity groups nourished by Islamic values, by focusing on Islamic economy in the post-Soviet Central Asian context.

Shaheed Tayob is a lecturer in the Department of Sociology and Social Anthropology at Stellenbosch University, South Africa. Shaheed's research focuses on the Anthropology of Islam with a focus on food practices and human-animal relations at the intersection of religion, politics, and economy in India and South Africa.

List of Figures

Fig. 2.1	Halal logos issued by halal certification agencies in the United States	31
Fig. 5.1	Republican-era *qingzhen* restaurant sign from Wuhan. Courtesy of Harvard-Yenching Library	96
Fig. 5.2	Contemporary *qingzhen* food sign. Author's collection	98
Fig. 5.3	Contemporary *qingzhen* food sign, Henan Province. Author's collection	99
Fig. 5.4	*Qingzhen* restaurant in Henan Province. Author's collection	100
Fig. 5.5	Official seal of Ningxia Halal Certification Center. Author's collection	103
Fig. 5.6	Example of Ningxia Halal Food Certificate. Author's collection	104
Fig. 5.7	Malaysian, Indonesian, Singapore halal logos. Author's collection	105
Fig. 9.1	Comparison of conventional, organic, natural, and halal chicken sold in markets based on 2016 prices in Carrefour national supermarket chain in Turkey. Here, 'conventional' refers to meat products from industrial feeding operations without any sustainability or health labels. Certified 'organic' fulfils organic production standards. There is no standard or regulation for 'natural' (*doğal*) in Turkey, but companies use the label generously	209

List of Tables

Table 9.1	Educational attainment of 2015 and 2019 focus group participants	199
Table 9.2	Economic status of 2015 focus group participants (n = 56)	205
Table 9.3	Economic status of 2019 focus group participants (n = 27)	205

1

Introduction: Religious Economies in Secular Contexts—Halal Markets, Practices, and Landscapes

Rano Turaeva and Michael Brose

Introduction

Religious economies have been studied mainly as types of moral economies using quantitative and economic approaches. However, religious markets are growing spaces across the world, increasingly accommodating more and more diversity in food production, food consumption, and notions of permissible food. As societies become more diverse and integrated into larger networks, consumers' approaches and reflections to what we consume and how food products are produced are changing—not only to reflect changing demands for environmental protection but also to reflect changing religious and moral categories. National

---

R. Turaeva (✉)
Ludwig Maximilian University of Munich, Munich, Germany
e-mail: r.turaeva@gmail.com

M. Brose
Indiana University Bloomington, Bloomington, IN, USA
e-mail: brosemc@iu.edu

© The Author(s), under exclusive license to Springer Nature Switzerland AG 2023
R. Turaeva, M. Brose (eds.), *Religious Economies in Secular Context*, New Directions in Islam, https://doi.org/10.1007/978-3-031-18603-5_1

boundaries that limited markets are being replaced by transnational markets and globalization of capital and production, and this trend is expected to continue once disruptions caused by the Covid-19 pandemic and regional conflicts are in the past.

Yet, halal food markets have not been spared from disruption. The challenges faced by halal market actors, interestingly, have made "halal" an even more important factor in food production and consumption around the world. Nor has the importance of halal food been limited to Muslim-majority nations. In fact, as the chapters in this book illustrate, halal markets in secular, non-Muslim-majority countries are increasingly important but are also sites of new competition between governmental and private food regulatory bodies. This struggle between competing regulatory bodies raises an additional question: What role should religion play in the economics of the food sector in secular societies? It is precisely this issue that this book seeks to examine in the case studies of halal food production, marketing, and consumption.

Muslims are the second largest religious group in the world. They constitute 24% of the global population. Moreover, fully one-fifth of this population (approximately 300 million) lives in non-Muslim-majority countries (World Population Prospects 2022). Indeed, the number of Muslims living in non-Muslim-majority countries is expected to increase due to the increasing mobility of populations linked to the globalization of capital, as well as to refugee crises (Bowen 2004; Grillo 2004). This demographic development has occurred in step with the globalization of markets, as producers and marketers of halal food products have courted the growing international Muslim consumer group and its standards, requirements, and demands.

Muslims living in non-Muslim-majority countries, like those living in secular states that have a majority of Muslim population such as Turkey, face particular challenges in trying to adhere to the religious rules that govern food consumption, doing business, and the daily practice of religion. The halal industry has become more relevant in their daily lives not only in the domain of consumption but also in the domains of religious belief and practice and in those of ethnic and religious belonging. Halal intersects with sectarian identity politics but also provides bridges. Both halal consumers and halal producers participate daily in the production

1 Introduction: Religious Economies in Secular Contexts—Halal...

of interpretation and values within halal and for halal as a lifestyle. Halal producers and authorities, for their part, participate in the process of defining the bargaining power and authority surrounding the definition of halal and access to the growing market in halal.

As a result of these dynamic processes, "halal" has become a kind of marketing brand used to market food, cosmetics, and other products. It is an effective marketing strategy. It appeals directly to Muslims but also increasingly to non-Muslims who seek pure, fresh products free from increasingly apparent industrial impurities. In this case, "halal" implies attributes similar to other labels, familiar in the United States and Europe, that promise to guarantee quality and purity—such as fair trade, bio, or organic—but with the additional appeal to prospective Muslim consumers that it satisfies Islamic norms and practices. This dual function of "halal" as a brand in the market and as an ideal of moral functions and qualities, however, raises an interesting contradiction that requires further investigation; to what degree does economic opportunity and profit-making contradict religiously based moral imperatives stemming, in this case, from Sharia?

At least at first glance, it would appear that there is some contradiction when "halal" is deployed to encourage consumption. It is precisely this apparent contradiction that we tried to puzzle out in an international workshop we convened in late 2019 where a diverse group of invited participants presented their research findings on various aspects of halal in non-Muslim and secular contexts. A small number of papers that emanated from that workshop were published in a special issue of the journal *Sociology of Islam*. Since that publication, other scholars who participated in the initial workshop were able to extend and develop their work, and others were brought into ongoing discussions about this topic, since it appears to be only growing in importance as a sector of the global economy. In order to provide wide access to this ongoing research, we have collected those papers in this book.

Here, we enquire further into specific practices and definitions of halal used by state and private businesses to define halal in legal, moral, and religious terms in several countries where the legal and administrative frameworks for consumer-oriented production and protection assume a non-Muslim, or at least a secular Muslim, majority population. For brevity, we sometimes use the formulations "non-Muslim majority" or 'secular,' despite their inaccuracies. Let us explain what is specific about halal in these countries, in opposition to those where the legal and administrative frameworks assume that the population consists of a majority of actively practicing Muslims.

As a first example, in countries—like Italy—where Muslims are a minority, it cannot be taken for granted that all food and other services are halal. In fact, Islam has so little public recognition in many of these countries that the appearance of a halal label is often perceived as an ethnic identifier and not necessarily as a religious marker. This is in stark contrast to the situation in most Muslim-majority countries where the consumer can assume and expect halal goods and services to be the norm (Bergeaud-Blackler and Lever 2016).

In some Muslim-majority countries, the majority of consumers are expected to be secular due to the historical developments in the region in question. This is the case in former Soviet countries as well as Turkey, albeit for different historical reasons. In these countries, the Muslim consumer cannot assume a halal marketplace as the norm, particularly for processed foods. In the post-Soviet context, in particular, one must account for the effects of seventy years of atheist ideology, the promotion of Russian cultural practices, and a generalized Soviet secularism on the daily practices of food consumption and production. Indeed, the secular systems of state services and infrastructure in the Caucasus and Central Asia predate the Soviets and were already established by the early nineteenth century from Russian imperial occupation of these regions.

In both types of countries under consideration in this volume, it will also be important to remember that while there is real or potentially significant domestic consumption of halal, a large proportion of certified halal production is also specialized for export. This raises interesting questions about the impact of an export economy on domestic halal markets and the degree to which there may be some kind of feedback loop between local Muslim populations and the global umma through the specific vectors of consumption and lifestyle.

Therefore, in this volume, we examine the interaction of the state's secular legal and religious systems within the processes for establishing and regulating the norms of halal. This includes halal certification

1 Introduction: Religious Economies in Secular Contexts—Halal... 5

processes; norms of food production, service, and delivery relations; consumption patterns, halal discourses, and halal practices; the morality of halal markets; and other social aspects of halal markets. We consider how the market economy in each state, with its particular manifestations of a global economic model based on capitalist principles, intersects with the secular legal basis to develop and expand religious-economic markets, both domestically and internationally. We also consider the morality discourses and practices that appear within the field of halal markets shaping a particularly "halal" moral economy that unites religious and secular aspects of economic practice.

The economic and legal incorporation of the religious needs of consumers in these modern secular economies does not go unnoticed by Muslims. As consumers and as believers, they raise other issues associated with halal: trust, religious authority, the ethics of branding halal, religious identity, social equality (when halal becomes a status marker), and finally the bureaucratization of Islam as it is manifest in the regulatory procedures of the halal market. At their widest, the issues associated with halal reach the dilemmas produced in the encounter between rational economic thinking and religious views about halal. All of the cases in this book address the apparent conflict between rational and moral action and decision-making. This conflict is faced on a daily basis by sellers and consumers, as well as regulators and certifiers.

Case studies from non-Muslim-majority societies put these dynamics in bold relief. This is because it can be assumed that here, alongside a system of morally correct and acceptable "Islamic" behavior, there is an opposing set of choices that are more "rational" in terms of strict economic benefit. For example, a Muslim businessman who owns a halal supermarket is assumed to face a choice in which he must decide whether to sell only products deemed halal or to gain higher profit margins from selling some *haram* products, such as alcohol and cigarettes. Certification only multiplies the perceived choices between religion and rationality. In this case, the Muslim businessman must decide whether it is more halal to do business only with other Muslim businessmen (regardless of whether their products are certified) or to insist on partners with certification. As certification is most common among larger more commercial enterprises, the second choice brings him into a more purely 'market' setting than the "religious" community of uncertified business partners. The examples multiply in the cases discussed in each chapter.

Importantly, qualitative studies of such situations reveal a number of active concepts producing local discussions of moral economy in and of the market. Some are drawn from English, like "sustainable" or local languages. Several are drawn from Arabic, such as *barakali* (with blessing), *risq* (sustenance), and *tayyib* (wholesome).[1] The multiplicity of terms shows that decisions required by businesses operating in halal markets are rarely simple decisions between rational choice and moral or value-driven choice. This strict dichotomy comes from Weber, who differentiates between two types of rationality: *zweckrational* (aim-oriented rationale) and *wertrational* (value-oriented rationale). While sociological views might be drawn to rely on such a dichotomy, the case studies presented in this book illustrate and reinforce the need for a more complex analytic frame to understand motives and choices in the intersecting domains of religion and economy. In non-Muslim-majority contexts, adequate analysis must include understanding specific legal and institutional constraints, local consumer culture, and access to information by those people who wish to sell halal products. The case studies in this book therefore examine the dual interaction of state secular legal systems with religious systems that regulate the halal market. Each of the chapters addresses one or more of the following three main issues or topics: (1) certification processes and rules in food production and the larger halal market; (2) principles and legal bases drawn on to expand the halal market among local Muslims, the national economy, and the global marketplace; and (3) ongoing creation of moral economy through discourses on trust, authority, branding, and status.

---

[1] *Risq* also covers the meanings of livelihood and divine provision, while *tayyib* can mean good, clean, wholesome, gentle, excellent, fair, and lawful.

Authority Over Defining Halal: Certification

The expansion of halal markets has led to a multiplication of centers authorized to certify products as halal, but this expansion also has entailed various games of power over Islam and within the Islamic market (Bonne and Verbeke 2008; Campbell et al. 2011; Lever and Miele 2012). Halal certification in non-Muslim-majority states is usually conducted by non-state agencies; however, standards and procedures for certifying halal must also comply with state forms of certification for food safety (Atalan-Helicke 2015). Thus, certification is entangled with other aspects of the state's relationship with religion, as well as its market regulations.

In the post-Soviet states, there has been stark bureaucratization and centralization of the administration of Islam. The states seek strong control over the Islamic influence from Arab countries and over the politicization of Islam. Post-Soviet states are secular, but they have seen religious revival and Arabic influence has been enormous in the Muslim majority countries. Currently, halal is an example also of the hybrid forms that Islamic practice has taken as traditional local practices, and their Soviet-influenced forms have come together with post-Soviet Arabic influences. Other secular countries with minority Muslim populations have more liberal and market driven principles towards the regulation of halal markets. Comparing transnational Muslim certification agencies versus local Muslim authorities offers an interesting field for considering certification of Halal products and services in secular legal systems. This section of the book includes case studies from the United States, Italy, and Russia.

Nurcan Atalan-Helicke's first chapter examines the processes of halal certification of food in the United States. With the changing demographics of the American Muslim population, halal-certified food has become more visible and mainstream in the United States in recent years, to the point that it now appeals to a broad range of millennial consumers, and some halal agencies advertise halal as a lifestyle that is accessible to "everyone," not only Muslims. Halal's regulation in the United States also provides a glimpse into the long duree of state-religion relations in food certification, as it follows paths previously developed around kosher regulation and navigates the complex intersections of federal and state laws.

Lauren Crossland-Marr's chapter examines the ways and spaces of negotiation of those who have an authority over local definition of halal in Italy. The author illustrates how the political, economic, and social dynamics of Halal Italia define authority over the definition of halal across Italy. She also shows how Halal Italia plays a central role within Islamic institution building process, even as its authority is challenged by some members of the broader Islamic community. Halal Italia represents a Sufi tradition and one that was promulgated by a convert from Catholicism. As Italy's Muslim population grows, especially with influxes of immigrants, Halal Italia's authority both increases in interreligious activities and becomes contested within intra-religious activities; both dynamics inform halal regulation and certification. As do others in this volume, Crossland-Marr makes the point that "far from [being] a universal standard, halal is created *in situ* and is never a finished process but an avenue to make and remake what Islam *is* in diasporic contexts." She argues further that it is necessary "to go beyond halal as an economic intervention or as part of a culture of foodways, but rather to delve into the moments in which the halal certification process generates new kinds of persons, communities, and worlds."

Izzat Amon's contribution is unique because we present it in its original form as a research report because the author is currently imprisoned in Russia and has not been able to complete his paper as he would have wished. Nevertheless, the trajectory of the argument he wanted to make is clear: He examines the double certification experiences of a meat production unit in Moscow by drawing from the experiences of business leaders of halal production in Russia. Especially valuable are the author's presentation of those leaders' opinions about the rationality of the double certification as well as discussion of the trust and religious values within halal production and marketing in Russia.

Growing Halal Markets and Authority of Labeling Halal

Wilson and Liu (2011: 28; see also 2010), citing Holt (2002 cited by Wilson and Liu 2011: 28), reminded us that "brands dictate tastes." Brands serve as symbols of prestige and class belonging, and they can result in monopolistic dynamics of market development, leading consumers to affiliate with certain social and status groups by choosing certain brands. These dynamics are signaled by Veblen's (1959) concept of conspicuous consumption. Conspicuous consumption refers to consumption practices, including knowledge about various products and their use, qualities, and meanings that are directed at making certain impressions. When brands are globalized, prestige categories travel beyond national boundaries having (often) the same effect as in the place where it first became popular. Brands also assume lives of their own, entering power games that change social and economic relations in various combinations within brand-based economies. Bourdieu (1984) provides another milestone in sociological thinking about the relations between taste and the (re)production of class.

Pink (2009) reminds us that the globalization of markets and capital has two sides. On the one hand, established global brands like Nestle or Coca Cola try to fit local tastes and culture better in order to win an increasing share of the global market. On the other hand, local producers try to fit into current trends of global consumerism to expand their reach (see also Miller 1998). To some degree, markets in and of "religious" goods and services (here, religious markets) exhibit similar patterns to those of any other market. Power, capital, competition, authority, and popularization are the keywords for such a comparison. Halal markets have not been spared from the dynamics that have characterized the development of other global consumption patterns. Halal has its popularity among certain groups, as well as its more and less popular brands (i.e., certification labels). Style matters, as does the social consciousness it conveys (see Ewen 1976, 1999). New brands have generated and been generated by new definitions of halal too as global halal economy has come into being (see also the contributions of the edited volume by Pink

2009). The growth of halal markets has even generated rebranding and subsidiary lines of popular global brands such as Turca Cola (Mutlu 2009), Halal Bavaria (alcohol-free beer in Malaysia), and Haribo halal.

The case study from China is another important contribution to this volume. China is home to a substantial but internally diverse population of Muslims (upwards of 40 million spread across 10 separate officially identified ethnic minority groups), and the connections of China's Muslims to other parts of the Islamic world are variable, changing, and almost always politically suspect in the eyes of the state. Yet, the situation of "halal" has been understudied until recently. Guangtian Ha shows how the state has become the final arbiter of whether "halal" is defined and has any place in local and national markets, especially starting in the late 1990s to the late 2010s when there was a critical transition in how halal food was identified in China and how the state as well as ordinary Muslims perceived these shifting signs. In these years, an older marking of products as *qingzhen* (clear and genuine) that had functioned more as a symbol of Muslimness than as a regulatory device and that had denoted places as much as foods for the Muslim community (especially ethnic Hui) was removed and replaced with a certification and labeling scheme for "halal." The change, at local state initiative, imagined the possibilities for increased trade and tourism with the Muslim world—but this goal, which coincided with national-level interests in economic development, soon diverged from state concerns with security. Still, Ha argues that "the current crackdown on Islam in China is as much about how Islam is to be visually represented as it is about concerns over sovereignty, ethnicity, and religious dissent."

Communist doctrines concerning religion uniquely shape the way that many of the states observed here have responded to Muslim residents' desires for halal, and anyone who wants to understand halal in those parts of the world must factor in that political legacy. However, the examples from states with a much reduced historical engagement with communism show the variability in state commitments to secularity. Thus, the growing numbers of Muslims living in multiple secular state contexts demand a highly qualitative approach to unpuzzle the dynamic and complex fields of religion, economy, and power.

1 Introduction: Religious Economies in Secular Contexts—Halal... 11

The work of Silvia Serrano deals with the rise of Russia's halal market through the scandals generated around them. Her paper is a case study of a scandal that erupted when certified halal meat products were found to contain pork DNA. Serrano shows how the scandal and its legal resolution in the courts reveal a preexisting order (based in state authority and technocratic regulation) which was put to test, confirmed, and strengthened.

Brylov shows the details of power games played out within the process of administering and bureaucratizing Islam in Ukraine and how global institutions also enter those games. The bureaucratization of Islam has been generally observed everywhere Muslims live, with respect to the administration of Islam, as power and authority are expanded over Muslims and Muslim spaces (Tasar 2017; Müller and Steiner 2018).

In the dynamics of halal branding, therefore, we see many sociological processes at work. The expansion and diversification of neoliberal market economies and the increasing consumption power of self-identifying Muslim consumers is an economic face of increased global attention to religion, its politicization, and religious identities. Economic actors cannot brand halal on their own but must rely on secular and religious authorities and institutions. Economic relations surrounding halal alter the balance between religion and the state, between consumption and belief, and between law and morality. Persistent discourses of trust, as well as the outbreak of scandals, show how societies realign their norms and values. Branding alone does not ensure the successful institutionalization of halal in the market. Below, we will try to further unpuzzle this doubt about halal in relation to identification, halal as practice, and the power of authority.

Moral Economies of Halal and Identity Politics

As indicated above, halal is directly linked to questions about identity and culture. The basic mechanism of identification through consumption has been recognized in the social sciences for many decades. That consumption practices link food and identity has also been qualitatively established across the academic literature (Fischler 1988; Poe 1999; Valentine 1999; Wilk 1999; Shields-Argeles 2004; Feffer 2005; Cwiertka

2006; Wilson 2006; Liu and Lin 2009; Rosenblum 2010; Counihan and Van Esterik 2013).

Max Weber recognized that consumption was employed to represent belonging to status groups (1946: 193; cf. Campbell 1987). But it is Veblen's (1959) "conspicuous consumption" that has dominated debates about class, modernity, identity, and self-reflection at the beginning of the twenty-first century (Zukin and Maguire 2004), perhaps because it underwrites a fundamentally positive valuation of consumption that is well-aligned with the burgeoning and dominant market research and business development studies (Kettle 2019).

In the 1990s, consumption was still viewed largely from a more critical Marxist approach (which emphasized value), even as pro-modernization theorists tried to integrate a consideration of modern technologies, self-reflection, and identities with the study of consumption (Giddens 1991; Warde 1994; but compare Roseberry 1996). The "consumption culture" and "mass consumption" appearing alongside twenty-first century global-ization, however, also support anti-consumption movements (Miele 2006). Even now, sociological studies that tie consumption with identification and group belonging along religious lines (as Weber did) are still scarce (Paterson 2006; see also Fischler 1988). Yet, religious iden-tity serves an important part of many people's self-identification and pro-vides them with membership in, and a sense of belonging to, a group of great significance in current sociopolitical contexts.

Like other ethnic and religious minorities, but perhaps more obviously so, Muslims in non-Muslim-majority countries face the prospect of social exclusion. The long-term ghettoization of migrant communities of Muslim background in the West has been well documented in scholarly works on interethnic studies and migration (Jargowsky 1994; Lamont and Molnar 2001; Chaddha and Wilson 2008; Hirsch 2009). Minority status implies also that the group's needs are not well represented in the majority of a state's agendas, regulatory procedures, or planning with regard to food and the provision of other basic material and social needs. These forms of exclusion are more poignantly felt now with the increase in xenophobic and right-wing movements.

Shaheed Tayob's contribution to this volume, for example, discusses "discourse and materiality of global trade and consumer growth within

1 Introduction: Religious Economies in Secular Contexts—Halal... 13

which halal certification obtains its demand." Tayob argues that "the intimacy of exclusionary politics and economic growth means that halal certification potentially partakes in the marginalization of Muslim labor and trade in the city." Furthermore, it is important according to Tayob that the questions of sustainability and halal consider "the ethical entailments of new formations of halal, in order to bridge between an ethics of intra-Muslim trade and exchange, and the conditions of global trade." In his contribution, Tayob shows that given "a discursive tradition of halal that centers intra-Muslim networks of labor, trade, and exchange, it is imperative to consider the ethical stakes of halal certification for marginalized and precarious Muslim populations around the world."

Nurcan Atalan-Helicke's second chapter deals with the morality of modern reflections on healthy food. In Turkey, she finds that the concept of *tayib* is invoked alongside that of halal. Consumers were concerned that animals are slaughtered properly, but they were more interested in being assured that the animal had lived well and that both meat and plant foods were "pure" and healthy. They were suspicious of genetically modified food. In this example, we see clearly how Muslim consumers are engaged in local-global and secular-religious debates simultaneously: A growing demand to label food with information about its quality and standards of production is a general global trend, connected to the changing environment and to discourses about global warming (see also Armanios and Ergene 2018: 191). Muslims everywhere engage increasingly with such global discourses on food through an Islamic lens—halal.

In such contexts, halal markets in non-Muslim countries are not only about satisfying "basic needs" (i.e., they offer religiously permitted products and services) nor only about a brand-oriented consumer identity. These markets also offer spaces for identity politics, spaces for socialization, and safe spaces in which Muslims as minorities can practice openly their religion. This dimension is most clear in the paper provided by Yana Pak. She details the transformation of solidarity groups in Kazakhstan which are known locally as Sulaymanchi. Pak shows how the "Islamic economy" offers a new framework for socioeconomic organization and redistribution of wealth through the mobilization and valuation of private initiative and solidarity outside of the still-dominant secular networks of the country's political and economic elite. Yet, even these new forms of socioeconomic organization contain a distinct admixture of Islamic values with Soviet-made norms of morality.

Because the halal label indicates that a product satisfies Islamic norms for "permissable" consumption, it is taken to imply attributes of quality, purity, ecological responsibility, and social justice—like fair trade, bio, and organic imply in the United States and Europe. As a brand, however, halal is more than a principled rejection of excess, luxury, and their attendant ills (see Frank 1997, 1999); it is also a distinct appeal to a religiously grounded morality. This dual appeal to potential buyers as "Muslims" and as consumers, however, raises an interesting contradiction between the rationality of making profits and the morality of following religious prescriptions (cf. Fourier 1998). Islamic teachings hold that some forms of economic opportunity and profit-making contradict religiously based moral imperatives—but, in the contemporary context, which ones? Can a halal café serve halal food during the day and turn into a disco in the evening? Can a halal shop sell vodka? How can one delineate the boundary between religiously acceptable profit-making and profit-making that adheres too much to market rationality? When one is doing business in the context of a non-Muslim-majority country, the complexity of these questions is related to the dynamic processes of identity politics, religious belonging, economic challenges, and cultural diversity of the new secular contexts.

As we proceed to the chapters produced by the contributors, we believe the work presented here illustrates important new developments in the economy of halal in many non-Muslim-majority states and societies. At the same time, we realize that the trends presented by the authors here will be "old news" even before this book has been printed. New crises, new economic imperatives, and new waves of consumer desires are constant in human societies, and the halal economy will certainly be transformed by these changes. Nonetheless, we believe the work presented here is both prescient and illustrative of the state of being in the second decade of the twenty-first century across a large part of the world that few in the West understand deeply but that has growing impact on the global economy.

1 Introduction: Religious Economies in Secular Contexts—Halal... 15

Acknowledgements Our sincere appreciation goes to the editorial and content editing work performed by our colleague and friend Jennifer Cash without whose critical comments and language improvement of all the texts this book would not have made it to seeing publishing lights. We wish to acknowledge the substantial support from several sources that have made the publication of this book possible. The coeditors received substantial institutional support from the Max Planck Institute for Social Anthropology in Halle Saale in Germany, generous financial support from the Fritz Thyssen Foundation in Germany for organizing the event on which the book is based as well as other costs related to the publication of the book. We also would like to thank the Office of the Vice President for International Affairs at the Indiana University Bloomington for their support at the initial stage of the publication project. The generous support of these institutions allowed us to hold our initial international workshop at Indiana University's Berlin Gateway office, expertly staffed by Andrea Adam Moore and Annabelle Turk.

References

Armanios, F., and B.A. Ergene. 2018. *Halal food: A history*. Oxford University Press.

Atalan-Helicke, Nurcan. 2015. The halal paradox: Negotiating identity, religious values, and genetically engineered food in Turkey. *Agriculture and Human Values* 32 (4): 663–674.

Bergeaud-Blackler, F., J. Fischer, and J. Lever. 2016. *Halal matters: Islam, politics and markets in global perspective*. New York and London: Routledge.

Bonne, K., and W. Verbeke. 2008. Religious values informing halal meat production and the control and delivery of halal credence quality. *Agriculture and Human Values* 25 (1): 35–47.

Bourdieu, P. 1984. *Distinction: A social critique of the judgement of taste*. Trans. R. Nice. Cambridge: Harvard University Press.

Bowen, J. 2004. Beyond migration: Islam as a transnational public space. *Journal of Ethnic and Migration Studies* 30 (5): 879–894.

Campbell, C. 1987. *The Romantic ethic and the spirit of modern consumerism*. Oxford: Blackwell.

Campbell, H., A. Murcott, and A. MacKenzie. 2011. Kosher in New York City, halal in Aquitaine: Challenging the relationship between neoliberalism and food auditing. *Agriculture and Human Values* 28 (1): 67–79.

Chaddha, A., and W.J. Wilson. 2008. Reconsidering the 'ghetto.' *City & Community* 7 (4): 384–388. https://doi.org/10.1111/j.1540-6040.2008.00271_7.x.

Counihan, C., and P. Van Esterik. 2013. *Food and culture: A reader*. New York: Routledge.

Cwiertka, K.J. 2006. *Modern Japanese cuisine: Food, power and national identity*. London: Reaktion Books.

Ewen, S. D. 1976. *Captains of consciousness: Advertising and the social roots of consumer culture*. New York: McGraw-Hill.

———. 1999. *All consuming images: The politics of style in contemporary culture*. New York: Basic Books.

Feffer, J. 2005. Korean food, Korean identity: The impact of globalization on Korean agriculture. *Shorenstein APARC*. Accessed 4 December 2011. http://ksp.stanford.edu/publications/korean_food_korean_identity_the_impact_of_globalization_on_korean_agriculture/.

Fischler, C. 1988. Food, self and identity. *Social Science Information* 27 (2): 275–292.

Fourier, S. 1998. Consumers and their brands: Developing relationship theory in consumer research. *Journal of Consumer Research* 24: 343–374.

Frank, T. 1997. *The conquest of cool*. Chicago: University of Chicago Press.

Frank, R.H. 1999. *Luxury fever: Why money fails to satisfy in an era of excess*. New York: Free Press.

Giddens, A. 1991. *Modernity and self-identity: Self and society in the Late Modern Age*. Stanford University Press.

Grillo, R. 2004. Islam and transnationalism. *Journal of Ethnic and Migration Studies* 30 (5): 861–878.

Hirsch, A.R. 2009. *Making the second ghetto: Race and housing in Chicago, 1940–1960*. Chicago: University of Chicago Press.

Jargowsky, P.A. 1994. Ghetto poverty among blacks in the 1980s. *Journal of Policy Analysis and Management* 13 (2): 288–310. https://doi.org/10.2307/3325015.

Kettle, K.L. 2019. Identity salience: understanding when identity affects consumption. In *Handbook of research on identity theory in marketing*, ed. I.I. Americus Reed and M. Forehand, 30–43. Cheltenham: Edward Elgar Publishing.

Lamont, M., and V. Molnar. 2001. How blacks use consumption to shape their collective identity. *Journal of Consumer Culture* 1: 31–46.

Lever, J., and M. Miele. 2012. The growth of halal meat markets in Europe: An exploration of the supply side theory of religion. *Journal of Rural Studies* 28 (4): 528–537.

Liu, Haiming, and Lianlian Lin. 2009. Food, culinary identity, and transnational culture: Chinese restaurant business in Southern California. *Journal of Asian American Studies* 12 (2): 135–162.

Miele, Mara. 2006. Consumption culture: The case of food. *Handbook of rural studies* 15: 344–354.

Miller. 1998. Coca-Cola: A black sweet drink from Trinidad. In *Material cultures: Why some things matter*, ed. D. Miller, 245–262. London: Routledge.

Müller, Dominik, and Kerstin Steiner. 2018. The bureaucratisation of Islam in Southeast Asia: Transdisciplinary perspectives. *Journal of Current Southeast Asian Affairs* 37 (1): 3–26. ISSN: 1868-4882 (online), ISSN: 1868-1034.

Mutlu, Dilek Kaya. 2009. The Cola Turka controversy: Consuming cola as a Turkish Muslim. In *Muslim Societies in the Age of mass consumption*, ed. Johanna Pink, 101–122. Newcastle upon Tyne: Cambridge Scholars Publishing.

Pink, Johanna, ed. 2009. *Muslim societies in the age of mass consumption: Politics, culture and identity between the local and the global.* Newcastle upon Tyne: Cambridge Scholars Publishing.

Poe, T.N. 1999. The origins of soul food in black urban identity: Chicago, 1915–1947. *American Studies International* 37 (1): 4–33.

Roseberry, W. 1996. The rise of yuppie coffees and the reimagination of class in the United States. *American Anthropologist* 98 (4): 762–775.

Rosenblum, J. 2010. *Food and identity in early Rabbinic Judaism.* Cambridge: Cambridge University Press.

Shields-Argelès, C. 2004. Imagining self and the other: Food and identity in France and the United States. *Food, Culture & Society* 7 (2): 13–28.

Tasar, Eren. 2017. *Soviet and Muslim: The institutionalization of Islam in Central Asia.* New York: Oxford University Press. https://doi.org/10.1093/oso/9780190652104.001.0001.

Valentine, G. 1999. Eating in: Home, consumption and identity. *The Sociological Review* 47 (3): 491–524.

Veblen, T. 1959. *The theory of the leisure class.* New York: Viking.

Warde, A. 1994. Consumption, identity-formation and uncertainty. *Sociology* 28 (4): 877–898.

Weber, M. 1946. Class, status, party. In *Max Weber: Essays in sociology*, ed. H.H. Gerth and C.W. Mills, 180–195. New York: Oxford University Press.

Wilk, R.R. 1999. 'Real Belizean food': Building local identity in the transnational Caribbean. *American Anthropologist* 101 (2): 244–255.

Wilson, T.M., ed. 2006. *Food, drink and identity in Europe.* Rodopi: Brill.

Wilson, J.A.J., and J. Liu. 2010. Shaping the *halal* into a brand? *Journal of Islamic Marketing* 1 (2): 107–123.

Wilson, Jonathan A.J., and Jonathan Liu. 2011. The challenges of Islamic branding: Navigating emotions and halal. *UK Journal of Islamic Marketing* 2 (1): 28–42.

World Population Prospects. 2022. published online by The United Nation Department of Economic and Social Affairs. Accessed 19 January 2023. https://www.un.org/development/desa/pd/sites/www.un.org.development.desa.pd/files/wpp2022_summary_of_results.pdf.

Zukin, S., and J.S. Maguire. 2004. Consumers and consumption. *Annual Review of Sociology* 30: 173–197.

Part I

Halal Certification

2

Halal Certification in the United States and the Expansion of Halal Markets

Nurcan Atalan-Helicke

Introduction

Meat is one of the most regulated food items in the United States, due to food safety and sanitary concerns, the importance of "packer strikes," other elements of politics and everyday life, and—not least—the continued frequency of disease outbreaks[1] (Kantor 1976; Jacobs 1997;

I would like to thank Brook Heston for research assistance, Angela Warner for opening the doors of Church of St Vincent de Paul to visit the food bank, and Sayeed Noor for translation assistance.

[1] There are about 48 million cases of foodborne illnesses annually in the United States that affect almost one in six Americans each year. There are about 128,000 hospitalizations and 3,000 deaths. Several of these illnesses are attributed to meat and poultry products. (See Foodborne illness-causing organisms in the U.S. https://www.fda.gov/media/77727/download. Accessed 20 December 2021.) The economic burden, particularly health costs, associated with foodborne illness is estimated to be $90 billion (Scharff 2020).

N. Atalan-Helicke (✉)
Skidmore College, Environmental Studies and Sciences Program,
Saratoga Springs, NY, USA
e-mail: natalanh@skidmore.edu

© The Author(s), under exclusive license to Springer Nature Switzerland AG 2023
R. Turaeva, M. Brose (eds.), *Religious Economies in Secular Context*, New Directions in Islam, https://doi.org/10.1007/978-3-031-18603-5_2

Golan et al. 2004; Bennett et al. 2013; CDC 2021). Meat is also one of the most studied items in halal certification processes worldwide (Lever and Miele 2012; Fuseini et al. 2017; Majeed et al. 2019). There is an assumption for many Muslims living in non-Muslim-majority countries that nonmeat food products are inherently halal (Tayob 2020). There is a proliferation of voluntary standards, eco-labels, and social labels for consumer products particularly in the food industry (Starobin and Weinthal 2010). Some standards include quality requirements and credence attributes related to environmental and social interests. Certification may entail compliance with standards related to organic production (e.g., United States Department of Agriculture [USDA]), fair trade (e.g., Fair Trade), sustainability (e.g., Marine Stewardship Council), religious food laws (e.g., Islamic Food and Nutrition Council of America [IFANCA]), or requirements for a healthy diet (e.g., American Heart Association Certification Heart-Check Program). Religious food certification, such as kosher and halal, may also be perceived as an expression of "ethical" and "very safe" food (Della Corte et al. 2018). However, current debates about the organic certification of halal meat and poultry in the United States and the European Union raise interesting questions about the intersection of religious and secular food certification and about the governance of food certification.

In 2017, after a long alliance with a kosher certification agency (Star-K), two of the leading halal certification agencies in the United States, Islamic Food and Nutrition Council of America (IFANCA) and Islamic Services of America (ISA), have successfully secured a religious exemption and further clarification. Under the new standards, organic meat and poultry can also be labeled kosher and halal.[2,3] The decision

---

[2] USDA guarantees kosher and halal meat can be organic too. https://ofwlaw.com/usda-guarantees-kosher-halal-meat-can-organic/. Accessed 20 December 2021.

[3] As of December 2021, however, the debates in the European Union about ritual slaughter exemption from pre-stunning and its repercussions for animal welfare have not been resolved, and these debates have repercussions for halal and kosher meat and poultry to be organic certified in the European Union.

2 Halal Certification in the United States and the Expansion... 23

involves debates about the exemption of ritual slaughter from pre-stunning and how that fits with national regulations on animal welfare and raises several interesting questions: What is the intersection of the authority of certifying agents and state organic programs over review of records related to humane handling and slaughter issued by the federal and state authorities? What is the legacy of kosher regulation for halal certification in the United States? Why have kosher and halal certification agencies worked together for so long to affect the federal government decision? Are there different approaches to stunning among halal certification agencies? What are different concerns, if any, among halal certification agencies regarding animal welfare?

The USDA's statement recognized that requirements concerning animal welfare standards "would also not apply to ritual slaughter establishments (e.g., kosher or halal slaughter facilities) that are required to meet all the humane handling regulatory requirements except stunning prior to shackling, hoisting, throwing, cutting, or casting" (Federal Register 2017). It also recognized the authority of certifying agents and state organic programs to review records related to humane handling and slaughter (Federal Register 2017), which is foremost regulated by federal authorities. As in most Muslim minority countries, "the halal sector is not controlled by the government" in the United States (International Trade Center 2015: 29). However, halal slaughter facilities in the United States have to follow federal regulations so that halal-certified meat and poultry products can be sold commercially within the United States and for export. This is particularly important because the United States has been connected to global halal markets through food exports since the mid-1970s (International Trade Center 2015).[4]

---

[4] One such early company is Midamar Halal. https://midamarhalal.com/pages/about. Accessed 20 December 2021.

The United States exports halal meat to Organization of Islamic Cooperation countries (OIC)[5] and "halal certification has become a necessary, and indeed lucrative, component of international trade" (International Trade Center 2015: 2). Thus, there are a number of halal certification agencies in the United States catering to the interests of the business and the growing domestic Muslim population. These multiple private and nonprofit halal certification agencies cater to a very heterogenous Muslim population with diverse cultural, ethnic, and traditional backgrounds. Regardless of their backgrounds, many Muslims in the United States choose halal products over non-halal products. Changing demographics also expand market opportunities for halal food items. Indeed, multinational food companies such as Kentucky Fried Chicken (KFC), Burger King, and Taco Bell have all seen an increase in customers after being certified halal (Kagan et al. 2020). However, as "all matters relating to Islam have some inevitable social and political overtones, it is more difficult to view the halal market simply as a business opportunity" in the United States (International Trade Center 2015: 29). While the domestic market for halal products keeps growing in the United States, each certifying body is also connected to the global certification agencies. Certification usually takes 30 days, but it could take longer for more complex products and for completion of the additional compliance steps depending on the different country standards.[6]

This chapter examines the processes of halal certification of food in the United States, a Muslim minority country. With the changing demographics of the American Muslim population, and through the work of companies like Saffron Road, halal-certified food has become more visible and mainstream in the United States. As a food industry subsector, halal is still subject to the health and safety regulations at the federal and state levels. As of 2020, nine states have specific laws regulating halal to prohibit misrepresentations of halal and to ensure compliance with halal

---

[5] The United States is one of the top five non-OIC exporters of meat and live animals to OIC countries (Majeed et al. 2019).

[6] American Muslims can depend on halal food (US Embassy in Niger). https://ne.usembassy.gov/american-muslims-can-depend-on-halal-food/. Accessed 20 December 2021.

2 Halal Certification in the United States and the Expansion... 25

standards.[7] State-based halal protection laws often refer to the success of kosher protection laws in the United States (Minnesota Bill 2001). With over 300 certification agencies, kosher is well-institutionalized in the United States; the kosher industry, however, is also dominated by five certification agencies that develop and enforce industry standards (Lytton 2014). In contrast, the halal market is still a small and nascent segment of the American domestic market.

Compared to the total of $741 billion spent on food and beverages in 2014, halal food and beverage expenditures amounted to only about $12.7 billion (Latif 2016). Similar to the global trends showing that the halal market has expanded rapidly (Bergeaud-Blackler et al. 2016), there are positive economic predictions about the halal market in the United States (Technavio 2020). As the halal market in the United States expands, there are more calls to address regulatory gaps in the halal certification process and to streamline the process of halal certification.[8] These calls connect closely to the debates on the standardization of halal, where standardization can refer to several things as "part of the moral economy in the modern world" in which it "set[s] norms for behavior and create uniformity"; standardization also fulfils several roles and is used as an instrument of control, particularly in global trade (Lever and Fischer 2018: 11).

This chapter focuses on the broader context for halal meat regulation and certification and on state-specific halal protection laws. The aim is to understand the roles of the state, market, and other actors in the expansion of halal markets. In the United States, federal food safety regulations require halal certification agencies to work closely with state officials; the potential for exports also create opportunities for collaboration. Indeed, two US scholars, both affiliated with IFANCA, published the first guide to production and marketing of halal foods. Published in 2004, *Halal Food Production* is still widely used to understand and comply with the current transformation of halal (Bergeaud-Blackler et al. 2016). The

---

[7] These states are California, Illinois, Maryland, Michigan, Minnesota, New Jersey, New York, Texas, and Virginia (Alabsy 2020).

[8] Standardizing halal certification. American Halal Institute, https://americanhalalinstitute.com/standardizing-halal-certification/. Accessed 20 December 2021.

chapter argues that halal certification agencies address a broad range of issues: in contrast to the traditional view that halal was primarily related to slaughter methods, several certification agencies develop guidelines stipulating that "halal integrity must be maintained throughout the entire supply chain" (International Trade Center 2015). With the emergence of global trade, complex supply chains have now become the norm, and "the issues of end-to-end halal integrity have become increasingly important" (International Trade Center 2015). Whereas internal factors and increasing calls for integrating halal and *tayyib* (wholesome) are one of the main reasons, external factors including increasing concerns about animal welfare, pressure from animal welfare groups, and the rise of Islamophobia also urge halal certification agencies to pay more attention to end-to-end integrity (Armanios and Ergene 2018; Lever and Fischer 2018; Animal Welfare Institute 2019).

The findings of this chapter come from a literature review and a review of newsletters and online materials of halal certification agencies in the United States. The author reviewed the web-based materials of halal certification agencies that have been most active with a focus on the years 2014–2021: IFANCA, Islamic Services of America (ISA), Islamic Society of North America (ISNA),[9] Halal Food Council USA, and Halal Transactions of Omaha. The author also reviewed news stories and legislation from the states of New York, Texas, and Minnesota; conducted participant-observation in halal stores and supermarkets; and conducted participant-observation at a food bank serving Muslim refugees facing food insecurity. All fieldwork was undertaken in and around Albany, New York, during the spring and summer of 2021. Six of the stores were owned and operated by Muslim Americans (from South Asia and the Middle East); one was a national chain (Walmart); two were regional

---

[9] ISNA is an umbrella organization serving about 300 community and professional organizations in the United States and Canada. It expanded from the Muslim Students Association that was founded in 1963. ISNA met with the halal industry leaders in the United States in 2009 and initiated the American Halal Association, a trade association to promote institutionalization of the halal industry in the United States. It has taken the lead to become the American Halal Accreditation Body that would accredit and monitor halal certifying agencies in the United States (Halal Connect 2010). However, a current review suggests that American Halal Association no longer exists and that ISNA is no longer involved in halal certification.

Demographics of the Muslim Population in the United States

The demand for halal food began to increase in the United States from the 1960s as the Muslim student population grew (US Department of State 2012). The American Muslim population is estimated to be 3.85 million, comprising just 1.1% of the population as of 2020 (Pew Research Center 2021).[10] According to Islamic Services of America (2019), the halal market is expanding as the American Muslim population grows. Studies on consumption of halal in minority contexts argue that halal consumption is an expression of national, ethnic, minority, and consumer identity (Bonne and Verbeke 2008; Fischer 2011; Tayob 2020; Turaeva and Brose 2020). In 2018, American consumers spent $20 billion on halal food, a 33% increase from 2010. While supermarkets are the primary food distribution channel, halal sales through smaller grocery and convenience stores have also been increasing in the United States (Islamic Services of America 2019). The expansion of halal sales can be understood "as a process of institutionalization, rationalization and late-modern expert intervention" (Tayob 2020: 324). It can also be approached through the rising purchasing power of the consumers and increasing preference of Muslim American consumers for precooked and convenience foods. The halal food market in the United States is estimated to grow by $8.17 billion during 2020–2024, and the demand for halal meat, which is perceived to be healthier than other meat in the markets, is also expected to grow in the same period (Technavio 2020).

The changing characteristics of the American Muslim population also shape the growth dynamics of halal markets in the United States. According to Pew research reports, over 80% of American Muslims are

---

[10] There is no official government count of the Muslim population, and the United States Census Bureau does not ask questions about religion. There are several estimates about the Muslim population in the United States. Some halal certification agencies estimate the American Muslim population to be over 6 million, according to Halal Transactions of Omaha. https://halaltransactions.org/our-services/. Accessed 20 December 2021.

US citizens and about one-fourth are native born (Pew Research Center 2017; see also Lipka 2017). Among immigrant Muslims, about half have arrived since 2000. There are clusters of ethnic groups in different cities or states due to chain migration (e.g., Twin Cities, Minnesota; Dearborn, Michigan), but there is no single country of origin that accounts for a majority of American Muslims. Thus, they are racially, ethnically, and culturally diverse (Pew Research Center 2018). Demographically, they exhibit some similarities as well as differences to the non-Muslim population: Muslims are younger compared to the overall population—one-third of American Muslims are between the ages of 18 and 29; but marriage rates and family sizes are similar. Just over 50% of American Muslims are married, similar to the US average (Pew Research Center 2017), with 2.4 children per married couple. The broadest strokes of religious observance appear similar for immigrant and US-born Muslims: They exhibit similar levels of religious observance—"people in both groups are about equally likely to attend religious services at least once a week"—both US-born and immigrant Muslims have high levels of pride in their religious identity; and about half of each group state that "eating halal food is essential to being a Muslim" (Pew Research Center 2018). In terms of socioeconomic characteristics, immigrant Muslims are more likely to have a college degree than US-born Muslims Americans: 38% have a college or post-graduate degree (Pew Research Center 2018).[11] However, there is an income gap among American Muslims: While 24% of American Muslims have incomes over $100,000, similar to U.S. general public, 40% of all American Muslims have incomes lower than $30,000, higher than U.S. general public (Pew Research Center 2018).[12]

---

[11] Immigrant Muslims are better off, collectively, compared to US-born Muslims. They are more likely to own a home and have a college degree (Pew Research Center 2018).

[12] Low incomes within the Muslim population seem to have several explanations. One is related to the differences of US-born and immigrant Muslims, in which religion intersects with race. That is, African Americans "make up a much larger share of US-born Muslims than of Muslim immigrants" and accordingly are "less likely than people of other races to have a college degree or to make at least $100,000 in household income" (Pew Research Center 2018). Another explanation is related to the composition of the immigrant Muslim population. Some are refugees but probably far fewer than many readers would expect. The admission of Muslim refugees has been subject to fluctuations due to federal level political decisions on the refugees admitted and their country of origins as well as US priorities. The highest annual number of Muslim refugees, 38,900 people, entered in 2016; a majority of whom were from Syria (Pew Research Center 2019).

The young and diverse Muslim American population is also tech-savvy and brand conscious. While they participate in American lifestyles, they also "feel connected to a multinational audience through their part in the *Ummah*, the global Muslim nation" (Goodman 2015). As in other minority contexts, particularly middle-class Muslim, consumers survey halal information, check applications, conduct their own search, and regulate their own halal consumption (Tayob 2020). The youthful demographics mean that social media and Internet-based marketing "has increasingly become [an] influential and effective method" for successful marketing and expansion of halal markets. Indeed, Saffron Road's entire marketing strategy was "carried out through social media interaction with existing and potential customers" (International Trade Center 2015: 39).

Halal Accreditation Agencies

As the halal market expands in the United States, there are more organizations that certify food as halal. In the context of practices seen in the United States, the understanding of halal is plural and has a structure prioritizing trade development.[13] There are several halal certification organizations that have been operating in the United States since the early 1970s, including IFANCA (est. 1980), Islamic Society of North America (ISNA) (est. 1982–1983), Islamic Services of America (est. 1975), Islamic Society of Washington Area (ISWA) (est. 1973), Halal Certification Services USA (est. 2015), Halal Transactions of Omaha (est. 1992), USA Halal Chamber of Commerce (started halal certification in 1997, and endorsed by ISWA), and Halal Food Council (est. 1984) (Halal Connect 2009; USA Halal Chamber 2021).

The organizations established in the 1970s and 1980s have been connected to a mosque, Islamic center, or nonprofit organization serving the Muslim communities in their local area. These halal certification organizations have multiple goals: while the main goal is to "address the needs

---

[13] Halal regulations in the United States of America. https://english.hak.gov.tr/international-relations/halal-regulations-by-country/americas/united-states-of-america. Accessed 20 December 2021.

of the Muslim community" and to allow them "to live within the bounds of their faith," several have been engaged in initiatives to create an awareness and advocacy network so that Muslim consumers can demand halal alternatives from institutions, including the school system, hospitals, and prisons (Islamic Services of America 2020b; American Halal Institute 2021; Islamic Horizons 2021a). Some of these organizations also provide education and training to businesses, state officials, and consumers through workshops, fairs, conferences, and public lectures to promote halal products and services and to ensure compliance (Halal Focus 2011; IFANCA 2014; American Halal Institute 2021). Halal certification agencies, thus, play several roles. They act as a link between the halal producer and the halal-sensitive consumer. They also function as a supply chain partner in the halal producer's (quality assurance) value chain (Bergeaud-Blackler et al. 2016).

A few halal certification agencies also publish Islamic books in English or their own magazines and advocate for establishing a sharia-compliant public fund system to address the needs of the Muslim community broadly (American Halal Institute 2021; Islamic Horizons 2021b). In doing so, the halal certification organizations recognize the power of the Muslim consumers in making decisions about what they trust, but they also want to transform Muslims' consumption patterns. For instance, IFANCA, which prides itself for being "a global leader in halal certification and education," organizes international halal food conferences for the industry to discuss technical aspects of halal and the global state of halal certification. In recent years, it has also organized a Halal Lifestyle Festival (IHeartHalal™) in conjunction with an international halal conference to promote "halal food, fashion, beauty, health & wellness, sports & fitness, banking & finance, and travel products and service" (IFANCA 2018). According to IFANCA, the halal lifestyle festival serves consumers "who are embracing both their modernity and their faith in their purchasing decisions" and allows them to "meet and interact with producers and vendors of the products and services they seek and buy" (IFANCA 2018).

While Muslim consumers still rely on traditional trust networks as in other Muslim minority contexts (Tayob 2020), the presence of a halal logo, regardless of the company that produced the product, indicates that

2 Halal Certification in the United States and the Expansion...

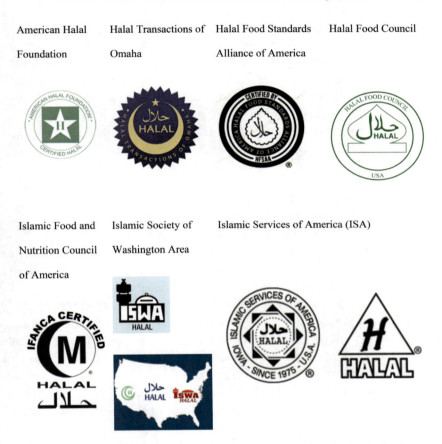

Fig. 2.1 Halal logos issued by halal certification agencies in the United States

consumers are more likely to purchase that product (Hashim and Hashim 2013). For customers, halal certification means that "they are able to access the convenience of public consumption," while for business it means that "they are able to compete in a world of increasingly complex local and global trade" (Tayob 2020: 337). Labeling and packaging are "important marketing issues" (International Trade Center 2015: 39).

American halal certification organizations offer different logos for their certification process, several of which use Arabic halal in the logo (Fig. 2.1). As Lever and Fischer (2018) explain, marking commodities with halal logos helps to personalize the exchange among the producer, trader, and consumer. While "the trader not only profits but also claims a measure of authority," the consumer and trader also share the symbolic content of the halal logo (Lever and Fischer 2018: 12). In restaurants and grocery stores where a wide variety of food options are served, visual representations of the halal logo provided by the halal certification agencies signify assurance of halal compliance (Kagan et al. 2020). However, the "lack of clear and transparent regulatory frameworks, and differences of opinion and interpretations" means that it may not be "always clear what a halal logo—or lack of it—actually represents" (International Trade Center 2015: 30). In small ethnic food environments, customers still rely on the personal trust relationships with the butcher and the shop owner rather than the requirement of a visual halal logo (Kagan et al. 2020). Yet, state-specific halal protection laws require even small establishments in the states with these rules (e.g., New York, Minnesota, Texas) to have clear and visual representations of the logo on their premises.

Halal certification agencies, like Islamic Services of America, also encourage the display of a 'visible Halal-certified logo' on product labels. Islamic Services of America (2020a) states that if the logo is not visible on the packaging, then "even when a product is certified Halal, it doesn't benefit the consumer." International Trade Center (2015) suggests considering halal product labels more carefully, instead of just using Arabic halal. Indeed, ISA uses three different logo options to choose from, explaining the differences between two of them: while "the standard circle seal is globally recognized and recommended," the letter "H" in a triangle with or without "Halal" inscribed beneath is more "subtle and usable in [the] domestic USA market" (Fig. 2.1). Islamic Services of America further encourages the display of a halal logo on packaging as it provides "another line of traceability of Halal standards" and provides "ease of purchase for consumers."

The use of multiple logos by Islamic Services of America and its suggestion for a 'more subtle' logo to use in the domestic market raises interesting questions. While it connects to the political and cultural context of halal certification in Muslim minority contexts, it can also help explain why some businesses may be hesitant about advertising their operations as

2 Halal Certification in the United States and the Expansion... 33

halal in the American domestic market.[14] They may worry about backlash and Islamophobia if they use a halal logo and announce that their operations are halal certified. Islamophobia can be defined as "a hostile attitude or behavior toward Muslims" (Çiftçi 2012: 3). Hate crimes directed to the halal industry in other Muslim minority countries, such as boycotts against halal-certified companies in Australia, or false claims about the unhealthiness of halal food in Europe can cause economic damage to companies. Several studies focused on the connection of Islamophobia to economic activities and halal markets in other countries, including Australia (Etri and Yucel 2016), Brazil, and New Zealand (Husseini de Araujo 2021). Misinformation campaigns on social media can also lead to lobbying against ritual slaughter and blocking ritual slaughter exemption from receiving other food labels (Ruiz-Bejarano 2017). Studies about Islamophobia in Western Europe and the United States discuss how different narratives helped construct Muslim immigrant identities as an antagonistic other in the West after 9/11, as an economic liability, and as not belonging culturally (Çiftçi 2012). However, there is a need for further research on how Islamophobia impacts halal economies, as halal food is not only marketed to Muslim consumers who exclusively prefer halal but also to a diverse community of non-Muslim consumers.

Turaeva and Brose (2020) suggest that halal has become like a brand appealing "directly to Muslims, but also increasingly to non-Muslims who seek pure, fresh products" (p. 296). Certainly, halal food consumption is increasing among young non-Muslim American millennials as "a healthier dietary alternative to fast food" (Halawa 2018: 57). Similarly,

---

[14] See, for example, You might be eating halal meat and not even know it. https://www.npr.org/sections/thesalt/2018/04/05/599520906/you-might-be-eating-halal-meat-and-not-even-know-it, 5 April 2018. Accessed 20 December 2021.

One of the largest lamb producers in the United States, Superior Lamb, slaughters and prepares all of its products as halal, but the company's website makes no mention of this. The company, which prides itself on "sustainably raised American lamb," provides lamb and goat to small ethnic grocery stores as well as grocery chains through three different brands (Superior Farms 2021). While initially halal slaughtering took place only one day a week in its Denver plant and slaughtering facility in California, after some time, the company converted all its operations to be halal. There are four practicing Muslims who slaughter the animals (Clyma 2016). One explanation for the switch was the increased burden to maintain inventory segregation and to avoid cross-contamination in the facility. The company switched all its operations to be halal certified as the halal slaughter did not slow their operations. However, the company's website does not announce its halal certification (Superior Farms 2021).

Adnan Durrani, the founder and CEO of American Halal Company, which is the parent company of Saffron Road, says a majority of people who buy their products are non-Muslim (Winston 2019). The success of Saffron Road to mainstream halal food demonstrates that the halal certification agencies and companies want to cater to any consumer regardless of faith, gender, ethnicity, nationality, or race and to give the message that anyone can "eat halal" and "lead a halal lifestyle" (Islamic Services of America 2021a).[15] Halal certification serves as a sign of quality and halal signifies that not only a certain set of standards is in line with Islamic law but also that food concerns related to health, environment, and quality are met (Olya and Al-Ansi 2018; Kagan et al. 2020).

The halal certification organizations in the United States follow slightly different criteria for halal certification than in some other countries. This diversity is due to the rules they must follow at the federal, state, and local government levels (e.g., ritual slaughter), the interpretive legal traditions they follow (i.e., Islamic schools), as well as the requirements of any global halal accreditation agencies with which they work. As Kurth and Glasbergen (2017) discuss through the case study of the Netherlands, halal certification organizations are aware of their own differences. Differences in meat certification and ritual slaughter have been one of the main topics that halal certification agencies have dealt with since their establishment. In the United States, meat slaughter is regulated at the federal level by the Food Safety and Inspection Service (FSIS), a public health agency within the United States Department of Agriculture (USDA).

Federal and State Level Regulations

Federal Meat Regulations

The United States has enforced federal level food regulations since 1865 to ensure the safety of commercially sold meat. The first agency, the Bureau of Animal Industry, had an initial function to prevent diseased

---

[15] Indeed, Islamic Services of America (2021b) suggests that "combining a Halal certification with other guarantees" can help a product stand out and thrive in diverse markets, particularly by attracting "younger consumers, Muslim, and non-Muslim alike."

2 Halal Certification in the United States and the Expansion... 35

animals from being sold as food. In 1906, with the Federal Meat Inspection Act (FMIA), the United States government placed federal inspectors in slaughterhouses for the first time. It was common for livestock to be cut by local butchers and sold locally in the early 1900s. After the Second World War, the US meat processing industry changed significantly. With the expansion of the poultry industry and development of refrigerated trucks, the Bureau of Animal Industry evolved into the Food Safety and Inspection Service (FSIS). Today, FSIS oversees "the processing, labeling, and packaging of commercial meat, poultry and egg products" (Harris et al. 2019: 10). Both FMIA and FSIS are under the authority of the US Department of Agriculture. The regulations expanded with the Poultry Products Inspection Act in 1957 to handle the expanding market for ready-to-cook and processed poultry products. Similarly, the 1967 Wholesome Meat Act and 1968 Wholesome Poultry Products Act defined the handling of meat products. These programs expanded the mandate of federal programs and required state level programs to be "at least equal to federal requirements" (Harris et al. 2019: 11).

Federal and state level regulations matter in relation to what are called 'amenable' and 'non-amenable' animals and products as these specify the authority to which they will be subjected. There are categorizations for domestic animals which are subject to USDA authority for slaughtering and processing. For instance, domestic livestock products "amenable to the USDA under FMIA are prepared from cattle, sheep, swine, goats, horses, mules, and other equines."[16] Amenable animals are more or less defined the same across states: For instance, in New York, amenable meat must be "slaughtered under USDA inspection," and these include cattle, sheep, swine, goats, horses, mules, and other equines, and the law also applies to the inspection of their carcasses and parts. In the state of New York, these animals must be processed at a USDA- or New York State-licensed facility that oversees food safety regulations. Food products from exotic animals, categorized as non-amenable species, are not subject

---

[16] "Livestock products amenable to the Federal Meat Inspection Act are prepared from cattle, sheep, swine, goats, horses, mules, and other equines. Poultry products amenable to the Poultry Products Inspection Act are prepared from domesticated chickens, turkeys, ducks, geese, ratites, and squabs. Egg products amenable to the Egg Products Inspection Act are prepared from shell eggs of domesticated chickens, turkeys, ducks, geese, and guineas" (USDA 2021).

to inspection under the FMIA. These non-amenable or 'exotic' species, as defined in federal law, include animals such as farm-raised deer, elk, bison, water buffalo, antelope, and rabbit and are subject to voluntary inspection by the Food and Drug Administration (FDA).[17] However, to legally sell the meat of non-amenable species, they also must be slaughtered and processed either at a USDA-inspected facility or a state licensed/registered processing facility and follow Good Manufacturing Practices (as specified in the Code of Federal Regulations) (Harris et al. 2019).[18]

For amenable species, federal level inspection by the USDA combines visual inspection of carcasses and periodic laboratory testing with a preventative program known as Hazard Analysis and Critical Control Point (HACCP) for all stages of processing. Under HACCP, the plant operator must identify all food safety and hygiene critical points along the processing and handling route. Federal inspection involves examination of animals prior to slaughter to ensure that diseased animals are slaughtered separately and that their carcasses are subject to a careful examination and inspection. Federal inspection also requires amenable animals to be slaughtered humanely (US Code 2014) according to the Humane Methods of Slaughter Act (HMSA) that originally passed in 1958 (see also USDA 1978). Through the inspection of meat and poultry products, the federal government aims to:

1) prevent the sale of adulterated, contaminated, or otherwise unsafe livestock products; 2) prevent misbranding; 3) ensure the safety of consumers by establishing minimum standards for the production, slaughter, processing, and marketing of these products; and 4) create a system of licensing, inspection and labeling to trace a product back to its origin if a public health problem should arise. (Harris et al. 2019: 11)

---

[17] Updates to the exotic animals eligible for voluntary inspection. https://www.fsis.usda.gov/policy/fsis-notice/46-21. Accessed 2 April 2022.

[18] While farm-raised game animals can be sold commercially, hunter-harvested game may not be sold commercially in New York. For poultry (including domesticated chicken, turkey, ducks, geese, guinea hen, and squab), there is an exemption for facilities processing and selling no more than 1,000 birds. The farmer who raises the animal can slaughter, process, and sell such poultry and products fresh or frozen without USDA inspection. (Harris et al. 2019)

2 Halal Certification in the United States and the Expansion... 37

Federally inspected slaughterhouse meat can be sold without restrictions anywhere and to anyone in the United States. FSIS seeks "to ensure that meat and poultry products for human consumption are safe, wholesome, and correctly marked, labeled, and packaged if they move into interstate or international commerce" (Institute of Medicine and National Research Council Committee 1998: 27).[19]

Ritual Slaughter Exemption

At the federal level, the First Amendment of the United States Constitution guarantees freedom of religion. In the context of food processing, this means that government agencies such as the USDA or FDA have to guarantee exemptions when it pertains to halal food. A ritual slaughter amendment was added to the original HMSA of 1958. The HMSA spells out that "the handling or other preparation of livestock for ritual slaughter are exempted" from the law's requirements (Animal Welfare Institute 2019). This exemption allows ritual slaughter facilities to perform a ritual slaughter without stunning, while they are still subject to all other humane handling requirements (Harris et al. 2019). While all halal slaughterhouses have to follow federally mandated food safety and hygiene standards, there is no federal mandatory labeling and certification for halal meat, and all halal standards are defined and audited by third-party certification organizations (Kagan et al. 2020).

In terms of halal meat certification in the United States, there are nuances as followed by different halal certification organizations: IFANCA, accredited by Indonesia, Malaysia, Singapore, and United Arab Emirates certification agencies (IFANCA 2021a), certifies meat

---

[19] FSIS shares federal authority with the Food and Drug Administration (FDA), another federal agency, which has authority under the Federal Food, Drug, and Cosmetic Act over food in interstate commerce (e.g., between New York and Texas) unless regulated by FSIS (Harris et al. 2019). There is a jurisdictional split along commodity lines: All amenable meat and products are subject to USDA authority. Thus, a pepperoni pizza will be subject to USDA authority, while a cheese pizza will be subject to FDA authority. Similarly, a canned poultry baby food product with product will be subject to USDA regulation (USDA 2005). In general, FDA has jurisdiction over domestic and imported foods that are marketed in interstate commerce, except for meat and poultry products.

products with a "Five Star Halal Identification System." This system gives consumers information about the practices used in the preparation of the meat: (1) The animal was slaughtered by a Muslim and following IFANCA's standard slaughter procedure. (2) The animal was slaughtered by a traditional horizontal cut across the neck. (3) The animals were fed an all-natural diet of plant origin. (4) The plant and slaughterhouse met animal welfare guidelines. (5) The animal was not stunned prior to or after the cut on the neck for bleeding purposes (IFANCA 2021b). Although controversial,[20] some certifying agencies allow stunning because most halal slaughterhouses in North America "use some form of stunning before slaughter" and "the impermissibility of the act of stunning does not influence the lawfulness of the animal which was stunned and does not necessarily mean that all stunned animals are also unlawful to consume" (Halal Food Standards Alliance of America 2021). Thus, from the perspective of these halal certification agencies, the legal status of an animal which has been stunned is dependent on whether the animal was alive at the time of slaughter.

Another halal certification body, Halal Food Council USA is accredited by Indonesia Ulema Council (MUI) and also follows FAO Codex halal standards to allow export. Halal Food Council USA goes through the meat and poultry certification process by inspecting "the facility to determine the compliance (of product, ingredients, equipment, production process, sanitation procedures, packaging, labeling, storage, and transportation) through halal standards, checking for possibility of cross-contamination." After registering the plant/slaughterhouse as a "bonafide Halal Slaughter Plant," it requires the presence and assignment of a

---

[20] The exemption of ritual slaughter from stunning is also a concern for animal rights activists (Animal Welfare Institute 2019). Use of stunning is controversial from a religious perspective. While there are numerous types of stunning (e.g., pneumatic stunner which delivers a blow to the head of the animal, captive bolt pistol which shatters the brain of the animal, electric water through which delivers an electric shock to poultry), some are irreversible, and the animal will die if it is not slaughtered within a few minutes. In theory, reversible methods of stunning would allow the animal to get up and walk around if not slaughtered in a few minutes. From a religious perspective, one concern about stunning is that it causes extra pain to the animal, above and beyond the pain experienced during the slaughter itself. However, from an animal welfare perspective, stunning and rendering the animal unconscious before slaughter is perceived to be more humane than its non-stun counterpart (Chaudry 2015, n.d.; Farouk et al. 2016; Pufpaff et al. 2018; Animal Welfare Institute 2019).

2 Halal Certification in the United States and the Expansion... 39

Muslim slaughter man "to perform the necessary procedures in accordance with the Islamic slaughter method."[21] However, in the application form, there is no specific mention of stunning or the animal's diet when it was alive.

ISA, accredited by several international halal accreditation agencies, including JAKIM (Malaysia), MUI (Indonesia), MUIS (Singapore), and World Halal Council, follows a "hard line approach" reflecting "accountability to Allah SWT" in its halal meat certification. ISA emphasizes humane treatment as well as standard USDA supervision. ISA procedures suggest that, in halal slaughter of an animal and poultry, "mercy should be practiced from beginning till end, knife must be sharpened so the animal does not feel prolonged pain, the slaughter cannot be performed in front of other animals, tasmia must be recited." ISA only accepts "capable Muslim slaughtermen" to complete the slaughtering process and thus halal certification process (ISA 2021b).

Some halal certification agencies are very careful about other activities in the processing facility and potential for cross-contamination. Halal Transactions of Omaha, also accredited by Indonesia MUI, asks very specific questions about the cross-contamination in the facility (e.g., type of animal and animal products to be processed, alcohol use,[22] and cross-contamination) as well as food safety certifications of the facility (e.g., HACCP) and inspections by federal authorities (e.g., Food and Drug Administration and United States Department of Agriculture).[23] There are specific questions about other certifications (e.g., organic) and the type of stunning used; however, the need for the presence of a Muslim person to slaughter the animals is not emphasized in the application. While none of the certification agencies emphasize the point, a general

---

[21] https://halalfoodcouncilusa.com/about/. Accessed 20 December 2021.

[22] Alcohol is one of the prohibited items in Islam. However, 0.1% alcohol in finished product standard has been used by IFANCA (Regenstein et al. 2003) and other halal communities, such as MUI. While it does not certify any alcoholic drinks as halal, irrespective of the alcohol content present (e.g., non-alcoholic beer would not be certified as halal), ethanol and ethyl alcohol presence in 0.1% amount is considered an "unavoidable impurity" in the manufacturing process. (See Synopsis on alcohol. Halal Digest, https://ifanca.org/HalalDigestNewsLetter/September%20 HD%202011/September%20HD%202011.htm. Accessed 20 December 2021.)

[23] https://bluecactustech.com/wp-content/uploads/2020/06/HTO-FRM-01-Application-for--Halal-Services.pdf. Accessed 20 December 2021.

understanding of halal criteria is that the blood of the animal must be completely drained before butchering may occur (Fischer 2016; Kagan et al. 2020).

The insistence that "the slaughter facility must be a United States Department of Agriculture (USDA) inspected one" is important for understanding compliance with federal level regulations. As certification bodies make approvals based on their own specific standards, USDA labeling indicates that the food or other agricultural product has been produced through the federal government's approved methods. The specific inspections[24] related to ritual slaughter exemptions are also outlined in revisions of FSIS in 2011 (Harris et al. 2019). These inspections allow accountability and transparency as well as traceability in case of a food recall (Brougher and Greene 2011). However, state level regulations about ritual slaughter and the absence of a designated halal slaughter facility may complicate practices. For instance, in Minnesota, there is no designated halal slaughtering facility, but only a few "custom exempt, equal to, and USDA-inspected slaughterhouses" have filed paperwork to perform halal slaughter (Kagan et al. 2020). In New York, state-level exemptions for direct marketing allow producers to have animals slaughtered on their farm following ritual practices for "personal use" after the consumer purchases the animal. This is exempt from USDA inspection (Harris et al. 2019). However, it is important to remember that any meat subject to commercial distribution and sale in the United States is subject to federal level regulation. Multiple states have enacted statutes in recent years to regulate the labeling and sale of halal food and to prevent deceptive practices.

State Halal Protection Laws

There are nine states in the United States (California, Illinois, Maryland, Michigan, Minnesota, New Jersey, New York, Texas, and Virginia) with specific halal food protection laws. These laws emphasize the protection

---

[24] All amenable animals slaughtered and processed for human consumption are subject to ante-mortem and post-mortem inspections by FSIS (Brougher and Greene 2011).

2 Halal Certification in the United States and the Expansion... 41

of Muslim consumers and specify which businesses may use the word halal without the verification of a certifying agency. Rejection of certification is coupled with the explanation that trust and word-of-mouth are key to the halal sector (Kagan et al. 2020). However, the arguments in favor of state-level bills for halal food protection laws reflect on the benefits of additional protection that kosher laws provide to the Jewish community. They also give reference to the increasing Muslim population in that particular state and the need "to protect the interests of the Muslim community by preserving the integrity of Islamic dietary (halal) requirements" (Minnesota Bill 2001). Regulation from three states, New York, Minnesota, and Texas, illustrates these state-specific processes.

All three states have significant Muslim populations for whom halal food is important. For instance, Texas is known for the availability of masjids and restaurants serving halal food from touristic websites addressed to American Muslim travelers.[25] New York is known for popularizing halal food through food carts.[26] These three states have also integrated halal food into hospital and higher education dining hall systems, complementing the wide availability of halal food in the retail and food service industries.[27] There are also farm-to-fork fresh and local halal food options available in these three states (Krishna 2019; Kagan et al. 2020; New Hira Halal 2021; Halal Pastures 2021). Both Texas and New York have more than 1300 restaurants, more than any other state, listed on the Zabihah website.[28] Both Texas and New York are also top refugee settlement states (not limited to Muslims) (Pew Research Center 2019). Minnesota has the largest Somali immigrant community in the United States, while it hosts other Muslim populations of Middle Eastern, North African, South Asian, and Southeast Asian descent (Kagan et al. 2020).

---

[25] Houston visitors' guide for Muslim travelers. https://www.hijabiglobetrotter.com/houston-visitors-guide-for-muslim-travelers/. Accessed 20 December 2021.

[26] Halal Guys started in 1990. It has 100 franchises open all across the United States and plans to open 400 more. http://fransmart.com/The-Halal-Guys/. Accessed 20 December 2021.

[27] Minnesota hospital adds halal options to patient menu. https://www.healthcarefacilitiestoday.com/posts/Minnesota-Hospital-Adds-Halal-Options-To-Patient-Menu%2D%2D25113, 8 September 2020; Halal food is now available at 11 more public schools. https://www.ny1.com/nyc/all-boroughs/news/2021/05/17/halal-food-is-now-available-at-11-more-public-schools, 17 May 2021. Both accessed 20 December 2021.

[28] See https://www.zabihah.com/com/media. Accessed 20 December 2021.

42 N. Atalan-Helicke

The laws in these three states demonstrate the range of liabilities of actors in the American halal food industry. There are several states without specific halal protection laws, but companies selling or certifying halal products may be liable under a state's general consumer protection statutes for selling mislabeled food.[29] While Texas and Minnesota laws specifically address the responsibilities of actors related to labeling and sale of halal food items, New York law also requires record keeping about halal certification.

Minnesota's halal food protection law was enacted into law in 2001. It applies to all the actors involved in the production and specifies that the processing and distribution of halal food relies on "good faith on the representation of the slaughterhouse, manufacturer, processor, packer, distributor, or person or organization which certifies food as being prepared under Islamic traditions" (Minnesota Bill 2001). The Minnesota law prohibits a person from serving, selling, or exposing for sale food, meat, or poultry falsely represented as halal. According to the Minnesota law, a food item cannot be labeled as halal, "unless it has been prepared and maintained in accordance to the laws and customs of the Islamic religion." The law also prohibits a person from making "an oral or written statement that deceives or leads a person to believe that non-halal food, meat, or poultry is indeed halal" (Minnesota Bill 2001). The law prohibits a person from willfully marking, stamping, tagging, branding, labeling, or "otherwise identify[ing] or caus[ing] to be identified as halal food that is not halal," and it outlines repercussions for willfully removing, altering, or destroying "the original halal sign, tag, or other means of identification affixed to food, meat, or poultry to indicate that the foods are halal." Another concern is about fraud, and the Minnesota law also has provisions that

> a person shall not knowingly sell, dispose of, or possess for the purpose of resale as halal any food, meat, or poultry that does not have the original, or contains a fraudulently affixed, halal sign, mark, stamp, tag, brand, label, or other means of identification.

---

[29] Cullen, Jeanne, and Furqan Mohammed. 2017. US halal food regulations. https://www.foodnavigator-usa.com/Article/2016/04/11/GUEST-ARTICLE-US-halal-food-regulations-Are-you-up-to-speed. Accessed 20 December 2021.

2 Halal Certification in the United States and the Expansion... 43

The New York Halal Food Protection Act took effect in 2005. It is one of the several sections of The Laws of New York under Chapter 69 (Agriculture and Markets), Article 17 (which pertains to "Adulteration, Packing and Branding of Food and Food Products") (New York Senate 2021). The New York Halal Food Production Act requires certain businesses and individuals to register or file certified information with the New York State Department of Agriculture and Markets. Similar to Minnesota law, it applies to a range of actors involved in the food system, including manufacturers and packers that produce and distribute food, as well as to food carts and caterers that sell food prepared on their premises or under their control. New York State has established a Division of Halal Enforcement under its Department of Agriculture and Markets and provides a halal registry for information by product name, certifier, or food establishment. The New York Halal Food Protection Act requires any person who sells both halal and non-halal food items to indicate to their customers at a location readily visible, such as "in [a] window sign, in block letters at least four inches in height," that "halal and non-halal meat [are] sold here" or that "halal and non-halal food items [are] sold here." According to the law, all food items must have a halal label affixed to them, and manufacturers, producers, packers, and distributors "must register their company with the Department and file the name, address and phone number of the person (e.g., individual, corporation, association, or organization), who certifies the food as halal" (New York Law 2020). Moreover, New York law specifically asks for the statement of qualifications for the halal certification agency's "background, training, experience, and any other information that justifies their qualification" in the case of certifiers of non-prepackaged food. New York law also requires record keeping for invoices and bills by the wholesale and retail firms selling halal food for a period of two years (New York Law 2005).

Texas passed House Bill 470 Subchapter 1 on Labeling, Advertising, and Sale of Halal Foods in 2003. The Texas law requires any company that sells halal and non-halal meat "to label each portion of halal meat with the word halal." According to Texas law, a person commits an offense if he or she knowingly sells meat that is not labeled appropriately. The law covers the sale of meat at restaurants as well. Moreover, a person is prohibited from 'knowingly or intentionally' selling a product that is misrepresented as halal, and "the person either knows the food is not halal food or was reckless about determining whether or not the food is halal food." Texas Law specifies that the violations of the law are subject to fines (Texas Bill 2003).

The state level consumer protection laws for halal-certified food products described above highlight the role of individual states in promoting consumer rights and business obligations regarding halal products. While they bring awareness about the halal products and certification process, they also aim to ensure the safety of Muslim consumers, both 'spiritual and physical.' In consuming food products, consumers are dependent on the information and the true representation of that information of these food products (Hermawan 2020). While the government of the United States has minimal interference with the halal industry, as the history of kosher protection laws in the United States demonstrate, government regulation can effectively satisfy demands for better consumer protection (Lytton 2014).

Growing Pains: Reaching to National and Global Markets

While there are federal level assurances to regulate meat to address food safety and humane handling concerns, there are also state level assurances for the consumers regarding sale and labeling of halal products. Unlike multicultural Muslim-majority contexts, such as Malaysia, where the state has taken the lead in pioneering standards and certifications, there is no specific oversight or accreditation for halal certification organizations at the federal level in the United States. Independent halal certification agencies can control the entire process of defining, auditing, and certifying domestic and export products (International Trade Center 2015). However, as the interest in the halal market grows, it exposes the gaps in the regulatory system, and several halal certification organizations advocate for standardization of halal processes. The standardization processes are connected to the consolidation and expansion of an audit culture around halal practice. While audit and inspection systems are a

2 Halal Certification in the United States and the Expansion... 45

feature of modern societies, they also "connect Islam, state and markets in novel ways" (Bergeaud-Blackler et al. 2016: 9). The American Halal Institute (2021) argues that "it is crucial for the American Muslim community to have a standardized system for halal certification" and to "streamline the process for consumers, manufacturers, suppliers and distributors alike." Similarly, Halal Food Standards Alliance of America (2021) promotes "higher and inclusive halal standards to accommodate all Muslims." IFANCA has been organizing halal food technical conferences since 1999 to address current and future issues of halal compliance and market development, as well as to offer "experiences and insight into the evolution of the market and regulations" (IFANCA 2018). The goals of the conference remind those of the World Halal Forum, a transnational economic forum organized annually by Malaysia. These international conferences were crucial in "intensified regulation and scientification of halal," particularly by the Malaysian state (Fischer 2016).

Standardization is presented as a solution to ease international trade, particularly among Organization of Islamic Cooperation countries (Halim and Salleh 2012). The fragmentation of the global halal industry due to differing halal standards between and within countries (as well as disagreements on animal meat, slaughtering methods, packaging, and logistics) is presented as a barrier to the further expansion of halal markets. Indeed, more than 30 countries signed a resolution at the World Halal Forum in 2006 to establish the International Halal Integrity Alliance and to have "mutual recognition of certificates issued by the respective certification agencies" in their respective countries. Some post-Soviet countries have adopted this resolution to be "exempt from re-certification" when they engage in trade among themselves (Botoeva 2020: 381). Standardization is market driven, but it is also contested (Bergeaud-Blackler et al. 2016): Halal standards are part of "global assemblages" and cannot be reduced to "a single logic" (Fischer 2016: 51). To be able to work closely with halal certification agencies, a business needs to be flexible and open to audit culture. Examining Nestlé, a global company that is "a respected and trusted company" with internal halal assurance, Fischer (2016) argues that processes of standardization create challenges for companies and that companies are "rationalized to deal with these challenges" (p. 51). For instance, Nestlé has developed and refined Islamic technoscientific solutions. While it adapted to increasing halal requirements in Malaysia, it was able to carry these experiences to a global level. However, this also occurred because the company has a long history of halal policy and compliance and was flexible (Fischer 2016).

As explained above, halal certification agencies in the United States are accredited by multiple global organizations. These accreditations can provide guidance and credibility for halal certification for global markets. However, there is fragmentation among companies that cater to the global and national markets. Cargill and American Foods Group are the largest halal meat exporters to Organization of Islamic Conference countries. In the domestic market, the key players are Al Safa Foods (one of the most established halal foods brands in the United States), Crescent Halal (one of the largest manufacturers of processed chicken in the United States), Midamar (a company operating since mid-1970s that has hundreds of distribution locations and, now, an online presence), and Saffron Road (one of the fastest growing halal food brands with dozens of frozen entrée food products) (Latif 2016).

There are also some retail companies in the United States that focus on both national and global markets. For example, Elevation Burger, a fast-growing organic fast food restaurant, has restaurant chains in major American cities and more than ten international locations. Indeed, halal market research emphasizes the potential to expand into global markets and suggests American companies to focus both on national and global markets. There is further potential to expand into organic markets, but in terms of barriers, these research bodies also emphasize the need to consolidate among small players "to create cost-efficient and scalable chains" (Latif 2016). Another consideration for the American halal food industry is upholding integrity of standards. For instance, Midamar was charged with "fraudulently shipping beef to Malaysia and Indonesia that did not meet the countries' import requirements" (Latif 2016). Scandals can damage a company's reputation but can also lead to questioning of halal integrity of products.

Conclusion

There are a number of halal certification agencies in the United States catering to both global and national markets, serving both the interests of business and the growing domestic Muslim population. While some of these halal certification agencies have been around since the 1970s, there is a proliferation of new agencies. Initially, these agencies were connected to a mosque or local Muslim American community. However, some of the newly established halal certification agencies are only involved with halal certification. While some of the halal certification agencies are involved in training the business sector, state officials, and consumers, they also engage in advocacy for the expansion of halal food and products in institutional settings (e.g., hospitals, prisons, schools). The halal certification agencies have been accredited by multiple international halal accreditation agencies and are well connected to global markets. However, there is a fragmentation of the business landscape as some companies, like American Foods Group, only cater to global markets.

The domestic halal market is growing and diversifying with new companies, such as Saffron Road, which emphasize halal and tayyib principles. The characteristics of the Muslim population in the United States are critical to understand these changes. Although a small percentage of the total American population, the American Muslim population is very heterogenous and ethnically and racially diverse. The young and diverse Muslim American population is also tech-savvy and brand conscious, open to social media marketing, which presents new opportunities for the expansion of halal markets. There are discrepancies among American Muslims in terms of social and economic status (particularly among immigrant and American-born Muslims), and understanding this gap provides a more nuanced reflection of the halal sector in the United States.

Halal certification agencies have focused mainly on meat and poultry, and they focus on not only on slaughtering processes but the integrity of the animal production system from beginning to end. Meat is also one of the highly regulated items in the United States at the federal level due to food safety concerns and connections to global markets. Current debates about exemptions for ritual slaughtering and about animal welfare have created more opportunities for halal and kosher certification agencies in the United States to work together and to think about the intersectionality of sustainability and ethics with halal certification more broadly. While there are still nuances among halal meat certification processes of halal certification agencies, as common in minority and Muslim-majority contexts, more halal certification agencies incorporate cradle-to-grave forms of integrity in the halal meat supply chain.

The last two decades has also seen a proliferation of halal protection laws in the food sector. These laws emphasize the success of kosher protection laws in the United States, which has a long history and undergird big business. These laws emphasize consumers' rights and aim to prevent mislabeling of halal products. These laws are critical for both business and consumers. They can lead to increased awareness about halal certification as they emphasize the visibility of halal. They can also add another layer of monitoring and enforcement of halal standards. They can also help with record keeping about halal-certified products and halal certification processes. However, the visibility of a halal logo is still a concern for some companies in the United States that may not openly declare their halal certification. Islamophobia and its relationship to halal markets, only briefly mentioned in this chapter, can be related to these concerns and should be the focus of future research. Other topics that merit further research include the opportunities for and barriers against expanding halal markets in the United States, new areas of opportunity such as religious certification of Military Ready-to-Eat Meals (MRE) and how halal MREs have become a foreign policy, and national security issues in recent years (due to American military operations and to humanitarian aid in post-conflict and post-disaster areas).

References

Alabsy, Jalot. 2020. Halal laws in the USA. Accessed 20 December 2021. https://halaltransactions.org/halal-laws-in-the-usa/.

American Halal Institute. 2021. Training. Accessed 20 December 2021. https://americanhalalinstitute.com/training/.

2 Halal Certification in the United States and the Expansion...   49

Animal Welfare Institute. 2019. Legal protections for farm animals at slaughter. Accessed 20 December 2021. https://awionline.org/sites/default/files/uploads/documents/fa-legalprotectionsatslaughter-12262013.pdf.

Armanios, Febe, and Bogac Ergene. 2018. *Halal food: A history.* New York: Oxford University Press.

Bennett, Sarah D., Kelly A. Walsh, and L. Hannah Gould. 2013. Foodborne disease outbreaks caused by *Bacillus cereus, Clostridium perfringens,* and *Staphylococcus aureus*—United States, 1998–2008. *Clinical Infectious Diseases* 57 (3): 425–433.

Bergeaud-Blackler, Florence, Johan Fischer, and John Lever. 2016. Introduction. In *Halal matters: Islam, politics and markets in global perspective,* ed. F. Bergeaud-Blackler, J. Fischer, and J. Lever, 1–18. London: Routledge.

Bonne, Karijn, and Wim Verbeke. 2008. Religious values informing halal meat production and the control and delivery of halal credence quality. *Agriculture and Human Values* 25 (1): 35–47.

Botoeva, A. 2020. Measuring the unmeasurable? Production & certification of halal goods and services. *Sociology of Islam* 8 (3–4): 364–386.

Brougher, Cynthia, and Joel Greene. 2011. The USDA's authority to recall meat and poultry products. *Congressional Research Service,* 6 January2011. Accessed 20 December 2021. https://nationalaglawcenter.org/wp-content/uploads/assets/crs/RL34313.pdf.

CDC. 2021. Estimates of foodborne illness in the United States. Accessed 29 December 2022. https://www.cdc.gov/foodborneburden/index.html#:~:text=Determining%20the%20sources%20of%20foodborne, year%20in%20the%20United%20States.

Chaudry, Munir. 2015. From the publisher's desk. *Halal Consumer* Fall: 3. Accessed 20 December 2021. http://china.ifanca.org/HCM/Halal%20Consumer%20Issue%2034/index.html#3.

———. n.d. Presentation to the Meat Institute. Accessed 20 December 2021. https://www.meatinstitute.org/index.php?ht=a/GetDocumentAction/i/11082.

Çiftçi, Sabri. 2012. Islamophobia and threat perceptions: Explaining anti-Muslim sentiment in the West. *Journal of Muslim Minority Affairs* 32 (3): 293–309.

Clyma, Kimberlie. 2016. Superior Farms unveils new lamb plant. Accessed 20 December 2021. https://www.meatpoultry.com/articles/19261-superior-farms-unveils-new-lamb-plant.

Della Corte, Valentina, Giovanna del Gaudio, and Fabiana Sepe. 2018. Ethical food and the kosher certification: A literature review. *British Food Journal* 120 (10): 2270–2288.

Etri, Manal, and Salih Yucel. 2016. Halal certification and Islamophobia. *Australian Journal of Islamic Studies* 1 (1): 1–22.

Farouk, Mustafa, Kristin Pufpaff, and Mohammad Amir. 2016. Industrial halal meat production and animal welfare: A review. *Meat Science* 120: 60–70.

Federal Register. 2017. Department of Agriculture Marketing Services (Document Number AMS-NOP-15-0012; NOP-15-06FR), Vol. 82, No. 12, January 19. Accessed 20 December 2021. https://www.govinfo.gov/content/pkg/FR-2017-01-19/pdf/2017-00888.pdf.

Fischer, Johan. 2011. *The halal frontier: Muslim consumers in a globalized market.* New York: Palgrave Macmillan.

———. 2016. Manufacturing halal in Malaysia. *Contemporary Islam* 10 (35): 1035–1052.

Fuseini, Awal, Steve Wotton, Toby Knowles, and Phil Hadley. 2017. Halal meat fraud and safety issues in the UK: A review in the context of the European Union. *Food Ethics* 1 (2): 127–142.

Golan, Elise, Tanya Roberts, Elisabete Salay, Julie Caswell, Michael Ollinger, and Danna Moore. 2004. Food safety innovation in the United States: Evidence from the meat industry. Accessed 20 December 2021. https://www.ers.usda.gov/publications/pub-details/?pubid=41636.

Goodman, John. 2015. Why brands cannot afford to ignore the U.S. Muslim consumer. Accessed 20 December 2021. https://www.campaignlive.com/article/why-brands-cant-afford-ignore-us-muslim-consumer/1347429.

Halal Connect. 2009. Pilot issue of the American Halal Association. Accessed 20 December 2021. https://issuu.com/kamarulaznam/docs/halal_connect_pilot_issue_2009.

———. 2010. Magazine of the American Halal Association. Accessed 20 December 2021. https://issuu.com/americanhalalassociation.org/docs/halalconnect2010.

Halal Focus. 2011. IFANCA organizes 13th international food conference. Accessed 20 December 2021. https://halalfocus.net/usa-ifanca%C2%AE-organizes-13th-international-halal-food-conference/.

Halal Food Standards Alliance of America. 2021. Stunning animals prior to slaughter. Accessed 20 December 2021. https://www.hfsaa.org/stunning-animals-prior-to-slaughter/.

Halal Pastures. 2021. Our philosophy. Accessed 20 December 2021. https://www.halalpastures.com/our-philosophy/.

Halawa, Abdelhadi. 2018. Acculturation of halal food to the American food culture through immigration and globalization. *Journal of Ethnic and Cultural Studies* 5 (2): 53–64.

Halim, Mustafa'Afifi Ab, and Mohd Mahyeddin Mohd Salleh. 2012. The possibility of uniformity on halal standards in organization of Islamic Countries (OIC). *World Applied Sciences Journal* 17 (17): 6–10.

Harris, Kathleen, Tatiana Stanton, Rebecca Thisthlethwaite, Peter Duryea, and Erica Frenay. 2019. Guide to direct marketing livestock and Ppultry: Regulations every producer should know to sell meat and livestock in New York State. Cornell: Cornell Small Farms Program. Accessed 20 December 2021. https://smallfarms.cornell.edu/wp-content/uploads/2020/05/Marketing-Livestock-Guide-2020.pdf.

Hashim, Puziah, and Mat Hashim. 2013. A review of cosmetic and personal care products: Halal perspective and detection of ingredient. *Pertanika Journals of Science and Technology* 21 (2): 281–292.

Hermawan, Agus. 2020. Consumer protection perception of halal products in Indonesia. *International Conference on Islam, Economy, and Halal Industry,* 235–246. https://doi.org/10.18502/kss.v4i9.7329.

Husseini de Araújo, Shadia. 2021. Desired Muslims: Neoliberalism, halal food production and the assemblage of Muslim expertise, service providers and labour in New Zealand and Brazil. *Ethnicities* 21 (3): 411–432. https://doi.org/10.1177/1468796821998369.

IFANCA. 2014. IFANCA talks halal in specialty diets workshop. Accessed 20 December 2021. https://www.newhope.com/managing-your-business/ifanca-talks-halal-specialty-diets-workshop.

———. 2018. 20th international halal food conference: Global state of the halal certification. Accessed 20 December 2021. https://www.ifanca.org/PressKit/PressKit030618.htm.

———. 2021a. Halal application. Accessed 20 December 2021. http://www.ifanca.org/Pages/HalalApplication.aspx.

———. 2021b. Five star halal identification system: Press kit. Accessed 20 December 2021. https://ifanca.org/presskit/presskit07112015.html.

Institute of Medicine and National Research Council. 1998. *Ensuring safe food: From production to consumption.* Washington (DC): National Academies Press (US); 1998. PMID: 24967491

International Trade Center. 2015. From niche to mainstream: Halal goes global. Joint Agency of the World Trade Organization and the United Nations. Accessed 20 December 2021. https://www.intracen.org/uploadedFiles/intracenorg/Content/Publications/Halal_Goes_Global-web(1).pdf.

Islamic Horizons. 2021a. Halal on the menu. Accessed 20 December 2021. https://issuu.com/isnacreative/docs/ih_july-august_21, p. 10.

———. 2021b. Islamic Horizons Magazine. Accessed 20 December 2021. https://isna.net/islamic-horizons-magazine/.

Islamic Services of America. 2019. Scope of the halal food industry in USA. Accessed 20 December 2021. https://www.isahalal.com/news-events/blog/scope-of-Halal-food-in-USA.

———. 2020a. 3 Reasons why you need a halal mark on your product packaging. Accessed 20 December 2021. https://www.isahalal.com/news-events/blog/3-reasons-why-you-need-halal-mark-your-product-packaging.

———. 2020b. Halal certification and prison foods. Accessed 20 December 2021. https://www.isahalal.com/news-events/blog/halal-certification-and-prison-foods.

———. 2021a. What is halal? Is halal for Muslims only? Accessed 20 December 2021. https://www.isahalal.com/halal-information.

———. 2021b. Why non-Muslims buy halal. Accessed 20 December 2021. https://www.isahalal.com/news-events/blog/why-non-muslims-buy-halal.

Jacobs, M. 1997. 'How about some meat?': The Office of Price Administration, consumption politics, and state building from the bottom up, 1941–1946. *The Journal of American History* 84 (3): 910–941.

Kagan, Ariel, Kathyrn Draeger, and Ren Olive. 2020. Halal and kosher Minnesota meat market assessment: Analysis, implications and recommendations. UMN Extension Regional Sustainable Development Partnerships. Accessed 20 December 2021. https://conservancy.umn.edu/handle/11299/210220.

Kantor, Arlene F. 1976. Upton Sinclair and the Pure Food and Drugs Act of 1906: 'I aimed at the public's heart and by accident I hit it in the stomach.' *American Journal of Public Health* 66 (12): 1202–1205.

Krishna, Priya. 2019. Deep in the Muslim heart of Texas, a farm family provides halal meat. 3 June 2019. Accessed 20 December 2021.https://www.nytimes.com/2019/06/03/dining/halal-meat-texas.html.

Kurth, Laura, and Pieter Glasbergen. 2017. Serving a heterogeneous Muslim identity? Private governance arrangements of halal food in the Netherlands. *Agriculture and Human Values* 34 (1): 103–118.

Latif, Haroon. 2016. Overview: The $10 billion U.S. halal food market (Salaam Gateway). Accessed 20 December 2021. https://www.salaamgateway.com/story/overview-the-10-bln-us-halal-food-market.

Lever, John, and Johan Fischer. 2018. *Religion, regulation, consumption: Globalising kosher and halal markets.* Manchester: Manchester University Press.

Lever, John, and Mara Miele. 2012. The growth of halal meat markets in Europe: An exploration of the supply side theory of religion. *Journal of Rural Studies* 28 (4): 528–537.

Lipka, Michael. 2017. Muslims and Islam: Key findings in the U.S. and around the world. Accessed 20 December 2021. https://www.pewresearch.org/fact-tank/2017/08/09/muslims-and-islam-key-findings-in-the-u-s-and-around-the-world/.

Lytton, Timothy. 2014. Jewish foodways and religious self-governance in America: The failure of communal Kashrut regulation and the rise of private kosher certification. *The Jewish Quarterly Review* 104 (1): 38–45.

Majeed, Imran, Husseini Al-Zyoud, and Naved Ahmad. 2019. Jurisprudence and demand for halal meat in OIC. *British Food Journal* 121 (7): 1614–1626.

Minnesota Bill. 2001. Minnesota Halal Protection Law, House Bill 5480 (Substitute H-2). Accessed 20 December 2021. https://www.legislature.mi.gov/documents/2001-2002/billanalysis/House/htm/2001-HLA-5480-a.htm#:~:text=Minnesota's%20halal%20food%20protection%20law,poultry%20falsely%20represented%20as%20halal.

New Hira Halal. 2021. About us. Accessed 20 December 2021. https://newhira-halal.com/index.php?route=information/about_us.

New York Senate. 2021. Article 17: Adulteration, Packing and Branding of Food and Food Products. Agriculture and Markets (AGM), Chapter 69. Accessed 2 April 2022. https://www.nysenate.gov/legislation/laws/AGM/A17.

New York State Act. 2020. New York State Halal Foods Protection Act of 2005. Accessed 29 December 2022. https://agriculture.ny.gov/system/files/documents/2020/02/halalfoodsprotectionactbrochure_0.pdf

Olya, Hossein, and Amr Al-Ansi. 2018. Risk assessment of halal products and services: Implication for tourism industry. *Tourism Management* 65: 279–291.

Pew Research Center. 2017. Demographic portrait of Muslim Americans. Accessed 20 December 2021. https://www.pewforum.org/2017/07/26/demographic-portrait-of-muslim-americans/.

———. 2018. Muslims in America: Immigrants and those born in U.S. see life differently in many ways. Accessed 20 December 2021. https://www.pewforum.org/essay/muslims-in-america-immigrants-and-those-born-in-u-s-see-life-differently-in-many-ways/.

———. 2019. Key facts about refugees in the U.S. Accessed 20 December 2021. https://www.pewresearch.org/fact-tank/2019/10/07/key-facts-about-refugees-to-the-u-s/.

———. 2021. Muslims are a growing presence in U.S., but still face negative views from the public. Accessed 20 December 2021. https://www.pewresearch.org/fact-tank/2021/09/01/muslims-are-a-growing-presence-in-u-s-but-still-face-negative-views-from-the-public/.

Pufpaff, Kristin, Mian N. Riaz, and Munir M. Chaudry. 2018. Halal production requirements for meat and poultry. In *Handbook of halal food production*, ed. Mian N. Riaz and Mihammad M. Chaudry, 105–124. Boca Raton: CRC Press.

Regenstein, Joe M., Muhammad M. Chaudry, and Carrie E. Regenstein. 2003. The kosher and halal food laws. *Comprehensive Reviews in Food Science and Food Safety* 2 (3): 111–127.

Ruiz-Bejarano, Barbara. 2017. Islamophobia as a deterrent to halal global trade. *Islamophobia Studies Journal* 4 (1): 129–145.

Scharff, Robert. 2020. Food attribution and economic cost estimates for meat- and poultry-related illnesses. *Journal of Food Protection* 83 (6): 959–967.

Starobin, Shana, and Erika Weinthal. 2010. The search for credible information in social and environmental global governance: The kosher label. *Business and Politics* 12 (3): 1–35.

Superior Farms. 2021. Our story. Accessed 20 December 2021. https://superiorfarms.com/our-story/.

Tayob, Shaheed. 2020. Trading halal: Halal certification and intra-Muslim trade in South Africa. *Sociology of Islam* 8 (3–4): 322–342.

Technavio. 2020. Halal food market in U.S. by product, end-user, and distribution channel—Forecast and analysis 2020–2024. Accessed 20 December 2021. https://www.technavio.com/report/halal-food-market-in-us-industry-analysis.

Texas Bill. 2003. Texas H.B. 470. Accessed 2 April 2022. https://capitol.texas.gov/tlodocs/78R/billtext/html/HB00470F.htm.

Turaeva, Rano, and Michael Brose. 2020. Halal markets in non-Muslim secular societies: Halal as brand, halal as practice. *Sociology of Islam* 8 (3–4): 295–306.

U.S. Code. 2014. Title 21 (Food and Drugs), Chapter 12 (Meat Inspection), Subchapter 1 (Inspection Requirements: Adulteration and Misbranding), Sec. 603 (Examination of animals prior to slaughter, use of human methods. Accessed 20 December 2021. https://www.govinfo.gov/content/pkg/USCODE-2014-title21/html/USCODE-2014-title21-chap12-subchapI-sec603.htm.

U.S. Department of State. 2012. Certified halal in the USA. Bureau of International Information Programs. Accessed 20 December 2021. https://static.america.gov/uploads/sites/8/2016/03/Certified-Halal-in-the-USA_English_508.pdf.

USA Halal Chamber. 2021. History. Accessed 20 December 2021. https://www.ushalalcertification.com/history.html.

USDA. 1978. Humane Methods of Slaughter Act. Accessed 2 April 2022. https://uscode.house.gov/view.xhtml?path=/prelim@title7/chapter48&edition=prelim.

———. 2005. Food standards and labeling policy. Food Safety and Inspection Service. Accessed 2 April 2022. https://www.fsis.usda.gov/sites/default/files/import/Labeling-Policy-Book.pdf.

———. 2021. What animals are inspected by USDA. Accessed 2 April 2022. https://ask.usda.gov/s/article/What-animals-are-inspected-by-USDA.

Winston, Kimberly. 2019. As halal food wins over new audiences, some fear it's losing its soul. 18 July. Accessed 20 December 2021. https://thecounter.org/halal-cuisine-faith-meat-slaughter-islam/.

3

Building Halal in Italy: The Case of Halal Italia

Lauren Crossland-Marr

Introduction

In this chapter, I look at the making of a distinctly Italian halal industry based on 18 months of research from 2015 to 2018 with halal certifiers operating in Milan and with an internship with one halal entity: Halal Italia. Like most halal certifiers operating in countries where Muslims are a minority, Halal Italia must grapple with a foodscape dominated by a non-Muslim majority as it positions itself as qualified to certify a good halal. Halal Italia is run by a community called Coreis, which has offices

---

I would like to thank and acknowledge the staff at Halal Italia for sharing their time and friendship with me. For many helpful insights, I thank John Bowen, Elizabeth Krause, and Glenn Stone. I would also like to extend thanks to the editors of this volume, Rano Turaeva and Michael Brose, for their help in developing this chapter. Research was supported by the Washington University in St. Louis Graduate School, The Department of Anthropology, and The Divided City Initiative.

L. Crossland-Marr (✉)
Dalhousie University, Halifax, NS, Canada
e-mail: l.marr@wustl.edu

© The Author(s), under exclusive license to Springer Nature Switzerland AG 2023
R. Turaeva, M. Brose (eds.), *Religious Economies in Secular Context*, New Directions in Islam, https://doi.org/10.1007/978-3-031-18603-5_3

58   L. Crossland-Marr

across Italy, but is headquartered in Milan where the community has about 40 regular followers.

In November 2017, one of my friends at Halal Italia called me. She was crying. Between sobs, she told me, "the Shayk left with a smile on his face." I told her how sorry I was. After I hung up, I thought to the first time I met Shaykh Pallavicini. It was 2015 and I remember thinking how his tall stature was probably enhanced by his long white robe and long, white beard. Since moving to Milan for my extended fieldwork, I had seen the Shayk often, at Jumu'ah and at community events.[1] Shayk Pallavicini was the leader of the Sufi group Coreis. Coreis was the religious entity behind the halal certification, Halal Italia.

On the day of the funeral in mid-November, my husband and I walked with mourners past security guards and photographers. Those of Muslim faith were in the main prayer area; my colleagues from Halal Italia who were also part of the Coreis community were there. Those of non-Muslim faith, like me and my husband, sat in the back on folding chairs. The Shaykh's raised wooden casket faced Mecca. Draped on top of it was a blanket with Qur'anic scripture. It stood between the men's prayer area and the non-Muslim area, a material bridge between religions, I thought. It was Friday Jumu'ah and the Shayk's son, Imam Pallavicini gave a short sermon (*khutbah*). He discussed the life of the Shaykh (his father) as one who resurrected Islam in Italy after the time of Dante Alighieri and Frederick II.[2]

At the end of the prayer, the Muslims greeted each other: "*As salamu alaikum wa rahmatullahi wa barakatuh*" (May the peace, mercy, and blessings of Allah be with you). After that, Imam Pallavicini asked to hear three testimonies about the life of the Shaykh. He asked a representative from the Senegalese Murid community to speak first. In Italian, the

---

[1] The Halal Italia office where I worked was connected to the community prayer space, where Jumu'ah was held weekly.

[2] Dante and Frederick are important historical figures to the community as they represent the decline of Islam in Italy. The Norman Emperor Frederick II (1194–1250) was king of Sicily, and he kept the Fatimid Caliphate at bay. The Fatimids were a Shia Islamic empire that ruled Sicily as the Emirate of Sicily from 831–1091. In *The Divine Comedy* (1320), Dante Alighieri represents Ali and the Prophet Mohammed in the eighth of hell's nine rings (sowers of discord). For Muslims in Italy, the late medieval period is thus marked as a point in which Christianity began to dominate Italy.

leader said that no one welcomed them in Italy except for the late Shaykh. They felt embraced by him and began to understand the importance of an agreement with the Italian state and Islam.[3] The second to speak was a leader of the French Ahmadiyya community, who delivered his testimony in French. Imam Pallavicini translated. He said that the Shaykh would live on through his words, actions, and life. The third person to speak was a member of the Moroccan community who lauded the late Shaykh's piety.

The multilingual, multiethnic, multinational, multi-racial, multi-denominational, and interdenominational assemblage of mourners at the Shaykh's funeral points to the complexity of alliances and potentials for contestation in Italy's halal market. In Italy, halal cannot be simply about the foods permitted to Muslims. Circumscribing and certifying halal is also an act of ordering relations among Italy's many kinds of Islam. There are few Muslims in Italy whose faith, knowledge, and authority can be taken for granted: The very ground on which we stood was bequeathed to the Shaykh by his Italian Catholic family.

Halal in the Global Economy

Shahab Ahmed's *What is Islam* (2017) captures the diversity of Islam in the opening vignette. He recalls how, at a dinner at Princeton University, he was joined by a non-Muslim European scholar and a Muslim scholar. The Muslim scholar ordered wine, which is widely considered *haram* or forbidden in Islam. Curious, the non-Muslim asked the wine-drinking man if he considered himself a Muslim. The Muslim man replied that he did, and to further clarify he said that he came from a long line of "Muslim wine drinkers" (Ahmed 2017: 3). The other man, now even more confused, replied that he didn't understand. The Muslim man ended the conversation with "yes, I know … but I do" (Ahmed 2017: 3). As

---

[3] Coreis is involved in seeking an *Intesa,* an official recognition of the Islam by the state. Other religions such as Mormonism have this distinction, which grants members of the religion certain rights including tax breaks and recognized places of worship. Due to the population's diversity, Muslim leaders have been unsuccessful in finalizing an Intesa agreement.

demonstrated with this vignette, static notions of Islam fail to capture actual diversity of practices and ideological frames.

Anthropologists have analyzed Islam as a discursive practice, a way in which moral selves come into being through interaction with others (Asad [1986] 2009). The Islamic economy is a productive place to analyze this interaction, as religious markets in the context of global capitalism "[shed] light on how the halal market offers a new field of Islamic expression" (Pak 2020: 308). A noteworthy example of this type of analysis in the realm of halal certification is Shaheed Tayob's (2020) research in South Africa. His analysis of the discursive practices at play shows that practices are creatively "produc[ing] new expressions of Islam" (Tayob 2020: 324). Analyzing halal certifications based in Johannesburg, Tayob shows that when certifiers shifted to a new discourse of risk, they did not replace earlier forms of halal but rather expanded networks of consumption beyond the local community. Similarly, I argue that halal certification, as it is created within a context of neoliberal governance, is refashioning consumers, certifiers, and the materials they are exchanging.

In Italy, as elsewhere, businesses that wish to be halal certified can choose from among a handful of non-state halal certifiers. As others have shown, this does not mean that the state is not involved in managing certification entities (Turaeva and Brose 2020). In the case of Halal Italia, it was at the urging of the state that Halal Italia came into being. In addition to state support, the expansive networks of the community also made Halal Italia well positioned. Indeed, the global networks of religious institutions are critical to success in the halal economy (Pak 2020).

Although the peninsula we call Italy has been influenced greatly by Islam in the past (Clancy-Smith 2012), modern-day Italy and its secular state are influenced more obviously by the Roman Catholic Church. This means no food in Italy can be assumed to be halal. The development of certification in Italy, like elsewhere, is an amalgam of international, state, and local regulations, logics, and practices. Halal certifications in Italy developed, initially, to certify foods for export to Muslim consumers abroad. Halal certification, while meant to standardize processes and practices, is incredibly diverse (Atalan-Helicke 2015).

Broadly conceived, halal certification guarantees a Muslim consumer that the producer has avoided contact with or inclusion of certain

3 Building Halal in Italy: The Case of Halal Italia   61

materials—such as pork and alcohol—and processed foods and materials according to additional Islamic guidelines. Yet, any one certification system draws on multiple standards and regulations; each certification system differs from all others in some points. In Italy, halal certifiers incorporate a combination drawn from international halal accreditation standards, national and EU food safety guidelines, and international guidelines such as the Hazard Analysis and Critical Control Points (HAACP) and The International Organization for Standardization (ISO). Interpretations of each standard are diverse.

The authority of any halal certification system therefore also depends on factors that cannot be reduced to standards and guidelines. Faith itself becomes one of the qualifying factors for a certifier's authority. In non-Muslim-majority countries, credible certification agencies tend to be established and operated by Muslims; their personal faith confers them with authority vis-à-vis both co-religionists and non-Muslims (Bowen 2020). Interestingly, the minority status of Muslims vis-à-vis the overall market in such countries seems to result in a situation, described by Febe Armanios and Boğaç A. Ergene, in which "diasporic Muslims ... play an equal (and sometimes greater role) than their co-religionists in majority-Muslim countries with regard to how halal food is consumed and molded in today's world" (Armanios and Ergene 2018: 6). However, the particularities of Islam with which a certifier is established can also draw distrust.

Italian Islam[4]

Shayk Abd al-Wahid Pallavicini was born in Italy in 1926 as Felice Pallavicini. Initially trained as a musician, Pallavicini travelled to Singapore in his youth. There, he joined Abd Al Rashid ibn Mohammed Said's *tariqa*, the Ahmadiyya.[5]

Modernity and multiculturalism were important issues to Al Rashid's *tariqa* (Sedgwick 2009). While Al-Rahid was open to many different

---

[4] I am indebted to friends and colleagues at Halal Italia for much of this history as well as Mark Sedgwick's book, *Against the Modern World* (2009). In this chapter, however, I show that Coreis is far from operating against the modern world as the title of Sedgwick's book suggests.

[5] A different movement from that founded in nineteenth-century British India by the same name.

perspectives, he and Pallavicini disagreed on the universality of monotheistic religions. Despite their differences, Al Rashid gave Pallavicini an *ijaza*[6] to induct others into the order (Sedgwick 2009). Pallavicini also later received an *ijaza* from Ahmad ibn Idris al Idrisi (a relation of Ahmad ibn Idris, the founder of the Ahmadiyya). Although Pallavicini could induct followers into the order, he had no intention of founding a branch, upon his return to Italy. His new order was not established until much later, in a way that could only happen in Italy, through the Catholic Church.

Among its many achievements, the Second Vatican Council (1962–1965) established a secretariat for non-Christians with the aim to promote the view that all religions contain *semina Verbi* (seeds of the Word). Accordingly, Catholic authorities approached the Centro Islamico d'Italia in Rome for a spokesperson of the Islamic religion.[7] By this time, Pallavicini had returned to Italy and was attending regular Friday prayers. The Centro Islamico therefore recommended him—citing his Catholic upbringing and native Italian as additional merits. From his end, the council's vision seemed to very much appeal to Pallavicini's personal belief that there is a universal truth to all religions.

Pallavicini soon became well-known to the media and to other Catholic organizations, quickly gaining attention from Catholic Italians looking for spiritual guidance. He was, however, reluctant to start his own community, and for years he only ran a circle where he discussed his interpretation of Sufism. In the late 1970s, with a band of committed followers, he finally formed Co.Re.Is (Comunità Religiosa Islamica, hereafter Coreis). By 2009, the community was characterized as abiding devoutly by Sunni practice: eating halal foods, praying five times a day, hosting Friday Jumu'ah, and fasting during Ramadan. They are all well-educated and have a great knowledge of Islamic jurisprudence and philosophy.

The Italian press was favorable to Pallavicini and played a major role in spreading the Coreis message. In 1986, Pallavicini was included in the Vatican's interreligious envoy to promote dialogue across religions. By 1991, he was the most interviewed Muslim in Italy (Sedgwick 2009). However, this also created fissures with the broader Italian Muslim

---

[6] A formal authorization granting its bearer the ability to transmit Islamic religious teachings.
[7] This organization now directs the Roman mosque, which was built much later, in 1994.

3 Building Halal in Italy: The Case of Halal Italia   63

community. By the 1990s, Muslim immigrants were settling in Italy, but Coreis remained primarily a community of Italian Catholic converts and their own children. Eventually, relations between Pallavicini and other Muslims in Italy became irreconcilable, and his son stepped in to smooth relations.

By 2017, there were some 1.6 million Muslims living in Italy. Their social, cultural, and national backgrounds are diverse, and leadership is often found in informal prayer spaces.[8] Alongside Coreis, however, there are several other associations important in the Italian political arena; alongside Coreis, many are actively seeking official recognition of Islam as a religion. Unlike Judaism and Protestantism, Islam is not recognized by the state through what is known as an *intesa*. Ramifications of this ambiguous status affect many people: Muslim workers cannot ask for religious holidays off, mosques are not considered official places of worship, and these informal mosques cannot obtain public funding. The most visible organizations today are the Italian Islamic Association (CII), Union of Islamic Communities and Organizations of Italy (U.CO.II), and Islamic Cultural Centre of Italy (Roman Mosque).

Italian Halal

In 2009, because of Shayk Pallavicini's notable Western ideals of interfaith dialogue, the Milan Chamber of Commerce asked Coreis to participate in a pilot project to set up a halal certification body. During the pilot project, Halal Italia certified five companies. In less than a decade, when I began my internship in 2017, Halal Italia certified over 100 companies; the staff, like that of other institutes and businesses run by members of Coreis community, was drawn internally from original members and their families (Crossland-Marr 2021).

Halal Italia faced few initial hurdles in its founding. An interministerial agreement was signed almost as soon as the pilot project ended. On

---

[8] "Muslims pray at Colosseum, protesting against Rome mosque closures," 21 October 2016. https://www.reuters.com/article/cnews-us-italy-mosques-idCAKCN12L2AU. Accessed 26 July 2022.

30 June 2010, ministers of the Organization of the Islamic Conference (OIC) were present for the signing. Largely ceremonial, the occasion meant that the Italian government and the international Muslim community officially recognized Halal Italia. The event comprised representatives from several ministries: Foreign Affairs; Economic Development; Agriculture, Food, and Forestry Policies; and Health (Ministry of Foreign Affairs 2010).[9] A press release about the event titled "Made in Italy: 'Halal' mark of quality compliant with the Koran" reported:

> The halal certification project is particularly important within the context of the [Ministry]'s support for the internationalisation of the Italian productive system through activities aimed at facilitating 'Made in Italy' products' access to Islamic markets, and could contribute to strengthening the bond between Italy and Muslim majority nations. (Ministry of Foreign Affairs 2010)

It communicated a sense that, for the government, Halal Italia was an ideal representative of Islam and had an important role to play in the export of national products to Muslim-majority countries. Among Italy's Muslims, however, Halal Italia's authority could not be taken for granted.

Certifying halal foods requires authority that is recognized within capitalist market dynamics. While religious commitments may seem opposed to profit-making, this opposition is eased in halal certification practice. Indeed, many active in the halal industry outside of Italy have noticed parallels between it and other nonreligious third-party certifications. Maryam Attar et al. write, "halal food should be produced—much like organic food—in ways that are good for human, animal, and environmental health" (Attar, Lohi, and Lever 2015: 56). Florence Bergeaud-Blackler et al. (2015) have argued that, from a technical point of view, the standardization of halal is like that of organic foods. The two diverge, however, because organic foods are enforced by international agreements and governmental departments (Bergeaud-Blackler, Fischer, and Lever 2015: 122). Halal speaks to the complex relationship between ethical production, religiosity, and consumers; it "is more than a principled

---

[9] For Coreis, this was also an important step in their fight to make Islam an officially recognized religion in Italy.

3 Building Halal in Italy: The Case of Halal Italia 65

rejection of excess, luxury, and their attendant ills" (Turaeva and Brose 2020: 298).

However, uncovering legitimacy was more difficult than I thought. Because my position working with Halal Italia was well known, I had trouble interviewing other halal certifiers. Few would speak to me about the perception of Halal Italia and its certification within the broader Muslim community. Certainly, there were some who doubted its authority. Assessments of authority and reliability, when I was told of them, seemed always to focus on the practices of Coreis and whether they were "correct" or followed Sunni practice.

For example, one of my friends, a practicing Muslim whose parents immigrated from Algeria, said to me over tea one afternoon, "You know, [Coreis] aren't really Muslims." I asked her why she thought this. She replied that her brother had attended Jumu'ah at the Coreis prayer space. He had reported that women sat in the back of the hall during prayer and men sat closer to the *minbar* (pulpit) and that there was no curtain or wall separating the male and female prayer areas. For my friend and her family, this was not correct practice; men and women should have been more separated.

Conversely, a colleague from Halal Italia had reported that representatives from a major certifier in the Americas had refused to talk to him at a conference until he had spoken about how the Coreis community operates. Whether he spoke to them of male-female relations is unclear, but his account of daily Islamic practice within the community convinced his counterparts that they could trust him and Halal Italia.

Yet, even if Halal Italia were accepted widely, it is hard to gauge whether their certified foods would be accepted as such by Italian Muslims. Almost all certified products are meant for markets abroad. In-country halal products are hard to come by. Indeed, some certified manufacturers sell their products in local grocery chains *without* the halal label because they fear non-Muslim Italian consumers will stop buying their products if they are marked.

Halal Certification in Context

Halal certification in the Italian context is analogous to post-Soviet countries in that the impetus for the industry was to export goods to Muslim-majority countries in the Middle East and Southeast Asia (Brylov 2020; Serrano 2020). The potential market for halal Italian products, however, is more diverse than that of the post-Soviet producers because artisanal food products from Italy are globally desirable alongside staple goods. The desire for Italian foods is complex, but certainly recent publicity from governmental bodies (as a healthy Mediterranean diet) and from movements like Slow Food has expanded the appeal beyond heritage communities (Laudan 2004; Parasecoli 2014). As a result, many halal-certified products are artisanal goods like pastas, cured beef-based meats, cheeses, coffee, and gelato. Thus, certifiers work across a broad product range, with both large and small producers.

This diversity in production is a challenge. Halal certifiers must ensure the directed use of regulations across small family-owned businesses and large companies, and most producers and their managers are not Muslims themselves. The seriousness with which a producer undertakes the work of maintaining halal varies widely. Larger companies usually have quality control staff who implement all relevant standards: halal, kosher, bio, etc. Smaller companies have no such specialized person—often electing a family member to take on the duty. Certification can be revoked if standards are not implemented, but more often certifiers would ask the producer to make adjustments. There was only one instance I heard of in which Halal Italia revoked a certification. Because producers are usually non-Muslims, issues with production were an expected part of the certification process. Severe issues were rare and were usually the result of a smaller producer not taking halal procedures seriously. Yet, as much as production sites are influenced by halal certification, so too are halal certifications influenced by producers. To untangle this further, let's look at standards surrounding genetically modified organisms (GMOs) and the use of kosher in halal certification. In the case of GMOs, many Italians are against genetically engineered foods, and this is reflected in Italian halal standards.

3 Building Halal in Italy: The Case of Halal Italia   67

GMOs possess genetically added traits, such as the capacity to produce insecticide within plants themselves. The food sources grown out of this process are known as GM crops, of which the most common are corn, rapeseed (canola), and soy. In Italy, GMOs have raised concerns and many halal certifiers do not allow GM crops in halal-certified products. As Nurcan Atalan-Helicke (2020) shows, there is no global consensus on permissibility of GM foods in animal feed despite attempts by international Islamic organizations to do so (344). While there is no "global" consensus on the permissibility of GMOs in the halal domain, the main halal certifying body in North America, the Islamic Food and Nutrition Council of America (IFANCA), certifies foods made from GM soy and corn. This is not surprising in the context of the United States where GM-derived plants are ubiquitous in the food system (Ackerman 2009).

Italy's halal standards have also been distinguished from other national systems by a close connection with kosher certification. There is often overlap between the two systems, and, at the time of my research, the Jewish and Muslim communities joined forces to advocate for a religious exception for non-stunning during slaughter. For several years, Halal Italia certified allowed producers to use meat that was slaughtered in the Jewish tradition (*shechita*).[10] However, this became complicated by politics on the global stage, as the some states pushed back on food products made from kosher meat. Yet, in Italy, many Muslim consumers told me that, if they couldn't find halal meat, they would buy kosher meat. Halal Italia still allows kosher certification in upstream production of yeasts and other microbes. A Halal Italia colleague explained that additives and flavorings during the upstream inspection must meet one of the following conditions: halal certified, kosher certified, and/or vegetable, microbial, or synthetic origin. He said microbes were allowed to be kosher but that, if the company had kosher certification, he recommended that they not include the symbol on products going to abroad because the products "will come under more scrutiny."

---

[10] The major difference between Jewish ritual slaughter (*shechita*) and Islamic ritual slaughter (*dabihah*) is principally that Jewish slaughter blesses the production area, while the blessing much be spoken over each animal in Islamic ritual slaughter.

The two examples elaborated here show that halal is created as much within the procedure of halal as it is outside of it. In other words, the boundaries of what is halal and what is not halal are constantly in flux, and these boundaries are only enforced in extreme cases. In the multi-faith context of Italy, politics on a global scale can clash with local alliances, which are ameliorated through further discussion. It is due to the unsettled nature of standards that halal certifications can succeed.

Concluding Remarks

Anthropologists have long shown that objects are not detached from the people who own, produce, and, in this case, certify them. This chapter is intended to push us to think about how the interaction between the global circulation of goods and the particularity of knowledge produces a world that creates value within many contexts (see Husseini de Araújo 2019). This chapter is meant to turn "toward Islam as a set of texts, interpretive conventions, internal debates, and social institutions that are increasingly part of the life worlds of Europe's Muslims" (Bowen 2020). I hope to expand notions of what Islam is by allowing for diversity in practice and in ideological frames across time and space. At Shaykh Pallavicini's funeral, I thought of him and the community he built as a bridge between Islam and Catholicism. However, in a broader scope, this community is more than a bridge within Italy; it also represents the diversity inherent to the global halal industry. Like the producers they certify, Halal Italia employees are artisans drawing on and blending religious commitments, standards, and practice through the institution they are fashioning.

Halal in non-Muslim-majority countries is an increasingly relevant economic and moral project. Diversity is not a barrier to this project but central to it. In Italy (as elsewhere, though perhaps less strikingly), Muslims are diverse in background and beliefs; Islamic institutions are similarly diverse; and halal certifiers employ different standards. Yet certifiers, like Halal Italia, still succeed in producing and defining halal. Their oversight not only eases the movement of products to Muslim-majority countries; it creates *Italian halal* products. Halal, as an institution, is co-constituted, created in interactions between Muslims and non-Muslim regulators, producers, and consumers. Beyond the market, Halal Italia and other certifiers create visions of Islam through their work. The work of certification not only checks the veracity of a 'material output,' but it also creates new pathways for living Islam.

Acknowledgments I would like to thank and acknowledge the staff at Halal Italia for sharing their time and friendship with me. For many helpful insights, I thank John Bowen, Krause, Glenn Stone, and the editors of this volume. Research was supported by the Washington University in St. Louis Graduate School, The Department of Anthropology, and The Divided City Initiative.

References

Ackerman, Jennifer. 2009. Altered food, GMOs, genetically modified food. *National Geographic*, 9 October. Accessed 26 July 2022. https://www.nationalgeographic.com/environment/global-warming/food-how-altered/.

Ahmed, Shahab. 2017. *What is Islam?* Princeton: Princeton University Press.

Armanios, Febe, and Bogac Ergene. 2018. *Halal food: A history*. New York: Oxford University Press.

Asad, Talal. 2009 [1986]. The idea of an anthropology of Islam. *Qui Parle* 17(2): 1–30.

Atalan-Helicke, Nurcan. 2015. The halal paradox: Negotiating identity, religious values, and genetically engineered food in Turkey. *Agriculture and Human Values* 32 (4): 663–674.

———. 2020. Sustainable halal? The intersection of halal, organic and genetically engineered food in Turkey. *Sociology of Islam* 8 (3–4): 343–363.

Attar, Maryam, Khalil Lohi, and John Lever. 2015. Remembering the spirit of halal: An Iranian perspective. In *Halal matters: Islam, politics and markets in global perspective*, ed. Florence Bergeaud-Blackler, Johan Fischer, and John Lever, 55–71. New York: Routledge.

Bergeaud-Blackler, Florence, Johan Fischer, and John Lever, eds. 2015. *Halal matters: Islam, politics and markets in global perspective*. London: Routledge.

Bowen, John. 2020. Placing Islam in European studies. *Europe Now Journal*, 3 June. Accessed 26 July 2022. https://www.europenowjournal.org/2020/06/02/placing-islam-in-european-studies/.

Brylov, Denys. 2020. Halal industry of Ukraine in the period of independence. *Sociology of Islam* 8 (3–4): 409–422.

Clancy-Smith, Julia A. 2012. *Mediterraneans: North Africa and Europe in an age of migration, c. 1800–1900*. Berkeley: University of California Press.

Crossland-Marr, Lauren Virginia. 2021. Working with(in) kinship: Value in Italian family businesses. *Modern Italy* 26 (4): 445–455.

Husseini de Araújo, Shadia. 2019. Assembling halal meat and poultry production in Brazil: Agents, practices, power and sites. *Geoforum* 100 (March): 220–228.

Laudan, Rachel. 2004. Slow food: The French terroir strategy and culinary modernism. *Food, Culture & Society* 7 (2): 133–144.

Ministry of Foreign Affairs. 2010. Made in Italy: 'Halal', mark of quality compliant with the Koran. Government. Ministry of Foreign Affairs and Insternational Cooperation. 21 June. https://www.esteri.it/mae/en/sala_stampa/archivionotizie/approfondimenti/20100621_halal.html.

Pak, Yana. 2020. Making halal business in Southern Kazakhstan: Combining the Soviet and Sufi legacies? *Sociology of Islam* 8 (3–4): 307–321.

Parasecoli, Fabio. 2014. *Al dente: A history of food in Italy*. London: Reaktion Books.

Sedgwick, Mark. 2009. *Against the modern world: Traditionalism and the secret intellectual history of the twentieth century*. Oxford: Oxford University Press.

Serrano, Silvia. 2020. Bacon or beef? 'Fake' halal scandals in the Russian Federation: Consolidating halal norms through secular courts. *Sociology of Islam* 8 (3–4): 387–408.

Tayob, Shaheed. 2020. Trading halal: Halal Certification and intra-Muslim trade in South Africa. *Sociology of Islam* 8 (3–4): 322–342.

Turaeva, Rano, and Michael Brose. 2020. Halal markets in non-Muslim secular societies: Halal as brand, halal as practice. *Sociology of Islam* 8 (3–4): 295–306.

4

Halal Business in Russia: Standards of State and Non-state Certification

Izzat Amon

Editor's Note on the Unique Nature of This Contribution

Izzat Amon (Kholov) became very popular both offline and online through the important work he did for Tajik and other migrants in Moscow for many years. He devoted his life to helping people, organizing charity for prisoners and their families in Russia, and helping to provide legal support to migrants in Russian courts. He did not fear the Tajik government but expressed critical opinions against the regime and eventually openly joined and initiated opposition activities. His active opposition work was not tolerated by Tadjikistan, and his work defending migrants against Russian state authorities brought him additional problems. Izzat Amon was therefore a perfect target in both countries for abduction and imprisonment. He disappeared from Russia on 25 March 2021 after distributing his short video addressed to President Vladimir Putin (uploaded in YouTube on 23 March), in which he asked for protection from abduction and imprisonment in Tajikistan as a Russian citizen. He reappeared in Tajikistan on 27 March (announced by Tajik authorities as being detained in pretrial detention) where he was sentenced initially to nine years on 19 October 2021 and later to an additional three years of prison. He was deprived of his Russian citizenship without any court or any opportunity to defend himself and forced to return to Dushanbe at the request of Tajik authorities, who accused him of financial fraud. Amon and his supporters dismiss the charges as politically motivated.

The material he prepared for the international workshop on Halal markets we organised in Berlin in 2018 was collected in Russia in close collaboration with Dr. Rano Turaeva, and he had at that time expressed an interest to contribute his work to this volume. Unfortunately, he had no opportunity to edit his initial paper, which consisted exclusively of transcribed reports from the field, because he was deprived of any way to communicate with the editors upon his imprisonment. The paper remains in the form of raw data, which we decided to publish with only minor English language editing in order to honor his work as an activist on behalf of migrants and his important scholarly contributions that document the state of Islamic markets and fellow Muslims in Russia.

I. Amon (✉)

A prisoner of conscience, independent researcher and Human Rights activist, Moscow, Russia

© The Author(s), under exclusive license to Springer Nature Switzerland AG 2023
R. Turaeva, M. Brose (eds.), *Religious Economies in Secular Context*, New Directions in Islam, https://doi.org/10.1007/978-3-031-18603-5_4

Introduction

This chapter discusses the role of legislative institutions in the process of administration and control over existing commercial organizations engaged in halal business throughout Russia. The certification of food in Russia is standardized through normal food safety regulations to which additional halal certification creates double or triple standardization procedures which raises different questions for producers, business people, and customers. Sometimes parallel regulation systems (state and Islamic) complement each other in some ways, and in others they come into conflict. A large proportion of the migrant population is employed in halal economies and production in Russia, and I collected data throughout 2017 and 2018, including interviews with the managers and workers of various production units throughout Russia in the Caucasus and Tatarstan. I have also studied their documents and conducted interviews with certification offices, assessing the networks of distribution and halal shops and how halal products are distributed.

Before I present the data I collected on major halal production units throughout Russia, I will provide background information on various methods of obtaining certification and control over the certification processes throughout Russia, including Muslim regions such as Tatarstan, Bashkortostan, Dagestan, Chechnya, Ingushetia, and the northern part of Russia where Muslims are a minority. The procedure for obtaining halal certification in Russia is presented on the example of large meat producers. The work is based on the materials collected in the period from the end of 2017 to mid-2018. Since the topic of halal business in Russia is extensive, and according to analysts "the future of halal is Russia," the process of collecting materials is not yet over.

Halal and Trust

Halal in the general sense of the word refers to actions permitted in Sharia. In everyday life, this often means "allowed to eat" meat, but the concept of 'halal' is not limited to the former only. Halal markets offer food products, cosmetic products, Islamic clothing, tourism, health care, pharmaceuticals, Islamic education, banking, and insurance services, among others.

Halal products are products whose composition and manufacturing techniques correspond to Muslim traditions and regulations. The prohibited products include primarily: pork, blood and some animal organs, meat of predatory animals and birds, meat of dogs and eagles, meat of animals killed in an inappropriate way and not with the name of Allah, alcohol, and products containing all of the above. In order to assure the quality of halal of these products, one trusts the producer and distributor or the label of halal with which the products are stamped.

The problem of trust in halal products among customers is tremendiously important. Muslims have a vested interest to receive halal food, and non-Muslim customers believe the food or meat has a biological (i.e., organic) quality and is fresh. One can also trust a person without the certificate of halal as it is the case with smaller producers and businessmen who buy meat from within entrusted networks. However, when the product is in larger quantities, then it is difficult to follow trust only, and the certificate becomes necessary.

Halal Certification

Halal certification has existed in Russia since 2004. With the massive increase in the number of Muslims in Russia, there is a need to regulate the turnover and control of products and services under the brand halal. The spiritual administrations of Muslims [ed.note, *dukhovnie upravlinnia musul'man*, DUM] are the authorities issuing halal certificates for the production of halal products. The practice of issuing certificates is also carried out in Dagestan, Chechnya, Ingushetia, and Kabardino-Balkaria. Accurate statistics on the Muslim population in Russia do not exist, but estimates vary from 20 to 30 million people. Of course, the seasonal migration of Muslims from Central Asian countries who work in Russia is not taken into account.

During the Soviet period, halal meat was usually sold in villages inhabited by Muslims. There, Muslims slaughtered and sold the meat of animals they had raised. Industrial production of meat for Muslims under Islamic law in the atheist Soviet country was not organized. Also, there was no need for this, since most then-Soviet Muslims used the so-called store meat, that is, non-halal. In the Soviet Union, there were few who could distinguish halal from haram. In larger cities, some kinds of halal product were only available in the small stalls at mosques.

The first products of halal corresponding to the Islamic canons began to appear en masse in the 1990s in the regions with a predominant Muslim population—in Tatarstan, Bashkortostan, and the republics of the North Caucasus. Since the early 2000s, there has been a rapid increase in the production of goods under the brand halal. The influx of a huge number of migrant workers from Muslim countries, mainly from the republics of Central Asia to Russia, made the business under the halal brand attractive.

During the period of rapid growth of the market and the need for halal products, certain violations were done: Sometimes products of poor quality, overpriced, and produced without compliance with Islamic standards were offered. Some producers of meat, knowing that the meat branded halal is better sold in the market, also managed to present and sell non-halal meat, tricking buyers to get a good profit. In order to prevent discrediting and deception, and to monitor the standards of production, transportation, storage, and trade of these products, special certification centers have been created by the spiritual administrations of Muslims.

For full and detailed information about the process of certification of halal products in Russia, I traveled to Muslim regions of Russia, visited large factories for the production of halal meat, talked with the management and staff of factories, and appealed to the spiritual administration of Muslims of Moscow and the Central region of Russia, where manufacturers receive certificates.

As one mufti in Moscow explained, halal certification is the process of confirming compliance of products and services with the standards and requirements of "halal," and it requires subsequent documented examination. According to the mufti, this procedure is carried out by officially authorized halal certification bodies, such as the Halal Standard Committee. Halal has a direct relationship to religion, and the development of the industry can bring considerable benefits to the economy and other spheres of activity.

According to the mufti, "One of the main advantages of certification is the expansion of the market of consumers of products. The manufacturer, which has a certificate of 'halal,' in an ideal order or in theory [has] more trust [from] buyers, including the most demanding."

Major Manufacturers of Halal Meat

In Russia, there are large producers of halal meat which have recently started to export halal meat into the Middle East and Southeast Asia to countries such as Iran, Malaysia, Bahrain, and Dubai. One of the largest exporters of halal poultry meat to the Middle East is the company which employs up to 15,000 people. The company produces up to 300 tons of halal meat daily. It also has shops in 55 regions of Russia that sell finished goods of the company. We were told by company representatives that animal slaughtering occurs exclusively in manual mode. Each employee of the slaughterhouse is obliged before entering the shop to wash thoroughly and put on special clothes. I was surprised by the collective prayer of the employees of the slaughterhouse. Before the start of their work shift, the employees lined up in several rows, one of them became an imam, and they began to pray. The mandatory prayers and other prayers are read collectively. After the namaz, employees pass face-control, where a special employee—after a thorough check—allows the employee to the slaughterhouse. At the slightest detection of violations in working clothes, the employee is obliged to eliminate them and is then allowed to work.

At the entrance to the slaughterhouse, employees are given special sharpened knives for slaughtering. These knives are also carefully checked by the warden. Employees of the slaughterhouse must read the obligatory prayer just before cutting the trachea of the bird and only then has the right to slaughter. The process of honoring a special prayer is also controlled by the warden. In addition, the process of work is recorded by surveillance cameras and then inspected by members of a specially organized commission.

The state of birds for slaughter is controlled by state bodies such as Rospotrebnadzor, sanitary epidemiological stations, and veterinary and sanitary examinations. At those stations, veterinary and sanitary examination of meat is carried out before and after slaughter. There are also state agencies that control the state of manufacture, transportation, storage, commercialization, and recycling of meat. I asked a question to my informant about the need and problems of obtaining a halal certificate to which he replied:

> We produce halal meat exclusively for the consumption of followers of the religion of Islam. Also, halal meat as healthy and quality food is popular among non-Muslims. Halal certificates give us the right to use the halal icon and produce meat under this brand. Halal—first of all provides the trust of our customers. We spend a lot of money to get a halal certificate. We pass a double test by state and religious orders so that customers trust us. Consultants and supervisors on the part of the mufti are permanently with us and receive official salaries. We work closely with the mufti. Also, we participate in many social projects initiated by the mufti. We build mosques, help orphanages and low-income families. From all this we get great pleasure.

Of course, to my question about how much the company annually spends on obtaining a halal certificate, no one answered, referring to that information as a trade secret. Yet, one employee anonymously said that every year the company spends tens of thousands of dollars to obtain a certificate.

Meat Processing Plant

The second largest company producing halal meat in Russia is located in city suburbs: meat processing plant. Three poultry farms of this company received the right to produce halal poultry. The company produces halal meat mainly for export to Arab countries. Their brands became the second most popular brands among buyers from Arab countries. The management of this company refused to meet with me in spite of several requests. I was also denied permission to enter their slaughterhouses and speak to the staff. When all hope for an interview was lost, suddenly I accidentally met an acquaintance who told me on the condition of anonymity that he did not advise Muslims to buy the products of this

4 Halal Business in Russia: Standards of State and Non-state... 77

company because the slaughter is done mainly by non-Muslims. Thus, one important condition of slaughtering of halal meat is violated. Also, one shop produced and stored *halalniy* (halal) with *nehalalniy* (non-halal) *nehalallnie* products. That, I was told, might be why the management refused to meet me and let me inside the production facilities. If this is so, then the question arises how the company managed to get a halal certificate and how the production process is controlled by the mufti?

A Meat-Packing Plant in the Republic of Dagestan

Regarding the marketing and manufacturing of Halal meat in the Caucasus, there is a company that has been a leader for over 18 years. The company mainly produces canned meat such as pâté, tongue in jelly, beef stew, and various sausages. The equipment in the meat processing plant is mainly European in origin, but the slaughter takes place according to the canons of Islam and in manual mode. The director of the meat processing plant told me in an interview that he received the halal certificate only in order to export his products to other Muslim regions of Russia, because in Dagestan everyone knows that the company produces exclusively halal products. Products manufactured by this company are also popular among Jews living in Dagestan and living according to kosher regulations.

The conditions for obtaining a halal certificate from the Dagestan Muftiat are no different from the Moscow or Kazan Muftiats. As in other regions, the company is undergoing double standardization and double check. Representatives of state bodies together with representatives of the Muftiat participate in all production processes.

In the slaughter shops of the Dagestan company along with Dagestani workers, there are migrant workers from Central Asia, especially Tajiks, Uzbeks, and Kyrgyz. An informant working in the administration stated:

> I trust the workers from Tajikistan and Uzbekistan to do the main work on slaughtering, because they do their work in good faith. The problem of migrant workers in the company is that they will have to pay a lot. And I would not like to have problems with the migration service. Muftiat does not care if a worker is a migrant or a citizen; they require that production follows the canons of Islam.

The head of the Committee on Standard Halal in Dagestan said:

> In Dagestan, there are more than 30 companies that produce products under the brand halal. Unfortunately, there were cases of violation of the requirements of Islam in the production process [and they] even found pork in halal products. Therefore, it was necessary to create a body controlling this area. In 2011, the Muftiat was created by a Committee of Halal. Today, the Committee employs more than 30 highly qualified specialists. Our experts go and inspect the production. If they find violations, they will fine the company. Repeated violation deprives the company of the permission to mark their products halal. That is, the first time we warn or fine, the second time we forbid the company to produce products under the brand halal.

Every year in April, the Muftiat holds an exhibition called the Dagestan-Halal Expo. In the framework of the exhibition and all-Russian scientific-practical conference on the theme "Islamic Finance in the Russian Context," it was discussed that halal is not limited to food consumption, but also covers all activities of Muslims. Furthermore, participants discussed that in Islam, all aspects of consumption, even the thoughts of Muslims, should be halal.

With regard to the conditions for obtaining the certificate, it is no different from other regions of Russia. If the production meets all the requirements of Islam, there is no reason not to give the certificate to this company. The price of the certificate depends on the capacity of the company. If this is a huge company, it is natural to pay more than a small one. The amount paid for the certificate also includes staff training.

A Meat Factory in the Chechen Republic

The factory is considered to be one of the largest companies for the production of halal products in the Chechen Republic. The meat packing plant has been operating since 1964, and it is a regional brand with products under the brand name halal. According to the director of the plant, during the war, the factory was almost completely destroyed. The first

4 Halal Business in Russia: Standards of State and Non-state...

launch of the slaughterhouse began in 2011, and it produces annually around 30 tons of halal sausages, working with slaughter shops operated with staff trained by the Muftiat of the Chechen Republic. The products of the plant are exported to many regions of the Russian Federation. It is interesting to note that in the slaughterhouses of the plant hangs notification in two languages: Russian and Chechen, and sometimes you can see inscriptions in Arabic. Apparently this is done for Arab guests, importers of halal meat from countries of the Middle East.

The director of the plant said that they intend to import finished products to Iran, Malaysia, and other foreign countries, but the capacity is not enough. The director of the company said:

> It is not difficult to get a halal certificate from the Committee of Halal under the Chechen Muftiat. Representatives of the Committee come and offer their services. After all, to get a certificate is not a forced case. We certainly pay them a symbolic price for their services. But this is not a large amount. Specialists of the Committee come to inspect, train, and always keep in touch with us. If any problems arise in the production they quickly solve. So we are very pleased with the cooperation.

The Halal Committee under the Muftiat of the Chechen Republic was organized in 2015. The task of the Committee is to protect the rights of consumers and manufacturers of halal products. As we were told by the Muftiat:

> The Committee of Halal of the Chechen Republic closely cooperates with the supervisory state bodies. Only after receiving a positive opinion of the state bodies, we get to work. If the company complies with all the rules and requirements of sharia for the production of halal, only then begins the process of issuing a certificate.
>
> Since Chechnya is a Muslim republic and in the territory of the republic live exclusively Muslims, people buying meat somewhere in the market absolutely do not worry about its origin. Nevertheless, in order to enter the markets of other entities, we receive a halal certificate and use this brand in our products.

Discussion

All the production units I have mentioned above had to go through the certification process to validate their product as halal through the administration of a Muftiat which has an authority to issue halal certificates. Businesses spend very high prices for obtaining and renewing halal certificates. Consumers end up having higher prices for their halal products. Some businesses expressed an opinion that a certificate would only be necessary for the export of the products abroad and not for the internal markets. Internal markets or smaller sales are often based on trust and personal knowledge about the seller. However, without a certificate it is challenging to sell the products as "halal" when they are without the halal label.

Financial interests within the business sector of halal certification and higher incomes from this economy provides a space for corruption. The field of halal certification is very young in Russia, and therefore this field is not well institutionalized as in other countries. The procedures and works of certification and following the rules are chaotic and poorly organized. The question of trust came up very often due to the lack of trust in Muftiat, and the corrupt character of bureaucrats and administrators. There were also varying discourses regarding trust in officials or authorities of halal authorization as well as trust between producers and customers of halal products.

Depending on the locale—if it was in Dagestan, Tatarstan, or Chechnya—the negotiation and necessity for a halal certificate, as well as the size of the production unit, was also decisive for discussions of halal certification, its necessity, importance, and the questions of trust.

Conclusion

The material presented in this paper covers a wide range of information, and some systematic analysis still needs to be performed to draw more conclusions. Nonetheless, I can make some initial working conclusions regarding the findings presented above.

First, halal business for Russian manufacturers, especially when compared to their counterparts in other countries such as Brazil, India, and the United States, is a new segment of the economy. Second, well-defined and developed mechanisms of interaction of state bodies with halal committees created for control and certification of halal products have not yet been developed. Third, many manufacturers interviewed do not like having to pass two separate rounds of inspection, especially when the manufacturers need to pay for those inspections and they appear to be duplicative. Fourth, relatively higher prices must be charged for halal products because they do not receive any state subsidies for production and processing. Fifth, the state refuses to officially recognize the established committees for the control and certification of halal products under the spiritual directorates. Finally, the conditions of sanctions make it impossible for large producers of halal products to enter the foreign market.

Part II

Halal Market Growth

5

Between Religion and Ethnicity: The Politics of Halal in China

Guangtian Ha

Introduction

It need not be repeated that religious freedom is a delicate matter in China, despite the stated commitment to its safeguarding in the country's constitution. The history of 'actually existing socialism' not only leaves an enduring legacy of totalitarianism reinforced by recent tides of nationalism and the rise of high-tech surveillance apparatuses; it has also created some terminological haze reflecting conceptual ambivalence in the governance of ethno-religious minorities. One such ambivalence pertaining to this chapter is lodged at the very hyphen that connects 'ethnic' and 'religious.' While its political and social ramifications arguably differ for each ethno-religious minority in China—for instance, the global repercussions of Tibetan politics and their religious convictions would likely render devout Tibetans more of a target for enforced assimilation than would be a Sinophone secular Manchu—here I focus, in particular, on its impact

---

G. Ha (✉)
Haverford College, Haverford, PA, USA
e-mail: gha@haverford.edu

© The Author(s), under exclusive license to Springer Nature Switzerland AG 2023
R. Turaeva, M. Brose (eds.), *Religious Economies in Secular Context*, New Directions in Islam, https://doi.org/10.1007/978-3-031-18603-5_5

on China's management of *qingzhen/halal* as an industry among its Muslim populations.

There are ten officially recognized Muslim groups in China. The Uyghurs, for instance, have of late made international headlines due to the severe surveillance and persecution imposed by the Chinese government. Similar, if less harsh, clampdowns have taken place among other Muslim minorities too. Newspaper articles and academic essays that investigate or celebrate ethno-religious difference have been withdrawn from online databases; some journals have circulated internal memoranda instructing its editors not to accept new submissions on Islam; and whole university programs have been accused—at first on social media, then panning out until the accusation reached the ears of senior university administrators—of stoking the fire of ethno-religious nationalism and have been quickly abolished. When I revisited Ningxia Hui Autonomous Region in 2018 for follow-up research, the suppression was in full swing, to the extent that some Hui Muslim intellectuals found in it an ominous echo of the Great Cultural Revolution (1966–1976) that caused a complete devastation of China's religious landscape.

While crucial differences exist among China's linguistically and culturally diverse Muslim groups, the distinction is less pronounced when we turn our attention to state management and supervision of the halal industry. This in part has to do with the fact that sectarian differences and variations in interpreting Islamic law regarding the definition of *halal* rarely rise to the level where they may affect state policy, and in part has to do with the fact that the public representation of halal certification—printed on certificates issued by a variety of organizations or as logos on merchandise packages—utilizes visual and scriptural motifs often common to all Muslim ethnic groups in China. As this chapter will demonstrate, new standards imposed by the state while generating significant disruptions also build on earlier conventions. The government's very selectiveness in deciding which conventions to follow and which to discard—for instance, valorizing the Chinese term *qingzhen* while banning the Arabic word *halal*—reveals nuances and ambiguities that would escape us if we were to consider these acts as no more than official endorsement of Islamophobia. A crackdown on Arabic *halal* signage is not

5 Between Religion and Ethnicity: The Politics of Halal in China 87

equivalent to a blanket crackdown on the halal industry itself; likewise, widespread Islamophobia in society and state suppression of Islam could also coexist with a thriving domestic halal market. Understanding the conceptual slippage between religion and ethnicity may help us explain these apparent contradictions.

There is little doubt that if we are to examine the consumption of halal food among China's Muslims, we will find a wide range of practices and a wider range of interpretive stances (from whether prawns are halal to under what circumstances drinking alcohol may be permitted); the focus of this chapter, however, is on the Chinese state's response to a burgeoning halal industry as it manifests itself in the numerous and at times self-conflicting policies created by local governments. In 2018, when I visited Zhengzhou (Henan Province, China) to reconnect with my earlier interlocutors, an eminent Hui Muslim entrepreneur, whom I had long known to hold strong ties to the Henan provincial government, offered his own explanation of what seemed to me to be a conflict between, on the one hand, the Belt and Road Initiative laying stress on deepened collaboration with the Muslim world and, on the other, the ongoing suppression of Islam within Chinese borders. 'It is completely reasonable,' he remarked matter-of-factly. 'The more you wish to expand your ties to the Muslim world, the more you would want to be sure that this is not taken the wrong way by the Muslim minorities: internal unity is all the more essential if you are to expand globally.'

Whether the view is at all representative of the official position of the Chinese Communist Party (CCP) is perhaps of less import. It offers us a path to coming to grips with a critical ambiguity that undergirds the Chinese halal industry: namely, the contradiction between its commercial and strategic value for the Chinese state and the potential threats the CCP considers halal may pose to national security if its association with global Islam is left uncontained. It is at the crux of this ambiguity that we ought to locate the most profound ramification of the conceptual ambivalence between religion and ethnicity. This is also where we can begin to explain the range of economic factors that have so far remained largely unexamined in dealing with the Chinese halal market.

Ethnic Customs or Religious Beliefs?

The halal industry is not the only, nor perhaps the most consequential, location where we can observe the social impact of the Chinese state's attempt to separate the religious from the ethnic. One other place is the regulation on cremation. While the law stipulating how bodies are to be disposed of after death is insistent on the propagation of cremation and tolerates little deviation,[1] shortly after its promulgation in 1997, the State Ethnic Affairs Commission (Guojia minwei), along with the departments of Health and Civil Administration, issued a short memorandum documenting special cases where exceptions were to be made. 'In funeral services the freedom of ethnic minorities to preserve or reform their funerary customs needs to be respected.' So the memorandum proclaims, and it continues to specify the groups of minorities to whom this rider applies:

> In areas where cremation is to become the norm, the customs of burial (*tuzang xisu*) among the Hui, the Uyghurs, the Kazaks, the Kirghiz, the Uzbeks, the Tajiks, the Tatars, the Salars, the Dongxiang, and the Bao'an need be respected (*zunzhong*). There should be no compulsion for them to carry out cremation. Those who voluntarily opt to cremating their deceased family members should be allowed to do so; there ought to be no external intervention.[2]

Other forms of funerary service practiced—for instance, sky burial among Tibetans—receive no mention; the stress is laid almost exclusively on Muslim funerals. However, the language used is telling for what it omits: no religious terminology appears in this memorandum. It is almost as if by meticulously listing all the concerned minorities, the explanation

---

[1] 'Binzang Guanli Tiaoli', State Council 1997. Text is available at https://zh.m.wikisource.org/zh-hans/%E6%AE%A1%E8%91%AC%E7%AE%A1%E7%90%86%E6%9D%A1%E4%BE%8B_(1997%E5%B9%B4). We need to note that the state propagation of cremation did not originate in the 1990s but constituted an essential social measure imposed by the new secularist communist government in the 1950s. The administrative order issued in 1997 was only a reconsolidation of prior policies and a reaffirmation of state resolve in eradicating unlawful burial practices.

[2] *Zongjiao Shiwu Tiaoli Xiangguan Falvfagui Ji Zhengce Shouce*, 296. See also http://www.gov.cn/banshi/2005-07/22/content_16671.htm. Accessed 19 July 2021.

5 Between Religion and Ethnicity: The Politics of Halal in China   89

deliberately avoided mentioning Islam. Burial is characterized as a 'custom' and an 'ethnic' one at that; it is something minorities *do* and, as such, is a *practice* that can presumably be considered separately from any pronounced religious commitment. In no officially published document I have perused over the years has burial been associated overtly with religion.[3] 'If burial is linked to religion and thus converted to a matter of religious freedom,' a Hui official once explained to me, 'then what if the Han claim that their religion—for instance, Daoism—also requires them to carry out burial? Then the government will see the end of cremation for everyone in this country.'

It is in the same ambivalent space between ethnicity and religion, between 'ethnic custom' and 'religious belief,' that we find the controversy over halal food in China. If burial has to be recast as an ethnic custom to avoid throwing open the floodgate that will practically end all state efforts in promoting—and enforcing—cremation, labeling halal as religious creates a different set of problems. One problem, for example, has to do with recruiting minority cadres for the Communist Party. Most Hui government officials I worked with in fieldwork observed halal dietary restrictions, yet all of them were members of the party. Casting the observance of halal in food consumption as an ethnic custom enables them to both remain loyal party members—thus, in principle, committed atheists—and continue to comply with the traditional dietary rules that signal their membership to their families and communities.[4] The balance is no doubt delicate and fragile, yet it seems to have worked—so far.

---

[3] However, somewhat of an exception can be found on the official website of the Department of Civil Affairs http://www.mca.gov.cn/article/wh/whbq/lsqm/whjz/201212/20121215389103. shtml. The linked article draws no pronounced distinction between religion and ethnicity, only claiming that 'Muslim burials (*musilin zangli*)' combine 'national, religious, geographical, and customary' characteristics and that there are ten Muslim ethnic groups in China. It should also be noted that in some official discourses, the term Muslim (*musilin*) could at times acquire a certain ethnic sense, too, by being associated with 'custom' instead of religion. See, for instance, https://www.chinadailyasia.com/nation/2016-06/01/content_15442495.html.

[4] For the paradoxical position of minority cadres, see Harrell (2008) and Litzinger (2000). The Communist Party has agonized repeatedly over its members' relationship to religion. As late as 2016, *People's Daily* was still publishing opinion pieces instructing party members to repudiate any religious belief while remaining concerned with the party's official policies on religion. See http://opinion.people.com.cn/n1/2016/1227/c1003-28978419.html.

In what follows, I draw on more than a decade of fieldwork beginning in 2009 at two places in China—Henan Province and Ningxia Hui Autonomous Region—to examine the politics of religion and ethnicity as they pertain to the production of halal food in China. In Part I, I revisit a critical distinction between two key terms often associated with the matter in question, namely, *qingzhen* and *halal*. This distinction criss-crosses with the religion/ethnicity dyad, to the point where *qingzhen* has acquired a stronger ethnic association while *halal*, for the reasons to be laid out below, is increasingly considered a stand-in for global Islam. While recent work tends to blur the distinction between the two, even treating them as largely synonymous and interchangeable (e.g., Brose and Min 2021), I draw attention to their historical difference and divergent political ramifications in the present. Encoded in the difference between *qingzhen* and *halal* is a contested division between religion and ethnicity that exhibits both a legacy taken over into China from Soviet socialism (cf. Brubaker 1994; Martin 2001) and some affinity with the religion/culture dyad familiar to European colonial and civilizing missions (Keane 2007: 83–112).

Apart from this admittedly more conceptual aim, in the second part, I also provide a close-up view of the specific executive and legal practices involved in the governmental supervision of halal food production. The recent article by Matthew Erie (2018: 406–407) does an excellent job exposing the legal disputes and administrative predicaments derived from this work. This chapter, however, examines the specific impact of these predicaments on the routine work of halal supervision conducted by local governments. In 2010, I undertook an extensive work trip with two provincial officials in Henan—both ethnic Hui—to carry out a comprehensive inspection of the major *halal* food manufacturers in the province and to announce the establishment of Henan's government-organized center for halal certification.

This visit has a backstory: in 2008, the first provincial-level center for certifying halal food was established by the government of the Ningxia Hui Autonomous Region. Its creation reflected a general, though short-lived, effort by the government to throw its own weight behind the

5 Between Religion and Ethnicity: The Politics of Halal in China 91

certification of halal food in China.[5] Returning afresh to Henan after the inaugural conference on halal supervision organized by this center, the two Hui officials I worked with enthused about the promises it made and the potential economic value as well as the tax revenue that a state-regulated halal industry could generate for cash-thirsty local governments. Equipped with a generous dose of optimism, they set up their own counterpart office in Henan soon upon return: the Henan Provincial Office for the Management of Qingzhen Food (Henan sheng qingzhen shipin guanli bangongshi).[6] The work trip was to announce to all relevant enterprises in their jurisdiction that the Henan provincial government was now officially on a course to subject the whole halal industry to its systematic control. They were to demonstrate how the supervision was to work and how regulation on paper was to be implemented in practice. It was a rare opportunity for a researcher. As shall become clear in this chapter, participant-observation on this trip allowed me to understand the persistent dilemmas and administrative dead ends related to the certification process.

The relationship between the two parts of this chapter is both contrastive and synergetic. I wish to show how the conceptual ambivalence encompassing the religion/ethnicity dyad and the *qingzhen/halal* distinction animates much dispute over how Islam is to be seen in the public sphere. This ideological controversy, while hyper-visible, does not translate into a systematization of state regulation and supervision of the halal industry. Offices and departments responsible for certifying halal products, once established, were continually understaffed, with the result that, while local governments might coerce businesses into changing their

---

[5] The conference was part of a Ningxia international festival for *qingzhen* food and Muslim wares. See http://news.sina.com.cn/c/2008-04-28/190415444953.shtml.

[6] The office is later alternatively referred to as the Division for the Supervision and Inspection of Interethnic Relations (Minzu guanxi yu jiandu jiancha chu). See http://hnsmzzjw.henan.gov.cn/2020/12-18/2003451.html.

halal signage and erasing all traces of Arabic (Ha 2020b),[7] they did little to make good on their promises of creating a reliable certification process. Some Hui lamented the failure, citing the lack of regulation and its effective implementation, especially at the national level, as the main reason for the underdevelopment of China's halal industry and its negligible share in the international market.[8] Others were less disturbed. 'I don't eat out anyway,' a Hui in Ningxia once remarked to me. 'I raise my own poultry and livestock and have them slaughtered in front of my own eyes. I know quite a few who do the same.' However, for the vast majority of urban and urbanizing Hui, this option is no doubt out of the question. As much as the Hui officials are involved in the work of supervision, they also have to contend with a debilitating tension between pronounced ideological constriction and less visible administrative failure.

From Hui to Yisilan: Separating Religion from Ethnicity

Islam underwent an official alteration of name shortly after the People's Republic was established. While numerous names had been applied to this religion—from the transliteration *yisiliamu* to *qingzhen jiao* to *xiao-jiao*—for centuries, the commonest name was *huijiao*, 'teaching of the

---

[7] This ongoing crackdown has been widely reported in international media. See, for instance, 'Chinese authorities launch anti-halal crackdown in Xinjiang,' https://www.theguardian.com/world/2018/oct/10/chinese-authorities-launch-anti-halal-crackdown-in-xinjiang. The removal of Arabic signage dovetailed with the demolition of Islamic architecture, presumed to look too 'Arab' and not Chinese enough. The latest example, which has provoked much resentment among the Hui, was the demolition of the dome atop the grand Dongguan Mosque in Xining, Qinghai. The website Bitter Winter has published an internal document detailing how the rebuilding was to be carried out. See https://bitterwinter.org/wp-content/uploads/2020/06/Report-on-the-plan-to--rectify-Arabic-style-mosques-in-Chengdong-district-of-Xining-city.pdf. Only in 2016 did an eminent politician—a Sufi leader, as a matter of fact—in Ningxia raise the suggestion that China ought to have a national standard for halal food. He is known to have suffered vicious political attacks both in Ningxia and nationally ever since. See 'Officials in China call for national standard for halal food,' https://www.nytimes.com/2016/03/15/world/asia/china-halal-food-standards.html?.?mc=aud_dev&ad-keywords=auddevgate&gclid=CjwKCAjwgISIBhBfEiwALE19SQsQ4IDm7gOQmJNuAS8ZlwMRR6UO2WtApy5yl7NeuaCxDhyMLgyMvxoCJMcQAvD_BwE&gclsrc=aw.ds.

[8] The minimal market share of China-produced *halal* food is well acknowledged. See, for instance, https://cn.chinadaily.com.cn/2017ydylforum/2017-04/12/content_28889050.htm.

5 Between Religion and Ethnicity: The Politics of Halal in China   93

Hui.' Derived initially from the ethnonym Uyghur in medieval times when Uyghurs were still mostly Buddhists, the term Hui began to refer to Muslims from the fourteenth century onward (Li and Feng 1985: 226–246). The shift was gradual, and while the term seemed to have thus acquired a purely religious sense, it was never quite severed from an association with ethnicity—even a Muslim ethnicity. In 1926, at the height of modern nation-building among the Chinese, a Sinophone Hui Muslim intellectual was deliberately provocative when he pontificated (Li and Feng 1985: 263),

> Is there a difference between *huijiao* and *huizu* (Hui ethnic group)? … Who are the Hui anyway? Indeed, we are merely Han who believe in a religion called the Hui teaching (*huijiao*). In this world there are numerous religions, just as there are numerous nationalities and ethnic groups. Each religion may contain various ethnic groups while in each group one finds believers of diverse religions … [If those observing the Hui religion constitute a separate Hui ethnic group, then] since the Manchus, the Mongols, the Tibetans, being different, still all practice one and the same Buddhism, why do they not constitute one single Buddhist ethnic group? Among the Han people one finds Confucianism, Buddhism, Daoism, Christianity, and Islam, why do we not see the Han being divided into ethnic groups along these lines? Only the Hui claim that their Hui religion ought to endow them with a distinct ethnicity; this is total nonsense.

These comments set up quite a few strawmen—they both exaggerate the conceived homogeneity of the Buddhism practiced by different groups and downplay the pursuit of distinct ethnic, religious, and geographical identities among the Han, which as a group is as much a constructed entity as are the 'ethnic minorities.' They also display with remarkable vehemence the intensity of the controversy evoked by the enduring association of Islam with ethnicity in late imperial and modern China.[9]

The new communist regime deliberately removed the ethnic connotations from Islam. On June 2, 1956, the State Council issued a brief directive announcing that, effective immediately, references to '*huijiao*' were

---

[9] For a recent account of this controversy see Cieciura (2016).

94   G. Ha

to be replaced with the word '*yisilanjiao*' in all public communication.[10] 'Islam is a global religion,' the directive proclaimed, 'and *yisilanjiao* is thus an internationally recognized and widely used term.' The intention, as stated somewhat less overtly in the text of the directive, was to wrest ethnicity away from religion: *hui* as a name had been so closely associated with Islam that only a new and officially consolidated transliteration, *yisilanjiao*, could manage to draw a sharper distinction between the two, for if Islam is no longer the 'Hui teaching,' then anyone in principle could be a Muslim without being a Hui, and vice versa—a Hui could also be a non-Muslim.

Precisely the latter was stated unequivocally in a speech delivered in April 1958 by a high communist official and designer of party policies concerning ethnic and religious affairs, Li Weihan. Rather befitting to the present discussion, the statement was made citing the Muslim dietary restriction as a prime example (Li 1986: 354–355):

Religious faith (*zongjiao xinyang*) is not within the remit of our reform (*gaige*). We do not wish to reform religious faiths; our aim is to reform religious institutions (*zongjiao zhidu*). Does this mean that we will need to reform all religious institutions? No, it does not. We are to reform only those institutions that under today's condition have obstructed the development of the Hui—institutions that are particularly harmful and contradict state law. These need to be changed; otherwise the Hui will fight an uphill battle in their advancement. We shall divide all religious institutions into three categories: those that must be changed (*bixu gai de*), those whose change is not a necessity (*bubi gai de*), and those that can be left alone for now (*kekai kebugai de*). Solutions must be found for those in need of change; those whose change is not a necessity can remain; and those that can be left alone for now can enjoy their temporary status. Some things should not be considered as belonging to religious institutions; they ought to be seen as ethnic customs. In my opinion the abstinence from pork is an ethnic habit (*minzu de xiguan*). If a commune needs to rear pigs, the work can be assigned to the Han members, sparing the Hui members. Regarding the abstention from pork, it should be considered a matter of personal habit (*geren de xiguan*). There ought to be no interference from others.

---

[10] The directive can be accessed at https://www.neac.gov.cn/seac/zcfg/201006/1074312.shtml.

5 Between Religion and Ethnicity: The Politics of Halal in China

Li resorted to no Islamic sources in making these remarks, nor had he consulted any Hui Muslim intellectual versed in these sources. His opinion reflects less engagement with the Hui than the official position of the new communist government. It sounds almost as if, insofar as the observance of the dietary restriction is a matter of 'ethnic habit,' it could then be immediately reduced to the level of personal choice. The implication is that religion, on the other hand, is by definition collective—institutional, to borrow Li's own terminology—and thus more controlling, constraining, and more of a threat to the new state. Another concern specific to the new communist state seeking a wide social basis undergirded this deliberate conceptual move. Labeling the observance of halal a religious practice would in one stroke cast a large and growing number of Hui party members as religiously observant Muslims, likely to the latter's chagrin since party membership proscribed religious affiliation. It would also unduly expand the reach of religion: those with no particular religious fervor who still abstain from pork (a sizable portion among the Hui) would all of a sudden appear unwittingly religious—while the stated position of the new state was precisely that religion ought eventually to have no place in a communist society. The concept of habit or custom, in this context specifically, implies a lack of willful conviction; the matter then becomes one of inertia, something adopted from the past with no particular purpose and thus innocuous.

Qingzhen Before Halal

The concept of *qingzhen* aided the ethnicization of *halal* because it had already undergone historical indigenization. While likely of Daoist origin, the term was used since at least the fifteenth century to at first refer to synagogues, which were called *qingzhen si*, a moniker that soon afterwards, if not simultaneously, was also applied to mosques.[11] It is not clear how *qingzhen* was first adopted in this context and whether it was

---

[11] For the use of *qingzhen* among the Jewish inhabitants of China, especially in Henan, see Wei (1995: 25). A transcript of one of the steles found of the old synagogue (*qingzhen si*) in Kaifeng is accessible at https://collections.dartmouth.edu/teitexts/tenney/diplomatic/ms794-009cn-diplomatic.html. For English translations of this and other steles, see Weisz (2006).

originally an exonym only later accepted by Jews and Muslims. As the latter became more vocal and innovative in attributing philosophical and theological meanings to *qingzhen* in late imperial times (Ha 2020a: 332), there was no effort to disambiguate its multiple references and no mention of the fact that the term continued to be applied to synagogues even until the nineteenth century. A historical imbrication of Islam with Judaism thus became overshadowed by an increasingly Muslim-centric interpretation of *qingzhen*, to the point that in the early twenty-first century, the term was rendered uncritically as almost completely synonymous with *halal*.

However, we have little evidence that prior to the 2000s, the Arabic *halal* sign was ever in wide use among the Hui. *Qingzhen* signs, on the other hand, were ubiquitous, and they were often more than drab reproductions of the two Chinese characters. A photo from the mid-1930s taken by Reverend Claude Pickens Jr. in Wuhan (Fig. 5.1), for example,

Fig. 5.1 Republican-era *qingzhen* restaurant sign from Wuhan. Courtesy of Harvard-Yenching Library

5 Between Religion and Ethnicity: The Politics of Halal in China

shows a *qingzhen* shop sign: the characters for *qingzhen* appear at the top, framed by floral patterns. There is Arabic script below the Chinese characters *qingzhen*. The Arabic words are unfortunately illegible but seem too elaborate to be the simple '*halal.*' Below this appears the image of a ewer, which evokes ritual ablution. On the body of the ewer is written (again not *halal*, which would have been orthographically simpler)— *alhamdulillāh*, 'Praise be to Allah.' The sign is notable because it includes Arabic and Chinese script—indicating some degree of familiarity with Arabic Islamic terms, at least among sign-makers (we do not know how many ordinary Hui could decode the Arabic inscription)—but *qingzhen* is present, and *halal* is not. We can presume that *halal* was not a preferred term.

Well into the 1990s, the ewer was still a popular visual motif in many *qingzhen* signs. An old sign I managed to purchase from a local vendor in Henan (Fig. 5.2) displays a reshaped ewer in the image of a considerably less charming teapot, on the body of which is inscribed the name of the Prophet Muhammad. *Qingzhen* is written in traditional characters as an adjective for 'food' (*shipin*), while the Arabic above it says '*ṭaʿām al-muslimīn*' (the food of Muslims). The couplet that flanks the ewer reads 'respect [the Hui] ethnic customs; [we] forbid the forbidden food.' Both the couplet and the note at the bottom—'plate of credibility for [the sale of] *qingzhen* food'—give out an air of officialdom though no authority is specified. Another 'plate of credibility' I collected that presents a similar pattern (Fig. 5.3) has at its bottom, 'under the supervision of Henan Provincial Commission for Ethnic Affairs (Henan sheng minzu shiwu weiyuanhui jianzhi),' while on the body of the ewer is written MYZ; MZ standing for *minzu* (民族),[12] with Y being the initial letter of *yisilan*, the modern Chinese transliteration for Islam.

---

[12] The word *minzu* is notoriously difficult to translate into English. It has been rendered alternately as 'nationality' or 'ethnic group,' each with its distinct suggestion. The word *minzu* in its modern meaning was initially derived from the Japanese term *minzoku*, but its later application in the Chinese context was also heavily mediated by the Soviet politics of *natsia* (nationality). For a comprehensive treatment of *minzu*, see Mullaney (2010). In the late 1990s and 2000s, the debate about a 'second-generation' ethnic policy in China also began as a tinkering with term (see Leibold (2013); Roche and Leibold (2020) offer a good overview of the latest pertinent literature). Whether *minzu* is 'nationality' or 'ethnic group'—the former deemed to suggest a right to political independence while the latter was somewhat 'cultural' in nature and thus de-politicized—became a key site for grappling with a still controversial socialist legacy in the age of revived nationalism. For a critical review of this debate, see Elliott (2015).

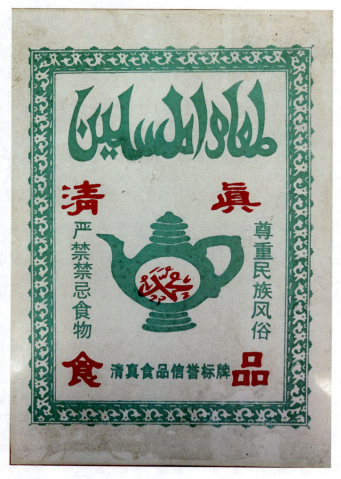

Fig. 5.2 Contemporary *qingzhen* food sign. Author's collection

Most Hui restaurants in the 1980s and 1990s used some sort of signage to exhibit their *qingzhen* status. A commonly used Arabic phrase was *ṭaʿām al-muslimīn*, 'the food of Muslims' (Figs. 5.2 and 5.3); two variants of it that had also been used widely were *al-maṭʿam al-muslimī* (the Muslim restaurant) and *maṭʿam al-muslimīn* (Muslims' restaurant). These phrases were often inscribed in such a manner that the letters were barely legible, and all geometrical rules that normally regulate Arabic

5 Between Religion and Ethnicity: The Politics of Halal in China

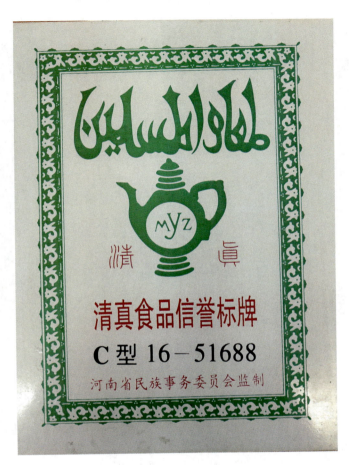

Fig. 5.3 Contemporary *qingzhen* food sign, Henan Province. Author's collection

calligraphy were defied most splendidly. By the 1990s, such phrases had largely become a sign *par excellence* in that it was the shape of the letters and their combination into an *image*, rather than the literal meaning of the words, that bespoke a *qingzhen* status. That *ṭaʿām al-muslimīn* had been rendered into an *image* is clearest when it is seen outside the context of food. For example, in summer 2018, as I walked down a street at the center of the Hui community in Zhengzhou, Henan, among all the newly painted plaques mounted on the façades of restaurants, there was

Fig. 5.4 *Qingzhen* restaurant in Henan Province. Author's collection

one bearing the name of a local residential community (Fig. 5.4). Above the Chinese name—星光小区 (xingguang xiaoqu, The Starlight Residence)—we read in Arabic, *ṭaʿām al-muslimīn*, 'the food of Muslims.' None of the Hui lulling about in the vicinity were able to read the Arabic words, and yet they all insisted that it meant that most residents living therein were Hui. It seems more plausible that those who had mounted this plaque had taken the phrase to be an *image* that indicated Muslimness or Huiness, as opposed to advertising the residents as human flesh for sale. In other words, while *qingzhen* was often written alongside *ṭaʿām al-muslimīn* in close proximity, it had never been a translation of the Arabic phrase. Ordinary Hui were not expected to understand the Arabic script; they were supposed to recognize the image composed of curled Arabic letters. Thus far, there has been no attempt to translate *qingzhen* into Arabic or *ṭaʿām al-muslimīn* into Chinese, nor to display this stricter translational correlation in the design of a sign. By the early twenty-first

5 Between Religion and Ethnicity: The Politics of Halal in China 101

century, *ta'ām al-muslimīn* had become so much of an image that its meaning as an Arabic phrase had largely been forgotten—only to be resuscitated, for good or ill, after the Arabic word *halal* began to appear en masse on *qingzhen* signs.

Qingzhen as Halal?

The equation of *halal* to *qingzhen* and the increase in halal's public visual prominence took place primarily in the 2000s. It received a major push in 2008 after the first governmental authority for halal certification was established in Ningxia. The new institution, officially a department of the Ningxia Commission for Ethnic Affairs, bore the name Ningxia International Centre for Qingzhen Food Certification (Ningxia qingzhen shipin guoji renzheng zhongxin, hereafter Ningxia Center), but its terms and conditions made it clear that *qingzhen* was understood as a direct translation of *halal*: '*Qingzhen* (halal [here in Latin script]) designates those actions and behaviors that accord with the law of Islam.'[13] The use of parenthesis indicates a complete equivalence of *qingzhen* to *halal* as though the latter offered merely a gloss on the former. Two years later in 2010, the inaugural session of the China-Arab Economic and Trade Forum (Zhong A jingmao luntan) featured a separate conference on reconciling (*duijie*) the divergent standards for halal certification between Ningxia and the international market. Boasting twenty-two high-level 'foreign guests' from Egypt, Kuwait, Australia, New Zealand, and Argentina—most of them involved in halal certification as government officials, academics, or entrepreneurs—the conference brochure included a piece that echoed the views of many Hui officials in Ningxia: it lamented the negligible amount of Ningxia export to the Muslim world and advised more consideration of the 'living habits' (*shenghuo xiguan*) of the Arab

---

[13] 'General Instruction on the Certification of Halal Food in Ningxia Hui Autonomous Region' (Ningxia huizu zizhiqu qingzhen shipin renzhen tongze) was issued by the Ningxia government in 2008. The instruction was officially abolished in December 2017 as the controversy over 'pan-qingzhen-ification (*qingzhen fanhua*)' intensified. For full bilingual text of the instruction, see Profile of Ningxia International Trade Certification Center for Halal Food [sic] (*Zhongguo Ningxia qingzhen shipin guoji renzheng shouce*), Yinchuan, Ningxia, September 2010, pp. 5–13.

world in future trade.[14] In the bilingual pamphlet distributed along with other conference materials, *qingzhen* never appeared in the English translation while *halal* was again used in parenthesis to gloss *qingzhen* in the Chinese text. They ran parallel to one another with no apparent friction.

Ningxia Center was founded in 2008 and upgraded in 2010 to become the new Ningxia International Trade Certification Center for Halal Food. Its responsibilities included, *inter alia*, 'undertak[ing] specifically the international trade certification duty of all halal food products within Ningxia to be exported to Islamic countries and regions.'[15] Prior to such official equation of *qingzhen* with *halal*, there had been more localized and non-governmental attempts to introduce the Arabic *halal* signs to a wider audience within China. In the early 2000s, for example, some new restaurants in Beijing and Yunnan had already begun to use *halal* on their signage; such deliberate choice often bespoke an allegiance to a specifically Islamic 'modernity' as opposed to the hegemonic Western version (cf. Gillette 2000). The subtle shift was double: as *halal* replaced or accompanied *qingzhen* in an increasing number of signs, Arabic script also gradually began to be recognized by more Hui as *words* rather than perceived as images. *Qingzhen* was old; *ṭaʿām al-muslimīn*, with its imagistic presentation of Arabic, was awfully verbose and outdated; what's with that peculiar *musulmānche*? Halal, on the other hand, was internationally recognized and beamed Gulf gold and Malaysian wealth. *Qingzhen* was the past, *halal* the future, and *ṭaʿām al-muslimīn* should be phased out once and for all. And yet none of these was official—until the government made it so.

The new officially advertised *halal* sign is remarkably bold (Fig. 5.5). Trilingual in Chinese, Arabic, and English, it depicts an orange-hued map of China with Ningxia marked at the exact geometric center. An oversized Arabic inscription of '*halal*'—even larger than the map of

---

[14] *Shoujie Zhong A jingmao luntan Zhong A qingzhen shipin renzheng jizhi duijiehui ziliao huibian* (Compiled documents for the reconciliation of certification processes for qingzhen food between China and the Arab countries during the Inaugural China-Arab Economic and Trade Forum), ed. Ningxia qingzhen shipin guoji maoyi renzheng zhongxin (Ningxia International Trade Certification Centre for Qingzhen Food), October 2010, p. 7.

[15] Profile of Ningxia International Trade Certification Centre for Halal Food, September 2010, p. 1.

Fig. 5.5 Official seal of Ningxia Halal Certification Center. Author's collection

China!—is partly superimposed on the map, translated into English below, with the whole image encircled by the words for 'halal food certification' in all three languages. Shamefully, the Arabic translation is grammatically incorrect: instead of *al-aghdhiyya al-halal* ('[the] halal [the] foodstuffs'); it is only *aghdhiyya al-halal*, missing the definite article in front of 'foodstuffs.' Considering the importance of this new logo, the error was especially confounding. No Hui officials in Ningxia I interviewed could read Arabic, and my question about a possible grammatical error in the sign often went unanswered. Interestingly, however, the same error was not replicated in a sample of the new halal certificate the Ningxia government offered for the viewing of its potential international collaborators (Fig. 5.6). The inconsistency most probably betrays the sloppiness of a government barely managing to meet the ambitious goal it had set itself. No doubt the design of the new logo and the new *halal* certificate had benefited from the counsel of experts with knowledge of

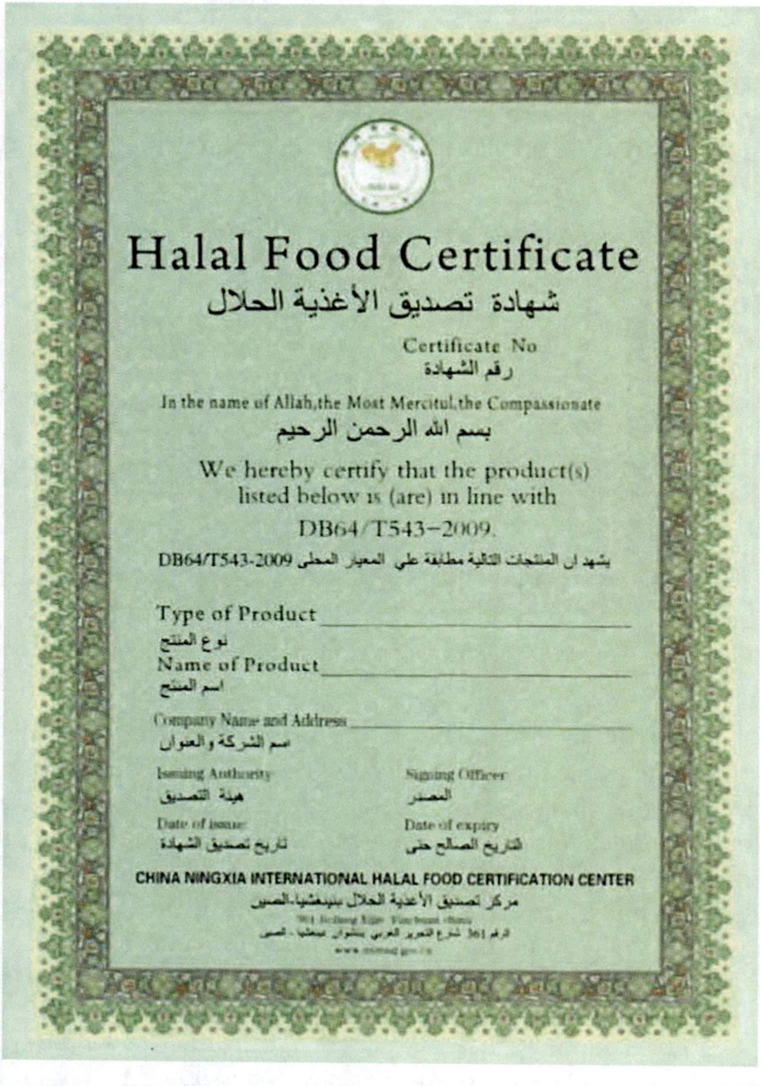

Halal Food Certificate

شهادة تصديق الأغذية الحلال

Certificate No

رقم الشهادة

In the name of Allah, the Most Merciful, the Compassionate

بسم الله الرحمن الرحيم

We hereby certify that the product(s) listed below is (are) in line with DB64/T543−2009.

يشهد ان المنتجات التالية مطابقة على المعيار المحلي DB64/T543-2009

Type of Product ____________

نوع المنتج

Name of Product ____________

اسم المنتج

Company Name and Address ____________

اسم الشركة والعنوان

Issuing Authority

هيئة التصديق

Signing Officer

المصدر

Date of issue

تاريخ تصديق الشهادة

Date of expiry

التاريخ الصالح حتى

CHINA NINGXIA INTERNATIONAL HALAL FOOD CERTIFICATION CENTER

مركز تصديق الأغذية الحلال بنينغشيا-الصين

Fig. 5.6 Example of Ningxia Halal Food Certificate. Author's collection

Arabic (I know some of these experts through fieldwork); yet the apparent inconsistency highlighted the small role such counsel had played, and it seems likely that the nod to Arabic was largely perfunctory. What is also clear is that in this new logo, the word for food is *aghdhiyya* instead

5 Between Religion and Ethnicity: The Politics of Halal in China

Fig. 5.7 Malaysian, Indonesian, Singapore halal logos. Author's collection

of *ṭaʿām*, and as such is a deliberate linguistic departure from the old ubiquitous *ṭaʿām al-muslimīn*. Neither the Malaysian JAKIM logo, nor the Indonesian or Singaporean *halal* logos, literally mentions 'food' (Fig. 5.7), thus its literality only renders the Ningxia logo all the more exceptional.

While *ṭaʿām al-muslimīn* was never verbalized in its Arabic pronunciation and invariably *qingzhen* stood in for it in nearly all daily parlance, toward the end of the first decade of the 2000s, *haliali* (哈俩里), a Chinese transliteration of *halal*, began to appear on Hui trademarks.[16] The word also slipped gradually into the daily parlance of some ordinary Hui. A Hui woman in Yunnan in her seventies once complained to me about the 'sudden eruption' of new terms in the around this time. It took her a while to grow comfortable with *haliali*; at times, she would say something was '*qingzhen haliali*' or add an explanation to clarify that *haliali* was *qingzhen*, for herself as much as for others. From the early 2010s, more Hui began to see a stronger and more literal equation between the idea of *qingzhen* and the word of *halal*.

This is the very time when the so-called *qingzhen fanhua*, or pan-*qingzhen*-ification—a term coined mostly by Han nationalists, Communist Party enthusiasts, and Islamophobes—began to attract wider attention online and in the government (Erie 2016). While in the next part of this chapter I will explain the reasons that might indeed have led

---

[16] See, for instance, the Haliali Qingzhen Food Inc. (http://www.halialifood.com/). Interestingly, despite the growing popularity of *haliali*, *qingzhen* refuses to give in. The coexistence of both terms in this company's name, as well as the owner's feeling of no sense of redundancy, shows *haliali* to be still new to Hui's daily language and thus different from *qingzhen*.

to a visible growth of *qingzhen*-marked products in the market, it is essential to note here that the governmental crackdown on *qingzhen fanhua* was again focused on the visual register: despite the fact that the campaign targeted pan-*qingzhen*-ification, it only enforced the removal of Arabic scripts in public signage—whether *halal* or the traditional *Ṭaʿām al-muslimīn*. In their place, it enforced using a uniform typeface—approved by the state—of the Chinese characters for *qingzhen*.

As state-sanctioned Islamophobia and widespread malice against Muslims are on the rise in China, the distinction between *qingzhen* and *halal* preserves some space for Hui identity to maintain its dual ethnic and religious character. This also means that the ethnicization—even a certain indigenization—of *halal* through *qingzhen* may offer a much-needed (though admittedly shrinking) space for an altered Islam to survive. Around 2017, if not earlier, a massive governmental campaign to Sinicize Islam (*yisilanjiao zhongguohua*) was launched with relentless violence across China (Miao 2020; Brophy 2019; Liang 2019). It began with the demolition of domes and the scraping of Arabic *halal* signage, presumed to be signs of unregulated 'Arabicization' indicative of a purported separatist anti-China stance, but soon expanded to cover other sectors. Whole university programs in Islamic studies were abolished overnight, and articles previously published on the topic were pulled from online databases (though they reappear now and again). When I visited Ningxia in 2018, nearly all Hui Muslim academics I contacted complained of ruthless attacks online, in their home institutions, and from backstabbing colleagues keen on exploiting the opportunity for personal gains. They had to file reports about their research, sit in excruciatingly long study sessions, and be prepared to explain the content of some obscure article they had published years previously that might evidence their conceived religious inclination. 'Guangtian my little brother (Guangtian *di*), we are friends,' a Hui academic messaged me before removing me from her contact list, 'but this is getting out of hand and I have to protect myself. I am sure you will understand. There is genuinely no way around this (*zhende mei banfa*)!'

In contrast to such vehement ideological work, however, the state seemed utterly uninterested in subjecting the halal industry to its control through effective administrative measures. A national-level

5 Between Religion and Ethnicity: The Politics of Halal in China 107

administrative regulation laying down the foundational framework for the governance of religious affairs regardless of local circumstances, the *zongjiao shiwu tiaoli*, had been issued by the State Council in 2005, but no comparative law was created for the supervision of the halal industry. Pertinent regulations abounded at the local level, with each province creating its own (though highly similar) rules governing the production and the sale of halal food; however, such commonality had not translated into a unified national policy. In the next part of this chapter, I draw specifically on my fieldwork in Henan and Ningxia to examine the administrative and legal intricacies, as well as the economic interests, that in combination made the supervision of halal an exceptionally difficult task for those local government officials keen on creating a regulated halal market.

Certification as a Secular Affair

In other locations, the production and sale of halal food has been surrounded by religious controversies, environmental concerns, technological dilemmas, and economic pitfalls (Bergeaud-Blackler et al. Bergeaud-Blackler et al. 2015; Fischer 2011, 2016; Shirazi 2016; Armanios 2018; Erie 2018). So far, I am not aware of similar debates gaining comparable attention in the Chinese public sphere. Casual comments concerning the reliability of some halal products were heard at times, and some mosques, invariably with no success, tried to take the matter into their own hands and to organize grassroots inspection squads. There is potential for additional debate. For example, in the 2010s, some Hui I interviewed recounted hearsay scenarios of massive halal slaughterhouses installing loudspeakers in their butchery to broadcast nonstop the *takbīr* (*Allāhu Akbar*) so the machinery carrying out the work would not violate the halal rule. But no one seemed to have contested the admissibility of such a strategy as conforming to the spirit of halal. And clearly missing were controversies over animal welfare and whether electric stunning is an acceptable practice in meeting the halal requirement. The certification of halal products seemed to have followed a different route in China.

Prior to the establishment of the Ningxia Center, the Islamic Association of China (IAC) had been offering paid halal certification services to Muslim businesses. While criticisms of the service were not in short supply—for example, that it was a sham and the certification was only money changing hands—IAC nonetheless carried its credibility for a long time as the only nationwide association for Islam, and its certification was still acknowledged and trusted by many Hui.

Why then, was a new center desirable? There are several possible reasons. One is that given the large number of halal food manufacturers across China, those pushing to establish new centers insisted that IAC did not have the capacity to ascertain on a regular basis whether the certified corporations had consistently met the standard of halal in their production process. A more important problem was seen to rest in the specifically ambivalent nature of IAC as an organization. Established in 1952, IAC is officially a 'patriotic religious organization founded to organize Islamic affairs for all Muslim minorities in China,'[17] according to its public self-definition (cf. Glasserman 2016). While there can be no doubt that IAC is under the control of the Communist Party and is practically an arm of the party in its governance of China's Muslims, it was precisely its officially religious—hence not ethnic—nature that was seized on by those disputing its unwanted intervention in halal certification.

After the inaugural conference on halal supervision organized in 2008 by the new Ningxia International Center for Qingzhen Food Certification, Wuqiang, a Hui official representing Henan at the conference, was unstoppably emboldened. He latched on to the argument that IAC and all its local branches—he had the Henan Islamic Association specifically in mind—were religious organizations and thus must refrain from halal certification, which, according to him, was a 'secular social affair' (*shisu shehui shiwu*). The argument was defendable because he was repeating the familiar mantra that the observance of *qingzhen/halal* was a matter of ethnic habit or custom instead of religious commitment. The shift from ethnic to secular further removed the matter from Islam; and Wuqiang thought his new division in the Henan Provincial Commission for Ethnic

---

[17] http://www.chinaislam.net.cn/about/xhgk/about132.html.

5 Between Religion and Ethnicity: The Politics of Halal in China 109

Affairs, one on which was only just conferred the authority to oversee the production of *qingzhen* products in Henan, could finally make its move.

I had met him weeks before the work trip he later invited me to join. At the time, he was working on a publication of his own initiative that offered a comprehensive overview of *qingzhen* businesses in Henan— these including, in addition to halal slaughterhouses, *qingzhen* food manufacturers, restaurants known for their *qingzhen* delicacies, hospitals catering to Muslim needs, Muslim funerary services, even kindergartens servicing Muslim families.[18] Perhaps reflecting the inconsistencies inherent to his insistence on the separation of the religious and the ethnic, the title of his book, after much agonizing on his end, was *Guide to Muslim Life in Henan* (Henan musilin shenghuo zhinan). Apart from an Arabic translation of the title (*dalīl al-ḥayāt lil-muslimīn fī khanān*), the cover also showcased a section from Qur'an 16:126: '[And if you punish, then punish in the same manner as you have been punished.] Yet if you are patient—it indeed is better for those with patience.'[19] Wuqiang knew no Arabic; the *sūra* from the Qur'an was selected likely because he found the calligraphic design aesthetically appealing. If he had known the meaning of the verse, he probably would have preferred to have it swapped for a different one or removed all Qur'anic references altogether. Presenting the Quran—partially superimposed on an image of Masjid al-Ḥaram in Mecca, no less—on a publication issued by the Henan provincial government was itself somewhat of a daring decision; this is all the more impressive since the official author whose name appeared on the cover, Li Zunjie, was at the time Vice-Director of the Henan Provincial Commission for Ethnic Affairs, one of the highest-ranking Hui officials in the province.

Wuqiang seemed unperturbed by such apparent disparities. Treating the supervision of the halal industry as falling within the ambit of secular ethnic affairs was for him consistent with a key policy thus far indisputable: that only a Hui Muslim could be the owner of a *qingzhen* business and any food manufacturers involved in such businesses need to hire a designated proportion of Hui employees. In the law promulgated in

---

[18] The book was later published in 2011 under the name of a more senior official under whose aegis the book was compiled. See http://book.kongfz.com/259891/1558662092/.

[19] Translation by author.

110   G. Ha

1997 that governs halal industry in Henan, the proportion of Hui employees in a halal food manufacturer was fixed at 15%, and the figure rose to 20% and 25%, respectively, for the sales and service industries. A similar law in Ningxia, with notable differences, was updated in 2011. Article 10 of the law stated thus:

> For those businesses applying for a permit to produce *qingzhen* food, their proportion of minority employees with the *qingzhen* dietary habit (*qingzhen yinshi xiguan*) must be no lower than the proportion of said minorities in the total population of the autonomous region. And the following personnel must be Hui or other minorities with the *qingzhen* dietary habit:
>
> 1) Person in charge of production, management, and food service
> 2) Person in key positions in procurement, storage, and manufacturing
>
> For small businesses applying for a permit to sell *qingzhen* food, the owner and the chefs must be Hui or other minorities with the *qingzhen* dietary habit.[20]

Wuqiang thus explained his logic to me: if the observance of *qingzhen* was a religious matter, then by definition any Muslim regardless of ethnic identity—a Han who converted to Islam, for instance—could be involved in the business of halal food manufacture, and the stipulation on the proportion of minority employees would have long become obsolete. That this had not happened meant that the halal food manufacturing business was also an enterprise designed to create jobs for disadvantaged ethnic minorities and thus was part of the state's alleged plan to enhance the economic well-being of minority populations. The policy killed two birds with one stone: it at once bound ethnicity to *qingzhen*, and it

---

[20] Notably missing in this version but present in an earlier version (2002) of this law is the stipulation that the proportion of minority employees with the *qingzhen* habit hired by a halal food manufacturer must be over 40%. See *Guoneiwai qingzhen shipin guanli falvfagui he zhengce huibian* (Collected Documents on the National and International Laws and Regulations in the Management of Qingzhen Food), Beijing: Law Press, 71, 90–91. It is not clear why this was removed in the 2011 update, but presumably the reason might have been the fact that, by 2010, only around 35% of the total population in the Ningxia Hui Autonomous Region were Hui, and in urban areas, the Han were even more in the majority. Data based on published information from https://www.chinanews.com/gn/2021/05-25/9485282.shtml.

5 Between Religion and Ethnicity: The Politics of Halal in China 111

converted what could have been a religious matter into one of economic equality. However, this does not necessarily translate into effective oversight of the *qingzhen* market. In both Henan and Ningxia, I have known cases—admittedly rare—where Hui butchers knowingly (or more likely unwittingly) put non-*qingzhen* beef and lamb on sale as *qingzhen* meat. In one case in Hebei, I also witnessed how duck meat—whether *qingzhen* or not—was reprocessed and repackaged and then resold as *qingzhen* lamb. A Hui official in Ningxia in charge of *qingzhen* supervision dubbed this practice 'meat-laundering' (*xirou*), inflecting the word 'money-laundering' (*xiqian*) to make the point that just as illegal money was laundered through apparently legal business operations, so was non-*qingzhen* food laundered by a Hui-owned business believed by policy-makers to guarantee the *qingzhen* quality of the food on sale.

A range of localized entities also purported to participate in the supervision of *qingzhen*. In a province as vast as Henan, certification of *qingzhen* food was doled out by practically every organization or institution claiming to possess the requisite authority. Some *qingzhen* products were certified by the local Islamic association at the county level; others by their county- or city-level commission for ethnic affairs; still others by a local mosque that enjoyed regional renown. In some rare cases, even the headshot of a locally trusted imam was printed on the package to bolster the *qingzhen* status of the salt beef on sale. This diversity of certifying institutions was compounded by the heterogeneity of the certified corporations; they hailed from a wide range of food industries.

A key change took place in October 2003, when the National Commission for Ethnic Affairs in Beijing issued an administrative order announcing the inclusion of *qingzhen* food in the category of 'products for the special needs of ethnic minorities' (*shaoshu minzu texu yongpin*).[21] The latter included a wide range of commodities and handicrafts: Tibetan dining sets, Uyghur musical instruments, Mongolian daggers, textiles with distinctly ethnic patterns, and so on.[22] In a list of the 1855

---

[21] The document can be found in *Shiyiwu qijian minzu maoyi he minzu texu shangpin shengchan zhengce wenjian huibian* (Compiled policy documents on minzu commerce and minzu specialized products in the eleventh five-year plan), Beijing: Minzu Publishing House, 2008, 173.

[22] A partial list of these products can be accessed at http://www.gov.cn/gzdt/2013-07/26/content_2455948.htm.

enterprises considered providers of such special goods that was published by the National Commission for Ethnic Affairs in 2007, further diversity is evident: carpet weavers, brassware manufacturers, textile plants, garment and hat factories, dairy producers, pastry shops, vegetable oil mills, *qingzhen* condiment makers, and manufacturers of incense and incense burners. It is also clear that the newly included *qingzhen* butchers and meat processing corporations varied in size, mechanization, and work routines. Fifty-nine corporations from Henan made the list, thirty-six of which were involved in the processing of halal food products. One enterprise, Henan Wanfu Youzhi (Wanfu Fat and Oil Co. Ltd.), was a manufacturer of edible vegetable oil with total assets at 2.3 hundred million RMB in 2021. At the time of the inspection carried out by Wuqiang and his colleagues, the corporation had just merged with Yangguang Jituan (Yangguang Group) and continued to produce edible oil using soybeans and rapeseed. Another corporation, Henan Huangguo Liangye (Huangguo Grain Co. Ltd.), was a manufacturer of edible rice products and in no way involved the use of meat, dairy, or other animal products that might raise questions concerning *qingzhen*. Both manufacturers were among the main targets for inspection, high on the list Wuqiang brought with him on the work trip; yet neither seemed to have a need to keep their *qingzhen* status.

One essential fact may help us unravel this puzzle. In 2006, China's central bank, the People's Bank of China, reissued an administrative order stating that all commercial banks in China ought to provide favorable financial policies for the benefit of businesses involved in the manufacturing of 'products for the special needs of ethnic minorities.' The centerpiece of these policies was a 2.88% reduction on the annual interest accrued to loans of liquid cash to such businesses. In 2009, Henan Huaying Agricultural Development Co. Ltd., one of the largest providers of duck meat and related products (such as down jackets and windbreakers), expanded an earlier workshop and established its first plant for processing *qingzhen* duck meat. All three corporations thus far mentioned were, by the time of my visit, in their fastest development since foundation, and all three, not surprisingly, benefitted greatly from the favorable loan scheme. When I interviewed a manager in 2011, Wanfu Fat and Oil had already received a loan of fifty million RMB from Bank of China in

5 Between Religion and Ethnicity: The Politics of Halal in China 113

the first quarter and had submitted proposals for additional loans later in the year. The annual amount of loans that Huangguo Grain received from the Agricultural Bank of China totaled over one hundred million RMB in the early 2010s. A *qingzhen* status thus meant genuine economic advantage in a competitive market.

While Huaying Agricultural Development only established its plant for processing halal duck meat in 2009—no doubt to take advantage of the new loan scheme—it soon grew into a listed company with numerous meat manufacturing plants, only one among them being a halal venue (they later built another two in Henan and Shandong). They paired up with a local mosque close to the headquarters and hired the only imam therein to be the halal supervisor. Enjoying regular pay from the company and his mosque's daily maintenance under the financial aegis of Huaying, the imam looked content and confident when we met him in person. In a video about its *qingzhen* branch published on the company's website, the camera caught a passing scene where the imam was apparently overseeing a few of his students slaughtering ducks hung head-down from suspended hooks on a production line; a few seconds earlier, they were seen praying together in a carpeted room that the video claimed was prepared by the company for daily prayer services.[23] A range of comparable measures were put in place to ensure that the slaughterers' religious life was not disturbed, though, admittedly, the only source we have in this regard are the words of the company managers themselves: the plant was shut down for two hours every Friday at noon so the imams could attend the weekly *jumuʿa* service. Indeed, the imams were required by the company to strictly observe the five daily prayers and missing one would cause immediate dismissal (!); they were generously remunerated for their work; and every Friday, the *qingzhen* cafeteria would reward them with special delicacies. Despite all these measures, however, the industrial scale of the manufacturing process and the small retinue of imams—the video showed around five imams at work on the production line—made such a stark contrast that one could not help but wonder how Huaying could have safeguarded the *qingzhen* status of their meat products. Yet the company, having benefitted from the favorable loan

---

[23] The video can be accessed at http://www.hua-ying.com/article/video.html.

114 G. Ha

scheme, was surely not willing to let go the financial advantages. The administrative order did not state unequivocally how the money ought to be spent and whether a group could invest the loan in non-*qingzhen* businesses while running its *qingzhen* component. A growing meat processing plant aspiring to become one of the largest in the industry worldwide was not likely to give up the opportunities for low-interest loans on an annual basis.

In the face of these massive forces at play, Wuqiang and his small team looked insignificant and powerless. He raised objections to what he considered was the undue intrusion of the local mosque into secular ethnic affairs and was abhorred and amazed in equal measure by the company's alleged enforcement of five daily prayers among the imams. Wuqiang was at a distinct disadvantage: while he came from the highest level of government in Henan, he still had to rely on his colleagues at the county and the township level for local information and for the implementation of whatever policy he promoted. 'We have little leverage in fact,' he remarked while we were driving on the inter-county highway. 'If those at the county and the township level do not collaborate and carry out the orders, or if they find some excuses to delay indefinitely their implementation, there really isn't much we can do about it.' When a company like Huaying Agricultural Development generated as much local tax revenue as over one million RMB in a year,[24] it was unlikely that the small county where it was based would fixate on whether the supervision of *qingzhen* ought to be a secular ethnic affair.

Further complicating the matter was what Wuqiang referred to as the policy of *suozheng suopiao* (demanding the certificates and the receipts) that had been put in place in Ningxia and was soon adopted by all provinces. Under this policy, the manufacturers of *halal* food products were supposed to provide detailed notarized documents showing the whole paper trail behind each ingredient that went into the finished product. At Wang Shouyi Shisanxiang (Wang Shouyi Thirteen Spices Seasoning), a prestigious manufacturer of *qingzhen* condiments founded in 1984,

---

[24] *Biannual report of Huaying Agricultural Development Co. Ltd.*, August 2015, p. 10. An online version of the report can be accessed at http://money.finance.sina.com.cn/corp/view/vCB_AllBulletinDetail.php?stockid=002321&id=1946856.

5 Between Religion and Ethnicity: The Politics of Halal in China 115

Wuqiang fastidiously noted down the information of every ingredient stored in the enormous warehouse and tried afterwards to ring the factories that provided them to verify their *qingzhen* status. Many of the calls went unanswered, and the 'certificates' he was able to get hold of were no more than a *qingzhen* sign on the package with the name of a local Islamic association or commission of ethnic affairs printed below. He pondered making more calls, yet soon realized, drawing on his experience only a few weeks previously at the conference in Ningxia, that his counterparts in other provinces might have faced the same problem, and their affirmation of the *qingzhen* status of said products offered no more assurance than his own. Roaming Wang Shouyi's warehouse, trailed by a small retinue of local officials keen on not offending the company, Wuqiang saw the limit of what his new division could accomplish. The irony is that while he was barely able to ascertain the *qingzhen* status of the products in question, all the corporations we inspected were insistent on retaining this status presumably because of the potential financial gains. When Huangguo Grain printed a *qingzhen* label on a 50-kilo sack of sticky rice, a non-Muslim might well wonder why this was necessary at all. What has since been referred to as *qingzhen fanhua*, or pan-*qingzhen*-ification, might have more to do with decisions made in the interest of increasing profits than with an Islamic revival portrayed by Han nationalists as a daunting threat to the state.

Conclusion

In this chapter, I have attempted to accomplish two goals. The first part examines the conceptual ambivalence of the religion/ethnicity dyad and inserts it into the distinction between *qingzhen* and *halal*. While in some places I have also used the two terms somewhat interchangeably, I hoped to demonstrate the extent of their historical difference and how this difference translates into divergent political ramifications. The most effective way of doing this, per recent events in the state clampdown on Arabic *halal* signs, is to pay closer attention to the visual representation of *qingzhen* and *halal* in the public sphere. A state-level ideological battle fought in the name of 'Sinicizing Islam' (*yisilanjiao zhongguohua*) and rooting out religious extremism perhaps could not avoid a certain obsession with the public representation of Islam—from the domes atop mosques, to the use of Arabic in signs. However, the specific context in question also requires us to be more cautious in comparing the controversy over *qingzhen*/*halal* to other debates around the public visibility of religion in Western secular contexts.[25] The legacy of socialism and its attendant ethnic policy continue to render ethnicity a potentially protective shell under which the *qingzhen* form of life remains possible while the *halal* signs are being removed. If in Euro-America and other analogous contexts, the terms of debate are often dual—the religious and the secular—in China, we will need a triadic framework, inserting the ethnic between the religious and the secular.

It is to these complexities that the second part of this chapter turned. My work trip with Wuqiang and his small retinue of officials showed the limitations of ideologically driven debates and the disparity between the state enforcement of Chinese *qingzhen* signs and the lack of effective governmental supervision in creating a reliable certification process. I showed the ways in which the expanded use of *qingzhen* signage, dubbed by some Han nationalists and Islamophobes as *qingzhen fanhua*, was less a reflection of a general Islamic revival than the outcome of pragmatic economic concerns of rapidly growing corporations involved in the production of halal food. As these businesses worked to retain their *qingzhen* status and enjoyed the consequent benefits derived from low-interest loans, the fine line between religion and ethnicity, between the religious and the secular, so carefully maintained by the state and insisted on by such local officials as Wuqiang, was crossed without much thought.

A caveat is in order before I conclude. While I purported to investigate the politics of *qingzhen* and *halal* in China, this chapter is based on fieldwork carried out exclusively among the Sinophone Hui Muslims, and the limited leeway ethnicity seems to have afforded them thus far—manifest in the continual use of *qingzhen* in lieu of *halal* signs—is thus specific to the Hui. Other Muslim minorities, such as the Uyghurs and the Kazakhs,

---

[25] These debates as pertain to Islam often revolve around Muslim women's veils: where they are allowed, why and how women ought to wear them, and so on. See, for instance, Macleod (1991), El Guindi (1999), Bowen (2007), Scott (2007), Elver (2012). The racial undertone of the veil, which has not received as much attention, is explored in Khabeer (2016: 109–138).

5 Between Religion and Ethnicity: The Politics of Halal in China

will no doubt experience the tension between religion and ethnicity differently, to the point where their ethnicity may offer no more protection than their association with religion. A Uyghur governmental official in Xinjiang would probably be considerably less likely to be as assertive in enforcing *qingzhen* rules as Wuqiang had been; instead of working to regulate the *qingzhen* food market, he would probably be fortunate enough not to be coerced into forgoing the abstinence from pork altogether. Whether that portends a future for the Hui is a question beyond the scope of this chapter.

References

Armanios, Febe. 2018. *Halal food: A history*. New York: Oxford University Press.
Bergeaud-Blackler, Florence, John Lever, and Johan Fischer. 2015. *Halal matters: Islam, politics and markets in global perspective*. New York: Routledge.
Bowen, John R. 2007. *Why the French don't like headscarves: Islam, the state, and public space*. Princeton: Princeton University Press.
Brophy, David. 2019. Good and bad Muslims in Xinjiang. *Made in China Journal*, 9 July. https://madeinchinajournal.com/2019/07/09/good-and-bad-muslims-in-xinjiang/.
Brose, Michael, and Su Min. 2021. Marketing as pedagogy: Halal e-commerce in Yunnan. In *Ethnographies of Islam in China*, ed. Rachel Harris, Ha Guangtian, and Maria Jaschok, 131–152. Honolulu: University of Hawai'i Press.
Brubaker, Rogers. 1994. Nationhood and the national question in the Soviet Union and post-Soviet Eurasia: An institutionalist account. *Theory and Society* 23 (1): 47–78.
Cieciura, Wlodzimierz. 2016. Ethnicity or religion? Republican-era Chinese debates on Islam and Muslims. In *Islamic thought in China: Sino-Muslim intellectual evolution from the 17th to the 21st century*, ed. Jonathan Lipman. Edinburgh: Edinburgh University Press.
Elliott, Mark. 2015. The case of the missing indigene: Debate over a 'second-generation' ethnic policy. *The China Journal* 73 (January): 186–213. https://doi.org/10.1086/679274.
Elver, Hilal. 2012. *The headscarf controversy: Secularism and freedom of religion*. New York: Oxford University Press.

Erie, Matthew S. 2016. In China, fears of 'creeping sharia' proliferate online. *Foreign Policy*, 15 September 2016. https://foreignpolicy.com/2016/09/15/in-china-fears-of-creeping-sharia-proliferate-online-muslims-islam-islamophobia/.

———. 2018. Shari'a as taboo of modern law: Halal food, Islamophobia, and China. *The Journal of Law and Religion* 33 (3): 390–420. https://doi.org/10.1017/jlr.2018.45.

Fischer, Johan. 2011. *The halal frontier: Muslim consumers in a globalized market*. New York: Palgrave Macmillan.

———. 2016. Manufacturing halal in Malaysia. *Contemporary Islam* 10 (1): 35–52. https://doi.org/10.1007/s11562-015-0323-5.

Gillette, Maris Boyd. 2000. *Between Mecca and Beijing: Modernization and consumption among urban Chinese Muslims*. Stanford: Stanford University Press.

Glasserman, Aaron. 2016. Making Muslims Hui: Ethnic bias in the new curriculum of the China Islamic Association. In *Hui Muslims in China*, ed. Rong Gui, Hacer Zekiye Gönül, and Xiaoyan Zhang, 47–61. Leuven: Leuven University Press.

Guindi, El, and Fadwa. 1999. *Veil: Modesty, privacy, and resistance*. Oxford: Berg.

Ha, Guangtian. 2020a. Hui Muslims and Han converts: Islam and the paradox of recognition. In *Handbook on religion in China*, ed. Stephan Feuchtwang, 313–337. Cheltenham: Edward Elgar Publishing.

———. 2020b. Specters of Qingzhen: Marking Islam in China. *Sociology of Islam* 8 (3–4): 423–447. https://doi.org/10.1163/22131418-08030004.

Harrell, Stevan. 2008. L'etat, c'est nous, or we have met the oppressor and he is us: The Predicament of minority cadres in the PRC. In *The Chinese state at the borders*, ed. Diana Lary, 221–239. Vancouver: University of British Columbia Press.

Keane, Webb. 2007. *Christian moderns: Freedom and fetish in the mission encounter*. Berkeley: University of California Press.

Khabeer, Su'ad Abdul. 2016. *Muslim cool: Race, religion, and Hip Hop in the United States*. New York: NYU Press.

Leibold, James. 2013. *Ethnic policy in China: Is reform inevitable?* Honolulu: East-West Centre.

Li, Weihan. 1986. *Li Weihan Xuanji (Selected Work of Li Weihan)*. Beijing: People's Publishing House.

Li, Xinghua, and Jinyuan Feng. 1985. *Zhongguo yisilanjiao shi cankao ziliao xuan bian* (Selected reference works for the history of Islam in China). 2 vols. Yinchuan: Ningxia People's Publishing House.

Liang, Lim Yan. 2019. China passes five-year plan to sinicise Islam, as Beijing tightens grip on major faiths in China. *The Straits Times*, 9 January 2019. https://www.straitstimes.com/asia/east-asia/china-passes-five-year-plan-to-sinicise-islam-as-beijing-tightens-grip-on-major.

Litzinger, Ralph A. 2000. *Other Chinas: The Yao and the politics of national belonging*. Durham: Duke University Press.

Macleod, Arlene Elowe. 1991. *Accommodating protest: Working women, the new veiling, and change in Cairo*. New York: Columbia University Press.

Martin, Terry Dean. 2001. *The affirmative action empire: Nations and nationalism in the Soviet Union, 1923–1939*. Cornell: Cornell University Press.

Miao, Ying. 2020. Sinicisation vs. Arabisation: Online narratives of Islamophobia in China. *Journal of Contemporary China* 29 (125): 748–762. https://doi.org/10.1080/10670564.2019.1704995.

Mullaney, Thomas. 2010. *Coming to terms with the nation: Ethnic classification in modern China*. Berkeley: University of California Press.

Roche, Gerald, and James Leibold. 2020. China's second-generation ethnic policies are already here. *Made in China Journal*, 7 September 2020. https://madeinchinajournal.com/2020/09/07/chinas-second-generation-ethnic-policies-are-already-here/.

Scott, Joan Wallach. 2007. *The politics of the veil*. Princeton: Princeton University Press.

Shirazi, Faegheh. 2016. *Brand Islam: The marketing and commodification of piety*. Austin: University of Texas Press.

Wei, Qianzhi. 1995. Zhongguo gudai youtairen de ishi Gongxian. *Shixue Yuek* 3: 23–29.

Weisz, Tiberiu. 2006. *The Kaifeng Stone inscriptions: The legacy of the Jewish community in ancient China*. Bloomington: iUniverse.

6

Bacon or Beef? 'Fake' Halal Scandals in the Russian Federation: Consolidating Halal Norms Through Secular Courts

Silvia Serrano

Introduction

On 13 March 2018, Andrei Maslov[1] bought a Tsaritsyno brand 'special beef' sausage (*Govyazh'ya osobaya*) bearing a halal label at an Auchan store in the city of Kazan (Tatarstan Republic, the Russian Federation). Since the store personnel refused to provide a document stating that the product complied with halal standards, he took it to the Tatarstan

---

Translated into English by Mary Schaffer. This chapter has been republished with minor changes from Serrano, S. (2020). Bacon or Beef? 'Fake' Halal Scandals in the Russian Federation, *Sociology of Islam*, 8(3–4), 387–408. https://doi.org/10.1163/22131418-08030002

[1] The name was changed.

S. Serrano (✉)
Eur'Orbem, Sorbonne University, Paris, France

Sorbonne University Abu Dhabi, Abu Dhabi, UAE
e-mail: silvia.serrano@sorbonne.ae

© The Author(s), under exclusive license to Springer Nature Switzerland AG 2023
R. Turaeva, M. Brose (eds.), *Religious Economies in Secular Context*, New Directions in Islam, https://doi.org/10.1007/978-3-031-18603-5_6

121

Interregional Veterinary Laboratory to undergo expert analysis. One week later, he received the results: the sausage contained DNA from *Sus scrofa* [*domesticus*], or pork DNA. Andrei Maslov considered that his rights had been violated and took the matter to court.

As illustrated by this example and many others, introducing halal certification has brought about complex changes with the increasing involvement of consumers, a market rational, and unprecedented calls for regulatory standards. In the Russian Federation (hereafter shortened to Russia), these changes are themselves part of a shift toward a capitalistic market economy, political pluralization, and multi-faceted religious renewal. A number of studies have explored the connection between the political and social transformations that followed the collapse of the USSR and the socialist system, the liberalization of religious beliefs in the 1990s, and changes to religion itself. However, relatively little research has been devoted to the economic dimensions of such changes (Gudeman and Hann 2015). Until very recently, research about Islam in Russia has been kept separate from the economic turn that renewed religious studies (Haenni 2005; Obadia 2017).

The crucial role played by the state in formatting Islam in the post-Soviet space, especially through the 'spiritual boards of Muslims' (further referred to with the Russian acronym as DUMs), is well informed (Braginskaia 2012; Bekkin 2017; Tasar 2017; Alikberov et al. 2019). But how does the tendency toward an 'economicization' of the world—the shift from a 'political regime [...] towards a global market regime' (Gauthier 2017: 94)—affect the relationship between the state and Islam? Indeed, the economic field provides opportunities for religious actors and believers to become more independent from the state. At the same time, the 'halal market', which presupposes routine and well-defined certification processes, is part of a trend to eradicate informality. Even more than the commercial aspects, could the primary characteristic of the halal market be said to derive from the 'bureaucratization of Islam' within and alongside the state as a form of modernization that is also shaped by other factors such as ethnicity (Müller and Steiner 2018)?

While arguing that practices and a market *imaginary* permeate the entire social dimension of halal, this chapter focuses on how state bureaucracy is impacted by the 'economicization' of religion. It investigates the

6 Bacon or Beef? 'Fake' Halal Scandals in the Russian Federation...

symbolic struggle for formatting the 'halal market' and argues that the penetration of an economic rational into the religious sphere strengthens the state's capacity to shape Islam.

It takes a case study approach—specifically, the case of the scandal over Tsaritsyno's 'mislabeling' of products as 'halal'—to explore the way in which the appearance of the halal market has changed the resources of religious actors, reshaped legitimacy within the Islamic field, and at the same time reformed relations with the state. Studying scandals makes it possible to go beyond the analyses which are focused on the marketing and organizational aspects of the halal market (Safiullin et al. 2016; Shovkhalov 2018) to understand its structuring effects. As pragmatic sociology would invite us to do, this chapter considers the scandal as both an observatory and a critical test: an observatory insofar as it uncovers the apparatus (*dispositif*) (Foucault 1975) on which trust is built, and a critical test insofar as it leads to the transformation of these *dispositifs*. It also causes the actors to reposition themselves and the roles played by institutions and their power to be redistributed (De Blic and Lemieux 2005).

This chapter is based on empirical data gathered in Moscow and Kazan in July and August 2018, in particular, the observation of the court trial mentioned above and the analysis of documents relating to its legal proceedings, as well as semi-structured interviews and online research—looking at websites of the spiritual boards, certification agencies, articles in the Muslim online media, and Muslim blogs. First, it looks at the factors that provide the context of the structuring of Russian Islam and the means used by the state to regulate it, which is essential for understanding the singular challenges of the development of the halal market in Russia. Next, it analyzes the mechanisms by which a 'strategy of scandalization' caused a shift in relations between religious actors and the secular authorities. The third and final section examines how, through legal arguments and capturing the attention of the media, the scandal contributed to the expansion, legitimation, and consolidation of the halal standard beyond the circle of pious Muslims. Although it looks at a single case in Tatarstan, similar dynamics of scandalization around halal certification have been occurring across Russia in recent years. Thus the more general dynamics revealed by scandalization—that is the simultaneous strengthening of religion and the state and their mutual

124   S. Serrano

dependency—can be said to be operating across Russia, even where Muslim populations are in a minority.

Islam in Russia: Between the State and the Market

Halal belongs to the Islamic tradition, but what it encompasses has changed considerably in recent decades and Muslims may not agree on how to define it. The halal market is intrinsically tied to changes in the capitalist economy and 'results from the proceduralization of halal that transformed a *discursive space* specific to the Muslim world into a *procedure-norm* for the "needs" of "individual" Muslims in the world' (Bergeaud-Blackler 2017: 22, original emphasis). Halal developed as an integrated standard in global commerce according to an identifiable genealogy in a system involving economic players (major meat exporters) and religious players. While dietary practices among Russian Muslims have always been influenced by Islamic tenets, the appearance of a halal market is a recent development, dating back to the mid-2000s.

Halal in Russia: From Practices to Market

Russia has the largest Muslim population in Europe after Turkey. Muslims represent between 11% and 14% of the population (between 15 and 20 million people, depending on the estimate) (Rosstat 2010).[2] Islam is a minority religion in Russia, but there are significant variations in different geographic areas. In the historic cradle of the Volga-Ural and in the northeastern Caucasian regions, Islam has been present for centuries (the oldest mosque in Russia, located in Derbent, Dagestan, was built in the eighth century). In these areas, Muslims constitute a majority—slightly

---

[2] The figures are based on the last census (2010) and other official statistics. Such statistics are controversial, however, and subject to manipulation because being registered as 'Muslim' does not necessarily mean that an individual is a practicing Muslim. As with declarations of Christianity and Russian Orthodoxy, declared adherence to Islam may be part of a broader identity without reflecting high adherence to official teachings or practices.

6 Bacon or Beef? 'Fake' Halal Scandals in the Russian Federation...

more than 50% in Tatarstan, over 90% of the population in the cases of Dagestan and Chechnya. The question of consuming halal product is different in Muslim majority regions from its appearance in major urban centers such as Moscow, where numerically large Muslim communities are still a minority and live among a Russian Orthodox majority in a highly secularized environment. Although migration from Muslim majority regions, including former Soviet republics in Central Asia, is reshaping Russia's religious landscape, Islam is not a recent import. In this way, Russia differs from other European countries where the increased presence of Islam can be linked to patterns of postcolonial migration. Rather, Islam is officially considered one of the 'traditional religions' of Russia.

During the Soviet period, Muslims did not seek out products that were labeled 'halal'. In predominantly Muslim regions and communities, 'traditional' foodways made it possible to obtain meat that had been slaughtered appropriately and to avoid certain forbidden foods. Even in Russia's big cities, the key role played by farmers' markets (not least in alleviating food shortages in state supply chains) contributed to maintaining short-circuit supply networks, often specific to a given ethnic group. In the 1990s, the Tatars of Moscow continued to have meat brought from the villages (Safarov 2015), while even today a number of Muslims buy halal products from producers they know personally. Diasporas play an important role in providing direct contact with Central Asian and Azerbaijani producers (cattle may be transported from Azerbaijan and slaughtered locally).

State Control and Financing Islam in Russia

For most Muslims, consuming halal means refraining from consuming pork and alcohol. For a majority of consumers, there is no need for a halal label. This 'simplified halal', according to the expression used by Safarov (2015), is different from the 'certified halal' that has developed over the last 15 years in parallel to Russia's expanded participation in global trade. The introduction of certified halal products into the Russian market took place in the context of a largely state-controlled Islam and a high degree of fragmentation of representative institutions.

The Russian Empire, the USSR, and then the Russian Federation administered Russian Islam within the scope of efforts to create a 'Muslim church' (Tasar 2017) subject to secular power. The system was based on creating Muftiates—the spiritual boards of Muslims (DUMs). Muftiates have considerable power to appoint, pay, and control imams and to organize pilgrimages. Currently, each mosque must be registered as a religious organization with the Ministry of Justice and placed under the control of a DUM.

During the Soviet period, there were just two DUMs for the entire territory of the USSR. In the 1990s, Muslim institutions underwent fragmentation along geographic and ethno-national lines, as well as according to personal rivalries. In 2018, there were more than 80 DUMs (*Atlas of Islamic Community of the Russian Federation*), theoretically governed by so-called federal umbrella DUMs, which also varied in number. Competition is fierce among the different spiritual boards and even within the same board. They are linked with clientelist ties to power, not with dogmatic or theological differences.

Secular authorities are directly involved in co-opting and appointing religious figures. Depending on the circumstances, they set their sights on one or another of the federal DUMs and may even encourage the creation of new DUMs. The state also plays a key role in financing the DUMs and, more generally, the mosques. The Constitution of the Russian Federation prohibits direct financing of religious organizations, yet public money is transferred to religious organizations via cultural or humanitarian programs and foundations. According to one imam, such funding, even in small amounts, 'has been sufficient to buy off everyone' (Interview 1, 2018), given the financial difficulties faced by mosques and the clergy and dwindling support from foreign sources.

Under the circumstances, it is hardly surprising that the different DUMs (and even the various administrative bodies and the dignitaries working for the bigger ones) should compete for the prestige and proximity to power that gives access to resources. The development of halal certification systems has changed the rules of the competition game among DUMs. Certification opens an avenue to a direct, market-based source of income that bypasses direct and indirect state support. Relatedly, it reorganizes the clientelist system by redistributing authority. Resources generated by DUMs' own activities reduce the importance of proximity to power and legitimacy in the eyes of the authorities. In addition, halal certification requires religious legitimacy that state institutions do not have. Finally, in the context of Russia's securitization of Islam and of the criminalization of non-coopted groups, the efforts of DUMs to bring the halal issue to the fore are also an attempt to depoliticize Islam. Promoting halal certification as a major activity allows DUMs to reinforce their support for a vision of Islam that is in line with the officially promoted values of the Russian Federation. The 'halal lifestyle' is fully consistent with the officially endorsed social model.

Development of the Halal Market and Transformation of the Clientelist System

The first certification body in the entire Commonwealth of Independent States was established in 2002 in Russia. The first halal labels began to appear on some products sold in the Russian market beginning in the first decade of the 2000s, and in 2009, the first halal standards were introduced. Demand for certification was motivated by a desire to export, especially after the Russian Federation joined the WTO in 2012. With the economic and political crisis following the annexation of Crimea in 2014, interest grew in redirecting a share of exports toward the Muslim world. Developing halal standards had become necessary to earn the trust of importers of Russian products in Muslim countries. Demands for a guarantee of authenticity did not come from the domestic market, but the introduction of a commercial standard altered the relationship of trust between consumers, producers, and distributers.

Little by little, a market for certification began to develop. Initially, dedicated agencies were in charge of guaranteeing that products complied with the characteristics they claimed to possess. Since it involves compliance with sharia, the certification process requires cooperation with religious authorities and expertise. All secular states face this challenge in combining regulation in the market with religious authority.[3] Russian legislation does not forbid bodies that are independent of DUMs to issue halal certifications, and some companies have developed their own certification system. It was not surprising, however, that the first halal standards and centers providing certification came from the spiritual boards. The standards provided by the International Center for Halal Standardization and Certification (ICHSC) of the Mufti Council and the Halal [Certification] System of the Halal Standards Committee of the DUM of the Republic of Tatarstan, both created in 2005, are two of the oldest and most important ones. Officially, they are legally distinct entities, but they are governed by the DUMs.

Halal's economic dimension is obviously important for producers and exporters as much as for certifying bodies. It is difficult to obtain information about certification fees and profits (a 'trade secret'). The head of the Halal Standards Committee of the Tatarstan DUM indicated that in the summer of 2018 there were 122 halal businesses working with the Committee and the fee for certification was about the same as the average monthly earnings of a resident of Tatarstan (around EUR 340, *Realnoe Vremja* 2018). In April 2019, the ICHSC provided certificates to 200 businesses, including 20 for export, compared to around 40 in 2010 (ICHSC Website n.d.). Certification was rapidly becoming a modest additional source of income for the DUMs, but one that does not depend on public funding.

These opportunities help explain the rise in the number of halal certification centers. In 2016, 12 centers were listed for Russia (Shovkhalov 2018). In the summer of 2018, there were 18 (Interview 2), in addition to halal certified producers from Belarus and Kazakhstan that are very active on the Russian market. In June 2019, 25 systems were registered in the single registry of 'voluntary certification systems' kept by Rosstandart, the Federal Agency on Technical Regulating and Metrology (Rosstandart Website n.d.). The certification market is also becoming increasingly competitive.

---

[3] In Russia, at the current stage, Rosstandart agency recognized halal standards as only 'voluntary certification'. A working group with Rosstandart and DUM representatives was set up to establish official state standards, but without any result so far.

The growth in food certification has also created the conditions for contestations over whether the food products actually respect the required criteria: market growth structurally leads to an increase in the number of scandals. The case presented here is but one among many examples in 2018 in which the compliance of halal products with requested criteria was challenged, but unlike other cases, it could be studied comprehensively because it involved a lawsuit. Moreover, this particular scandal unfolded against the broader backdrop of public concern within Russia to improve quality standards within the food industry—for example, the standards that apply to 'organic' food were also still underdeveloped in Russia. It was also when health risks received growing attention and consumer advocacy groups became more powerful. Moreover, it involved a company that had been in the spotlight of such debates before. In 2016, Tsaritsyno took Channel One Television to court because it had reported that Tsaritsyno sausages contained soy, although soy was not listed in the ingredients (Lenta.ru, April 2016). According to the independent consumer watchdog organization Roskontrol, 75% of sausages were fraudulent (Lenta.ru, March 2016).

The 'Strategy of Scandalization' and the Reconfiguration of Actors

In the present case, taking matters before the courts was part of a 'strategy of scandalization' (Offerlé 1998) in a fierce competition. Since the 2000s, the growing halal market has reset the configuration of actors and changed the nature of the competition game by bringing to the fore the question of the credibility of certification centers. The Tsaritsyno scandal may be seen as a play in three acts taking place chronologically. Each act follows its own distinct line of reasoning.

Act 1: The Courts

Andrei Maslov took the matter before the administrative court and filed a lawsuit in the civil court. After receiving the results of the expert

130 S. Serrano

analysis detecting swine DNA, officers from the Tatarstan Branch of the Federal Service for Surveillance on Consumer Rights Protection and Human Wellbeing (Rospotrebnadzor n.d.) made a surprise visit to the Auchan store. They seized more 'special beef' sausages and sent them to a different laboratory for analysis, which also detected the presence of pork (Judgment). Rospotrebnadzor fined the Tsaritsyno company RUB 100,000 (approximately EUR 1362) for violating administrative codes (Letter 2018).

Mr. Maslov did not stop there. He asked the civil court to award damages to cover the costs he had incurred. He wanted the Auchan store to reimburse RUB 119.01 (EUR 1.60) for the purchase of a defective product; RUB 1,495.01 (EUR 20) to cover the cost of analysis by the veterinary laboratory; RUB 86.96 (EUR 1.18) for postage; and finally RUB 500,000 (EUR 6810) for non-pecuniary damages (Judgment). The hearing took place on 2 August 2018 in a district court in Kazan, and the judge ruled that Auchan was responsible for merchandise sold in its stores and that the plaintiff should be reimbursed for the cost of the product, the laboratory analysis, and the postage, and that he should also receive symbolic damages amounting to RUB 1000 (EUR 13) (Judgment n.d.).

Act 2: The Media

At this point, given the modest financial stakes, almost no one seemed interested in the case. No representative of the Auchan store or Rospotrebnadzor attended the trial, nor did the plaintiff himself bother to appear. Among the few people in the court room were two representatives of the third party, the sausage manufacturer Tsaritsyno (a company lawyer and Dinar Sadykov, the director of the certification center of the company). Just one person representing the public attended: the author of this chapter.

The contrast could hardly be more vivid between the trial, the publicity it received, and—most of all—its future repercussions. A new campaign appeared on social media protesting against 'fake halal' products. Several articles published in a Kazan newspaper denounced what they called 'the Ostap Bender' (in reference to the con man in Ilf and

6 Bacon or Beef? 'Fake' Halal Scandals in the Russian Federation...

Petrov's novels)[4] of halal, who was interested only in getting rich (Buzines online). A few public figures with followers on blogs and social media were particularly vocal in accusing the center that had delivered the certificates to businesses that marketed illicit food products as halal products.

Information about 'fake halal' products quickly spread in the Muslim press and social media, especially on the website of the Mufti Council and in Tatarstan's newspapers. At the same time, expert analyses were conducted over the next few months in other republics (FoodNewsTime 2018). In each instance, pork DNA was found in beef products sold under the Tsaritsyno brand name.

At this point, the scandal was limited to the Muslim community. Several months went by before articles appeared in the general Russian press (autumn 2018), just when the international repercussions of this trial started to emerge (RBK 11-2018).

Act 3: International Repercussions

In October 2018, the World Halal Council (WHC), an international organization founded in Malaysia in 1999, held its conference in Istanbul. Three organizations in the Russian Federation were members of the WHC: the ICHSC, the Halal Standards Committee of the Tatarstan DUM, and Dinar Sadykov's Center for Halal Audit and Control. Their exchanges became so heated that some of the Russian representatives had to be called to order. A resolution was passed stating that the Assistant Secretary General of the organization (a member of ICHSC) had to apologize to the WHC for unacceptable and inappropriate manners (Islamnews.ru, RBK). The General Assembly of the WHC further stripped Dinar Sadykov of his position as Assistant Treasurer and suspended his membership from the organization for three years (Russia Council of Muftis website 2014). The Mufti Council publicly announced that it regretted that the actions of Dinar Sadykov 'had done irreparable

---

[4] An attractive and resourceful con man, Ostap Bender is the central character of the novels *The Twelve Chairs* (1928) and *The Little Golden Calf* (1931) written by Soviet authors Ilya Ilf and Yevgeni Petrov.

132   S. Serrano

harm to the authority of [the Russian Federation] on the international stage' (Islamnews.ru 2018).

This brief chronological account of the controversy throws light on the various actors' strategies, particularly the instrumentalization of judiciary procedures and the international dimension of the growing competition within the Islamic field. The rivalry driving this scandal was both commercial and institutional.

Competing Interests

Let's try to understand the relations among the protagonists of this affair. The certifying organization, the Center for Halal Audit and Control, along with its director, Dinar Sadykov, were specifically targeted by the Muslim press covering the scandal.

Sadykov entered the business of halal products in 2007. In 2011, he became the director of the Halal Standards Committee of the Tatarstan DUM (islamrf.ru). At the same time, he was put in charge of the affiliate of the Islamic Chamber Research and Information Center of the Organization of Islamic Cooperation that opened in Kazan (Tatar-inform.ru 2011). He later resigned, grew distant from the DUM (HCRT Website n.d.), and created the republic's first certifying agency. This was followed by a second one, the Center for Halal Audit and Control. The reasons for his dispute with the Tatarstan DUM are not entirely clear (they may have had to do with his opposition to the mufti appointed in 2012). The business reasons for the conflict are, however, easy to understand.

Tsaritsyno is one of the leading producers of halal meat products on the Russian market and one of the companies that had invested most heavily in halal production, using modern technology designed to limit the risk of contamination. To certify its products, the company initially used the services of the ICHSC. In 2013, a first scandal erupted, when some of the meat products manufactured by Tsaritsyno were suspected of not meeting halal standards. The following year, the ICHSC suspended its certificate. Some sources say that Tsaritsyno then sought to engage a different certification center: the Halal Standards Committee of the

6 Bacon or Beef? 'Fake' Halal Scandals in the Russian Federation... 133

Tatarstan DUM, which refused, as did the certification center of Kazakhstan (Russia Council of Muftis Website 2014; Biznes Online 2018). According to other sources, it was Dinar Sadykov (2011) who took the initiative to steal Tsaritsyno's business from the ICHSC (Muslim. kz 2018). At any rate, Tsaritsyno's halal products subsequently received certification from Sadykov's Center for Halal Audit and Control. As it turns out, the Mufti Council and the Tatarstan DUM became allies in the attacks on Dinar Sadykov. The scandal provided a way for both of them to discredit their competitor and adversary.

Concerning the individual at the origin of the scandal, some enthusiastically noted the civic spirit of 'an ordinary Russian guy' from Kazan who helped reveal the presence of swine DNA in products manufactured by Tsaritsyno (Regiony-online 2018). But how often does one request an expert analysis of a sausage before eating it? This is no ordinary civic spirit and, as we may have suspected, Andrei Maslov was no random citizen. He had ties to the general director of the ICHSC of the Mufti Council and appears to have done legal work for the ICHSC. The ease with which it is possible to trace the network of relations among these different players shows that the official Muslim field in the Russian Federation is indeed a small world.

The Stakes for Russian Institutions

Beyond commercial considerations, there were institutional stakes for those involved in the scandal. The market for Muslim goods, by altering the value of the financial and symbolic capital of the religious powers, transformed the clientelist relationship that they had formed with government representatives.

The scandal was also the outcome of the DUMs' struggle to assert their monopoly on halal certification. The Muslim press pointed out that Dinar Sadykov's certification center operated independently of any DUM, using this argument to discredit it. The website of the Mufti Council brought attention to the fact that the organization that had issued the certificate 'had no ties to a Muslim spiritual board' (Russia Council of Muftis website 2018).

Because the expanding market for Muslim goods and services generated new sources of funding, religious figures were able to gain a degree of independence from the state. The hegemonic position of the DUMs as institutions representing Muslims depended on being co-opted by the secular power—much more than it depended on their own material and religious capital. Bearing this in mind, it is easy to see why they might consider potential autonomy to be a threat. Yet if halal certification—and the resulting development of private certification centers—threatened to weaken the DUMs, it also provided the means to reinforce their proximity to the state. When the DUMs portrayed themselves as the only qualified certifiers, or as the most reliable ones, they became more valuable in the eyes of the authorities. In this sense, halal certification changed the balance in negotiations with public authorities and therefore increased the chances for the institution to obtain funding thanks to the state's clientelist networks.

We can see how the halal market transformed the relationship of trust by institutionalizing it—through the certifying bodies and through a combination of two sources of legitimacy: the market and the state. On the one hand, the ups and downs of the market ultimately validated the credibility of the certificate. Very few DUMs could boast, as the ICHSC did, that their halal committees certified products for export to Muslim countries. Market recognition for the legitimacy of a standard guaranteed by a religious institution ultimately strengthened the position of this religious institution in the eyes of public authorities.

At the same time, the religious institutions had access to financial and symbolic resources because they were close to the authorities, making it easier to obtain validation from the market. The certification bodies overseen by the DUMs cast themselves as 'more credible' to deliver halal certificates because of their quasi state-conferred status. This form of 'state legitimacy' depends on the bureaucratic capacity to control the standards and resources of government expertise and on the key role played by public bodies. Rospotrebnadzor is a public administration. The 'voluntary halal certification system' was developed jointly by the Mufti Council and the Russian Scientific and Research Institute for Certification which was then a state agency and the leader of quality management (Shovkhalov 2018), while the Halal Standards Committee of the Tatarstan DUM cooperated with public organizations, such as the Center for Hygiene and Epidemiology of the Republic of Tatarstan (Interview 3, 2018).

In discussions of the scandal, another derivation for this 'state-conferred legitimacy' is that the state appears to embody the common good, unlike commercial enterprises that serve private interests. A Muslim blogger, explained, for example: 'There are only two types of organization that deliver halal certification in Russia. The first were created at the Muftiates, and the others are private agencies.' (Biznes-Online 11-2018). For him, 'The difference has to do with the notion of responsibility. The centers overseen by the Muftiates bear the weight of responsibility before the ummah and also before the State'. At the same time, the state appears to be an arbiter among competing institutions. A member of the Council of Ulamas of the Halal Standards Committee of the Tatarstan DUM described it this way: 'How do Muslims know whom to trust, when each of the systems attempts to show that it's better than its neighbor?' (Interview 4, 2018).

Such is the paradox of halal certification: while it is an instrument of market-conferred autonomy, it needs the state insofar as the state has the capacity (although not without meeting certain conditions) to generate the trust of the market stakeholders that religious powers alone cannot provide.

Spreading the Halal Norm

While a strategic analysis makes it possible to describe the rationale underlying the actions in the religious sphere, it does not give us a measure of the social effects of the scandal beyond this very limited space. This next section looks at the scandal as a *test* and analyzes the mechanisms by which the halal certification norm was established, redefined, and disseminated.

As Eric de Dampierre suggested, a scandal is a test of transgressed values. It allows a community to determine whether or not it has become indifferent to these values (de Dampierre 1954). Scandal is not just a *revealer*, but it *establishes* something: either a collective reaffirmation of the transgressed values (and therefore their reinforcement); or, conversely, a collective demonstration of their obsolescence. In this case, the consolidation of the norm occurred simultaneously with the transformation of the group that reaffirmed the norm. A study of the arguments put forward during the trial, the way in which they spread from one sphere to another, and the way they took on different meanings according to the context of communications, helps us understand how a shared standard within a small group is transformed as it is being disseminated.

Reconciling Halal and the Secular: The Acrobatics of the Judicial System

Taking the matter before the courts is what made this scandal possible. Paradoxically, however, the administrative authorities and the Justice of the Peace avoided infringing on religious territory. The court's decisions remained within the scope of the secularism written into the Constitution of the Russian Federation. As is often the case in secular countries, the rules governing the labeling, safety, and quality of food products (i.e., the protection of consumers' rights) are what justified disciplinary measures, with no reference to a religious rule. The word halal did not appear in the report issued by Rospotrebnadzor, nor in the ruling of the civil court (except in the account of the plaintiff's reasons for bringing a lawsuit). What's more, reading through all of the documents, it becomes clear that as the administrative formatting went on, defining the issue as a halal problem gradually disappeared from the qualification of the charges.

The report written after the sample tested on April 28 mentions that the sausage was labeled 'halal'. The only information appearing in the report of the laboratory analysis on May 17, 2018 concerns swine DNA, which shows that this is the only information the laboratory sought to detect. The veterinary expert report (2018) dated May 18 confirmed that the presence of swine DNA was a violation of two Customs Union technical regulations: TR N° 022/2011 On Food Labeling and TR N° 034/2013 On Safety of Meat and Meat Products. This document mentions the presence of a mark indicating compliance with halal standards, yet it does not explain the connection with the violation.

The report of an inspection in the Auchan supermarket (conducted on 28 April 2018 and dated 30 May 2018) repeats the conclusions of the expert report stating that the sausage does not comply with Customs Union technical regulations N° 022/2011 and N°034/2013. It further states that in the case of the second regulation, the violation concerns 'the organoleptic indicators and the conformity of information appearing on the product label', but without mentioning the halal label.

Finally, the administrative offense report issued by Rospotrebnadzor on 21 June 2018 indicates that 'pork DNA was detected, whereas it does not appear on product packaging intended for the consumer [i.e. the label)]'. It is precisely this, along with other violations 'constituting a threat of harm to the lives and health of citizens', also established during the inspection, that made it possible to qualify the violation of the administrative code. Even though the violation is related to the presence of the halal label, the connection is not made explicit in the administrative documents.

The judgment in the civil court was also based on legislation concerning food safety and food labeling. The judge considered that Auchan was responsible for the products sold in its stores, referring to specific laws:

- Federal Law of January 2, 2000, On the Quality and Safety of Food Products, which requires the seller to ensure production controls of the quality and safety of food products
- Federal Law of March 30, 1999 On the Sanitary and Epidemiological Welfare of the Population, which stipulates that business owners and legal entities must provide controls, including laboratory analyses and testing, in order to guarantee safety and harmlessness for humans and for the environment where products are used (Judgment)

Concerning relations between the plaintiff and Auchan, the judge deemed they are governed by Russian Federation Law No. 2300-1 of February 7, 1992, On Consumer Rights Protection, which defines the obligations of the seller toward the consumer concerning quality and the sharing of information.

Finally, the judge awarded damages to the parties by referring to the explanations provided in the Resolution of the Plenum of the Supreme

Court dated June 28, 2012, On the Examination by the Civil Courts of Disputes Relating to the Protection of Consumer Rights, according to which the establishment of a violation of consumer laws is sufficient for the judge to award compensation for moral damages (Minutes).

All of these arguments seek to present the traces of pork in products with a halal label as a violation but without referring to a textual definition of the halal standard. As with the administrative court ruling, product quality and safety measures actually focused on labeling were therefore applied to a situation that had nothing to do with quality or safety.

Bringing the Halal Case Beyond the Religious Field

The court used euphemisms and did not define the halal norm in order to retain its jurisdiction as a secular authority. The court case maintained a separation of religion and state and did not bring state law to infringe upon religious territory; it made no comment on what Islam stipulates, authorizes, or forbids with reference to the term 'halal'. The lawyer for Tsaritsyno and Dinar Sadykov himself were aware of the importance of the social space in which halal-related questions could be discussed. During the trial, they sought to limit any such discussion to the religious sphere, arguing that 'the Quran is not a source of law [according to the Constitution of the Russian Federation], so it could not be used as a reference' (Minutes n.d.).

The scandal developed because their attempts to limit discussion of halal to the sphere of virtuous Muslims failed. As the third party, Dinar Sadykov claimed before the judge that there was an 'absence of proof that the plaintiff had suffered physical or mental harm justifying that damages should be awarded'. He also challenged the conditions under which the expert analysis had been performed (Judgment). In the months following the trial, he stressed that 'after the media hype targeting him, numerous consumers had sent him the results of various expert analyses showing that the composition of certain products did not match the product label' (RBK 12-2018). His line of defense actually supported the judge's ruling that consumers had been misled. It was therefore unlikely to convince people that the products he had certified were licit.

At the same time, Dinar Sadykov developed another argument, based on religious grounds. He claimed that there was no fatwa about the presence of swine DNA in halal products (tatar-inform.ru 2018). Although debatable, this argument was valid among his peers who were familiar with the technical challenges of halal manufacturing. In particular, if a production facility did not have separate production lines for products containing pork and for those that contained no pork, trace amounts of pork could be expected to appear in halal products.

Given the difficulty of all the technical and logistic information necessary to guarantee zero contamination (during slaughter but also during transport), someone who is determined to find pork DNA will, after several expert analyses, eventually succeed. While this might suggest that halal certification would become less meaningful to consumers, the opposite occurred. Since the accused certification center was unsuccessful in transforming the scandal into an 'affair' (Claverie 1994) by throwing the accusations of scandal back at the accuser (and since no other Islamic certifying bodies rose to its defense), the scandal was 'confirmed'. Not only did calls for punishment appear legitimate, but by the time it was over, halal as a certified standard (based not only on religious but also technical and commercial grounds) was made stronger.

Consolidating the Halal Standards and Reframing Collective Identities

The court's ruling had an impact on the religious field because of the question it was asked to answer but also because the parties decided to go to court and to attract the attention of the media to the case.

The very fact that the civil court did not declare itself to be incompetent removed the affair from the religious sphere and made it a cause of concern for all citizens. It is significant that the lawsuit was filed by a non-Muslim, although third parties attempted to use this argument to suggest that damages should not be awarded, as recorded in the Minutes: 'Moreover, there is no evidence that the complainant is a Muslim.' It was nevertheless the religious powers that were behind the lawsuit, aware that that court's ruling had the power to establish social order.

In a strategy of scandalization, the court ruling was given as much publicity as possible, including internationally, hence contributing to the extension of its focus beyond the religious field. Along with the judiciary, the media played an important role in this process of de-sectorization. When the arguments used in the court case were echoed in the media, their meanings changed. What had been implicit in the court's decision became, in the media, the very reason for the scandal—with numerous articles in the press focusing on 'fake' halal products (RBK 10-2018; Food Newstime 2018).

Those who were condemned publicly in the media were not the same as the alleged offenders in the court case. Auchan was required to pay a small fine and suffered little damage to its image. Tsaritsyno was in a more serious situation: not only did it have to pay a hefty fine, but it was involved in other scandals and began to lose the trust of Muslim customers in its halal products. Although it was not condemned in the court ruling, the certification center suffered the greatest blow to its image. Dinar Sadykov considered that his adversaries had 'discredited him, damaged his honor, his dignity and his commercial reputation', and had attempted to 'vilify him and harm his international authority' (RBK 12-2018). The press did not make a distinction between pork DNA and pork meat in the sausages. The scandal gave precedence to industrial purity over religious purity (Bergeaud-Blackler 2017). For halal non-specialists, trace amounts of pork were likened to fraud and generally attributed to money grabbing and profit seeking, even to 'profanation' (EurAsia Daily 2016). Indirectly, the government (through its judiciary branch) strengthened its capacity to designate the best certification center by directing public trust.

By moving the debate about halal products into the public arena, the scandal helped reshape the halal standard and made it more legitimate in a broader social space. At this point, little is known about halal consumers and their attitudes toward certification in the Russian Federation (Kapustina 2016). Available information suggests that, whereas most devout Muslims continue to rely on products from outside the certification circuit, inexperienced and inexpert believers in multi-faith contexts—such as big cities—turn to halal-labeled products that are clearly

6 Bacon or Beef? 'Fake' Halal Scandals in the Russian Federation... 141

intended for Muslims. Hence the development of the market in Muslim goods is part of a process of re-Islamization.

Scandals like the one examined here actually help spread the message that one should 'consume halal'. As a result of the scandal, certification appeared necessary to individual believers because it allows them to make the right choice—to consume products compliant with the tenets of 'their' religion. State institutions—namely the justice system—played a central role in reframing halal as the marker of a collective identity. Although the courts avoided using this term, a ruling about 'fake halal' *de facto* introduced a supposedly 'true halal' as legitimately recognized by an emanation of the state. Certification was validated by the state in its capacity to determine whether food products comply with the standard, therefore to classify them and to identify which ones are intended for Muslims. Paradoxically, the strategy of de-Islamization of halal through the court and media discourses stimulates a process of re-Islamization with collective identities constructed by the state.[5]

Conclusion

With the rapid development of a competitive halal certification market in the Russian Federation, the spread of a commercial rationale in the religious sphere extends beyond what market metaphors applied to religion might suggest. First, this rapid rise has transformed the nature of the norm. Halal standardization has taken place against a backdrop of a general rise in standards of compliance for products put on sale. Increasing standards are part of a transformation from a technical rationale to a market rationale, which is consumer-oriented and emphasizes quality and traceability (Cochoy 2000). Moreover, since the norms promoted by different actors follow a commercial rationale, their resources have been impacted profoundly. Certification has changed the rules of the game among competing actors, and recognition by the market has objectified differences in the credibility of religious institutions. In addition, it accentuates the process by which Russian Islam is becoming increasingly

---

[5] I thank an anonymous referee for this observation.

bureaucratic. Lastly, even though halal certification opens up a potential path to financial autonomy for religious organizations, the market rationale at the heart of halal legitimacy does not eliminate the role of the state. Instead, the demands and opportunities created by the growing halal market are such that all those involved must reposition themselves in relation to the state and redefine the role they expect it to play. The economic mindset impacts what people want from public authorities: not so much to assert and apply the principles of secularism laid out in the law, but rather to ensure that individual consumers and believers will have access to a certain category of products—Muslim products in this case. Halal market changes the relations between the Muslim religion and the state and secular arrangements because the state itself is impacted by commercial imaginary.

References

Alikberov, A.K., V.O. Bobrovnikov, and A.K. Bustanov. 2019. *Rossijskij Islam, ocherki istorii i kul'tury*. Moscow: Academy of Sciences.

Bekkin, Renat. 2017. The Muftiates and the state in the Soviet time: The evolution of relationship. In *Rossiyskiy islam v transformatsionnykh protsessakh sovremennosti: novyye vyzovy i tendentsii razvitiya v XXI veke*, ed. Z.R. Khabibullina, 54–75. Ufa: Dialog.

Bergeaud-Blackler, Florence. 2017. *Le marché halal ou l'invention d'une tradition*. Paris: Seuil.

Braginskaia, Ekaterina. 2012. 'Domestication' or representation? Russia and the institutionalization of Islam in comparative perspective. *Europe-Asia Studies* 64 (3): 597–620. https://doi.org/10.1080/09668136.2012.661920.

Claverie, Elisabeth. 1994. Procès, affaire, cause: Voltaire et l'innovation critique. *Politix* 7 (26): 76–85. https://doi.org/10.3406/polix.1994.1843.

Cochoy, Franck. 2000. De l'«AFNOR » à « NF », ou la progressive marchandisation de la normalisation industrielle. *Réseaux* 18 (102): 63–89. https://doi.org/10.3406/reso.2000.2258.

de Blic, Damien, and Cyril Lemieux. 2005. Le scandale comme épreuve. Éléments de sociologie pragmatique. *Politix* 71 (3): 9–38. https://doi.org/10.3917/pox.071.0009.

de Dampierre, Eric. 1954. Thèmes pour l'étude du scandale. *Annales ESC* 9 (3): 328–336. https://doi.org/10.3406/ahess.1954.2291.

Foucault, Michel. 1975. *Surveiller et punir*. Paris: Gallimard.

Gauthier, François. 2017. De l'État-nation au marché. Les transformations du religieux à l'ère de la mondialisation. *Revue du MAUSS* 49 (1): 92–114. https://doi.org/10.3917/rdm.049.0092.

Gudeman, Stephen, and Chris Hann, eds. 2015. *Economy and ritual: Studies of postsocialist transformations*. New York and Oxford: Berghahn.

Haenni, Patrick. 2005. *L'islam de marché: l'autre révolution conservatrice*. Paris: Seuil.

Kapustina, Ekaterina. 2016. Rynok islamskih tovarov i uslug v Dagestane: praktiki potreblenija i obshhestvennye diskussii [The market of Muslim goods and services in Dagestan: Practices of consumption and public debates]. *Gosudarstvo, religiia, tserkov' v Rossii i za rubezhom* 34 (2): 176–202. https://doi.org/10.22394/2073-7203-2016-34-2-176-202.

Müller, Dominik, and Kerstin Steiner. 2018. The bureaucratisation of Islam in Southeast Asia: Transdisciplinary perspectives. *Journal of Current Southeast Asian Affairs* 37 (1): 3–26.

Obadia, Lionel. 2017. Marchés, business et consumérisme en religion: vers un « tournant économique » en sciences des religions? *Mélanges de l'École française de Rome—Italie et Méditerranée modernes et contemporaines* 129 (1): 193–203. https://doi.org/10.4000/mefrim.3475.

Offerlé, Michel. 1998. *Sociologie des groupes d'intérêt*. Paris: Montchrestien.

Safarov, Marat A. 2015. Sovremennye tendencii sobljudenija tradicii «halal» v Moskovskoj Musul'manskoj obshhine [Compliance with halal traditions in Moscow's Muslim community: Modern Tendencies]. *Tatarica* 2 (5): 141–151. https://doi.org/10.26907/2311-2042.

Safiullin, L.N., G.K. Galiullina, and L.B. Shabanova. 2016. State of the market production standards, 'halal' in Russia and Tatarstan: Hands-on review. *Academy of Marketing Studies Journal* 10 (27): 6160–6164. https://doi.org/10.3923/ibm.2016.6160.6164.

Shovkhalov, Shamil A. 2018. *Formirovanie i razvitie rynka konfessional'nyh uslug v Rossii: teorija, metodologija, praktika* [The formation and development of confessional services in Russia: theory, methodology, practice]. Unpublished thesis, Federal University of Siberia.

Tasar, Eren. 2017. *Soviet and Muslim: The institutionalization of Islam in Central Asia*. New York: Oxford University Press.

Documents and Websites

Administrative offense report issued by the Rospotrebnadzor on 21 June 2018.

Atlas of Islamic Community of the Russian Federation, Presidential Grant Fund, Project No. 17-2-009700, Moscow, 2018.

Halal Committee of the Spiritual Board of the Republic of Tatarstan website. n.d.. http://halalrt.com/.

International Centre for Halal Standardization and Certification at the Council of Muftis of Russia (ICHSC) website. n.d.. http://halalcenter.ru/.

Interview 1 with the imam of a mosque near Kazan, July 2018.

Interview 2 with a former member of the Halal Standards Committee of the DUM of the Republic of Tatarstan, Kazan, July 2018.

Interview 3 with an employee of Test-Tatarstan, Kazan, July 2018.

Interview 4, with a member of the Council of Ulamas, Kazan, August 2018.

Judgment, case 2/2 1307/18, Justice of the Peace, court district 2, Moscow judicial district of Kazan city.

Letter of 7 August 2018 from the Head of the Territorial Department of the Directorate of the Federal Control Service, in the sphere of defense of consumer rights and human wellbeing of the city of Moscow, to A. Maslov.

Minutes of the hearing, case 2/2 1307/18, Justice of the Peace, court district 2, Moscow judicial district of Kazan city.

Report of the inspection in the Auchan supermarket by Rozpotrebnadzor (conducted on 28 April 2018 and dated 30 May 2018).

Report of the laboratory analysis, 17 May 2018.

Rosstat (Federal State Statistic Service) 2010. website: https://rosstat.gov.ru/free_doc/new_site/perepis2010/croc/perepis_itogi1612.htm.

Rosstandart (Federal Agency for Regulation and Metrology) website. n.d.. https://www.gost.ru/portal/gost/.

Rospotrebnadzor (Federal Service for Surveillance on Consumer Rights Protection and Human Wellbeing) website. n.d.. https://rospotrebnadzor.ru/.

Veterinary expert report, 18 May 2018.

Media Coverage

A branch of the Research and Information Center of the Islamic Chamber of OIC was opened in Kazan. *Tatar-inform*, 14 September 2011. Accessed 28 June 2019. https://www.tatar-inform.ru/news/2011/09/14/285697/.

6 Bacon or Beef? 'Fake' Halal Scandals in the Russian Federation...

A mass study of halal products to be launched in Russia. *RBK*, 4 December 2018. Accessed 28 June 2019. https://rt.plus.rbc.ru/pressrelease/5c066f417a8aa9777ceb9a68?from=newsfeed.

A member of the Muftis Council was expelled from an international organization for 'unethical conduct'. *IslamNews*, 2 November 2018. Accessed 18 June 2019. https://islamnews.ru/news-sotrudnika-soveta-muftiev-izgnali-iz-mezhdunarodnoj-organizacii-za-nejetichnoe-povedenie/.

Certification Centre from Tatarstan expelled from Halal World Council. *Muslim.kz*, 8 November 2018. Accessed 16 June 2019. http://muslim.kz/ru/news/sertifikatsionnyyi-tsentr-iz-tatarstana-isklyuchen-iz-vsemirnogo-soveta-khalyal.

Dinar Sadykov: 'It's time to start bringing our halal products to Muslim countries'. Former website of Halal Standards Committee of the DUM of the Republic of Tatarstan, 2 August 2011. Accessed 28 July 2018. http://www.halalrf.ru/.

Dinar Sadykov: 'There is no fatwa that makes a product haram'. *Tatar-inform*, 5 August 2018. Accessed 28 June 2019. https://www.tatar-inform.ru/news/2018/08/03/621493/.

Horns and hooves have proven to be untenable. *Regiony-online*, 31 August 2018. Accessed 28 June 2019. http://www.gosrf.ru/news/37995/.

Meat dispute: was pork in halal products by Tsaritsyno? *RBK*, 27 October 2018. Accessed 16 June 2019. https://rt.rbc.ru/tatarstan/27/10/2018/5bd3273f9a79471ca9a73aa0.

Pork was found in the halal sausage of the Tsaritsyno. *Food Newstime*, 9 November 2018. Accessed 15 June 2019. http://www.foodnewstime.ru/novosti-rynkov/russia-prod/v-xalyalnoj-kolbase-mk-caricyno-nashli-svininu.html.

Roskontrol called 75 percent of sausages sold in Russia a falsification. *Lenta.ru*, 16 March 2016. Accessed 31 July 2018. https://lenta.ru/news/2016/03/10/fake/.

Russian halal: Between growth and profanation. *EurAsia Daily*, 11 June 2016. Accessed 18 June 2019. https://eadaily.com/ru/news/2016/06/14/rossiyskiy-halyal-mezhdu-rostom-i-profanaciey.

Shame because they have no conscience. ... They are the children of Ostap Bender. *Biznes on Line*, 7 November 2018. Accessed 15 July 2019. https://www.business-gazeta.ru/article/401704?fbclid=IwAR33_prte3SvcYMvY_6ILb6Vbgp4yMDKSqOa0dS_nk52MWgLEL5hN_upmBc.

The Council of Muftis of Russia discussed the appearance of false certifiers in the halal market. Mufti Council website, 23 December 2014. Accessed 30 June 2019. https://www.muslim.ru/articles/285/8827/.

The deputy heads of the Halal Certification Center of the Mufti Council were expelled from WHC. *RBK*, 2 November 2018. Accessed 16 June 2019. https://plus.rbc.ru/pressrelease/5bdc72227a8aa936b19977df?ruid=NaN.

There is 0.4% of pork in halal products of Tsaritsyno. *Biznes on Line*, 13 October 2018. Accessed 15 July 2019. https://www.business-gazeta.ru/article/398774.

There was a scandal: A firm from Tatarstan was expelled from the Halal World Council. In *Kazan*, 7 November 2018. Accessed 18 June 2019. https://inkazan.ru/news/society/07-11-2018/ne-oboshlos-bez-skandala-firmu-iz-tatarstana-izgnali-iz-vsemirnogo-soveta-halyal.

The Russian certification center was expelled from the World Halal Council with shame. The meeting of the Halal World Council turned out to be a scandal. Mufti Council website, 6 November 2018. Accessed 30 August 2018. https://www.muslim.ru/articles/285/22458/.

The scandalous aftertaste: The story of 'halal pork' made Marat Akhmetov do the checks. *Realnoe Vremja*, 26 June 2018. Accessed 16 June 2019. https://realnoevremya.ru/articles/103820-chelny-myaso-izyali-ne-vsyu-halyal-produkciyu-s-narusheniyami.

Tsaritsyno defended doctoral sausages from Channel One in court. *Lenta.ru*, 26 April 2016. Accessed 31 July 2018. https://lenta.ru/news/2016/04/26/tsaritsino_sausages/.

7

Halal in Contemporary Ukraine: Markets and Administration

Denis Brylov

Introduction

The halal industry is actively growing all over the world. In order to satisfy the demands of Muslim customers, companies strive to certify their products as conforming with the principles of sharia (i.e., allowed to be consumed by Muslims). Meanwhile, the Muslim countries of the Middle East and Northern Africa are among the largest food importers in the world: imported goods cover approximately 50% of their food needs. Even 10% of the region's wheat, one of its own major food products, is imported. The demand for food in this region is expected to increase as the population there grows yearly at a rate of approximately 3%. This situation creates an opportunity for Ukraine to enter the Middle Eastern markets, the Gulf countries in particular, with its food products (Volovych et al. 2011: 5)—if they are considered permissible for Muslim consumption.

D. Brylov (✉)
Department of Modern Studies, A. Krymskyi Institute of Oriental Studies of the National Academy of Sciences of Ukraine, Kyiv, Ukraine

© The Author(s), under exclusive license to Springer Nature Switzerland AG 2023
R. Turaeva, M. Brose (eds.), *Religious Economies in Secular Context*, New Directions in Islam, https://doi.org/10.1007/978-3-031-18603-5_7

148   D. Brylov

Ordinarily, Ukraine is not thought of as a Muslim country, and it seems—at first glance—an unlikely contender in the global halal marketplace, even though it is a major producer of wheat, sunflower oil, and other staple foods, representing more than 30% of the total export of Ukraine. This chapter, however, draws attention to the ways in which the growth of Muslim communities in post-Soviet Ukraine has contributed to the development of a halal industry, with both domestic and export-oriented capacities.

After the break-up of the Soviet Union, religion has seen a growing role in Ukrainian society, and religious organizations that were not registered on the territory of Soviet Ukraine have entered the public sphere. These include Islamic communities. During Soviet times, certain Muslim communities (such as Volga Tatars) were illegal and functioned only underground in Ukraine. After independence, these resurfaced, and other Muslim communities appeared through such processes as the return of Crimean-Tatar Muslims and the transmigration of Meskhetians from Central Asia. These communities have led to the development of a visible Islamic infrastructure in Ukraine. It includes, in particular, the development of the halal industry, encompassing catering establishments that meet halal requirements, brands with the corresponding certification, and certification structures.

At the same time, the development of the halal industry in Ukraine has its own economic and sociohistorical characteristics. Among these are the to-date export orientation of Ukrainian halal producers; the long absence of Muslims from public discourse and consideration as a "market" with particular dietary needs and preferences; and a low level of religious knowledge, including of sharia and halal, among a significant part of local Muslims. Taken together, these factors mean that Muslims in Ukraine have not been the primary customers, real or imagined, for the local halal industry—although, of course, they could have been. Instead, it is Muslims outside of Ukraine who are the primary customers.

In my chapter, I analyze the activities of the two main halal certification centers associated with the most influential Islamic organizations among Muslims in Ukraine. These both have wide connections in the Islamic world. They are the Certification Center "Halal" by the Religious Administration of Muslims of Ukraine (DUMU) and the Center for

7 Halal in Contemporary Ukraine: Markets and Administration 149

Research and "Halal" Certification by the NGO Alraid Association. It should be noted that, since 2008, the Product Certification and Standardization Department "Elal" (Halal) functions also alongside the Crimean Muftiat, the Religious Administration of Muslims of Crimea (DUMK). However, this department issued its first halal certificate only in August 2013,[1] and, six months later, the Crimean Muftiat was absorbed within Russia's legal field with that country's annexation of Crimea. Therefore, I do not consider it here.

My chapter is based on data gathered during field research on Islamic infrastructure in Ukraine conducted in 2015–2020. It included participant observation, in-depth interviews with representatives of the Islamic community and the certification centers, and analysis of the press.

Halal in Ukraine: Economic and Sociohistorical Background

There is no precise data on the numbers of Ukrainian Muslims—that is, more precisely, Muslims in Ukraine—or on the ethnic and national composition of particular Islamic communities. According to the last national census of 2001,[2] there are 436,000 ethnic Muslims. The designation "ethnic Muslim" refers to members of ethnic groups predominantly associated with Islam (e.g., Tatars), irrespective of whether such individuals are believers or atheists). This amounts to about 0.9% of the overall population (Yarosh and Brylov 2011). Representatives of various Islamic religious administrative units, however, generally voice numbers that are three times higher than the census figures: 1–1.5 million people.

The largest Muslim ethnic groups are Crimean Tatars (248,000), Volga Tatars (73,000), Azerbaijanis (45,000), representatives of the North Caucasus ethnic groups (14,000), Uzbeks (12,000), and Turks/

---

[1] Muftiat dal pervoe razreshenie na elyal-produkciyu [The muftiat gave the first permission for elyal-products]. Avdet, 6 August 2013. Available online, https://avdet.org/ru/2013/08/06/muftiyat-dal-pervoe-razreshenie-na-elyal-produktsiyu/. Accessed 3 August 2021.

[2] The first Ukrainian census was carried out by the State Statistics Committee of Ukraine on 5 December 2001, twelve years after the last Soviet Union census in 1989. It has so far been the only census held in independent Ukraine.

150   D. Brylov

Meskhetians (approx. 10,000). All of these groups count their 'homelands' in the former Soviet Union; the census does not record any significant communities of Muslims who have arrived more recently in Ukraine. Geographically, the largest Muslim community of Ukraine was in Crimea (272,600, including Sevastopol), followed by the Muslims of the Donetsk region (36,000), Kharkiv (16,000), Luhansk (15,000), Dnipropetrovsk (now Dnipro, 15,000), Kherson (14,000), Odessa (12,200), Zaporizhia (11,700), and Kyiv (10,900) (Bogomolov et al. 2006: 24).

The most important Islamic institutions consolidating a huge part of Muslim communities are the Religious Administration of Muslims of Ukraine (Dukhovne upravlinnia musul'man Ukraïny—DUMU) in Kyiv; the Religious Administration of Muslims of Crimea (Dukhovne upravlinnia musul'man Krymu—DUMK) in Simferopol; the Religious Center of Muslims of Ukraine (Dukhovnyi tsentr musul'man Ukraïny—DTsMU) in Donetsk; the Religious Administration of Muslims of Ukraine 'Umma' (Dukhovne upravlinnia musul'man Ukraïny "Umma"—DUMU-Umma) in Kyiv; the Religious Center of Muslims of Crimea (Dukhovnyi tsentr musul'man Krymu—DTsMK) in Eupatoria; and the Religious Administration of Independent Islamic Communities Kievskii Muftiat (*Relihiine upravlinnia nezalezhnykh musul'mans'kykh hromad Ukrainy*—RUNMHU) in Kyiv.

Since 2014, DUMK and DTsMK (members from which founded the Central Religious Administration of Muslims "Tauride Muftiat") have been outside Ukraine's legal field. DTsMU remained in zones of armed conflict in the self-proclaimed Donetsk People's Republic and Luhansk People's Republic. The remaining religious administrations—DUMU, DUMU-Umma, and RUNMHU, as well as the Religious Administration of Muslims of the Autonomous Republic of Crimea (*Dukhovne upravlinnia musul'man avtonomnoi respubliky Krym*—DUM ARK, registered at the end of 2017) and independent Muslim communities that are not part of any of these spiritual boards—continue to function on the territory of Ukraine which is under Kyiv's control.[3]

---

[3] The religious, or spiritual, administrations of Muslims (DUMs) in Ukraine—also referred to as *muftiat, muftiate, muftiyat,* or *muftiyyat*—share a common historical background with those in Russia and Central Asia (see Amon, Pak, and Serrano; all this volume).

7 Halal in Contemporary Ukraine: Markets and Administration 151

The NGO Alraid Association (officially the All-Ukrainian Association of Social Organizations "Alraid"—AUASO Alraid) is ideologically, organizationally, and financially connected with the global Muslim Brotherhood movement (Brylov 2014: 73–74). Because of its charitable organization status, Alraid could not register as another Muftiat in Ukraine. The solution to this problem was the establishment in 2008 of DUMU-Umma, which is seen as a "front Muftiate" for Alraid in Ukraine (Izmirli 2012).

At present, it is difficult to assess the total potential of the domestic market for halal products. Available estimates are based on the total number of Muslims in Ukraine and range from $1–2 billion. The export potential of halal producers, however, is estimated at $4–5 billion.[4] The main and most promising direction of halal certification is with the certification of chicken meat. Ukraine is already a major producer, ranking 4th in the world for the export of this product,[5] and already has an established presence in the large Middle Eastern markets. Countries of the Islamic world import almost half of all chicken produced in Ukraine. The largest importer of Ukrainian chicken meat is Saudi Arabia.[6] Moreover, even with a general decrease in exports in the initial months of the COVID-19 pandemic, the supply of chicken increased by 5%, with Saudi Arabia and the UAE becoming the top three global importers of Ukrainian chicken.[7]

---

[4] Ukrainskaya Halyal industriya: tekushaya situaciya v strane, perspektivy razvitiya na mezhdunarodnyh rynkah [Ukrainian halal industry: Current situation in the country, development prospects in international markets]. *Ukrhalal* website, 3 August 2017. https://ukrhalal.org/ukrainskaya-halyal-industriya-tekushhaya-situatsiya-v-strane-perspektivy-razvitiya-na-mezhdunarodnyh-rynkah. Accessed 3 August 2021.

[5] Ukraina voshla v top-5 mirovyh eksporterov kuryatiny—Minekonomiki [Ukraine entered the top 5 world exporters of chicken—Ministry of Economy]. *Liga.Biznes*, 14 January 2020. Available online, https://biz.liga.net/ekonomika/prodovolstvie/novosti/ukraina-voshla-v-top-5-mirovyh-eksporterov-kuryatiny%2D%2D-minekonomiki. Accessed 2 August 2021.

[6] Saudovskaya Araviya stala osnovnym pokupatelem ukrainskoj kuryatiny [Saudi Arabia became the main buyer of Ukrainian chicken]. *Liga.Biznes*, 30 May 2019. https://biz.liga.net/ekonomika/prodovolstvie/novosti/saudovskaya-araviya-stala-osnovnym-pokupatelem-ukrainskoy-kuryatiny. Accessed 3 August 2021.

[7] Ukraine's chicken meat export went up in Jan–Aug (2020). *Latifundist*, 9 September 2020. Available online, https://latifundist.com/en/novosti/51866-ukraina-uvelichila-eksport-myasa--ptitsy-s-nachala-goda. Accessed 2 August 2021.

The prospects for entering the market of Muslim countries have led to the development of the halal livestock industry, which would otherwise be unpromising in Ukraine. Some firms are switching completely to the production of halal products. According to the director of one of these companies, the main consumers of the products are Azerbaijan, Egypt, and Turkey, and only 5% of the total volume is sold in the domestic market. What's more, halal meat in the domestic market is dominated by the residues suitable for the manufacture of sausages![8]

Another important area is the halal certification of sunflower oil. In terms of exports, Ukraine ranks first in the world for this product. As with chicken meat, the trade in sunflower oil has been unaffected by the COVID-19 pandemic. The export of sunflower oil in 2020 increased by 10% compared to the same period in 2019, and among the main buyers of Ukrainian oil there are also countries of the Islamic world: Iraq occupies the 4th position, and its share is 8.6% from the total volume of Ukrainian exports.[9] Other major buyers of sunflower oil include the UAE and Malaysia.

At the same time, the economic attractiveness of obtaining halal certification for export products plays a negative role in the formation of a domestic market. According to the head of one of the largest halal certification centers, many of the products that receive the halal certificate are not supplied to the Ukrainian market at all, as it is economically impractical, due to the low purchasing power of Ukrainian citizens and the instability of the national currency. For example, the largest producer of sunflower oil in Ukraine, KERNEL, which supplies several brands of halal sunflower oil (including premium ones) to Arab countries, does not sell any products with halal certification in the domestic market. Thus, we can say that the export orientation of the Ukrainian manufacturer has become an obstacle to the formation of the domestic halal market.

---

[8] Vostok—delo tonkoe: v Ukraine osvaivayut standard «halal» dlya govyadiny [The East is a delicate matter: In Ukraine they master the halal standard for beef]. *Ekonomika*, 20 September 2018. Available online, http://economica.com.ua/article/77715520.html. Accessed 3 August 2021.

[9] Ukraina ustanovila rekord po eksportu podsolnechnogo masla tankerami [Ukraine has set a record for the export of sunflower oil by tankers]. *Liga.Biznes*, 2 August 2021. https://biz.liga.net/all/prodovolstvie/novosti/ukraina-ustanovila-rekord-po-eksportu-podsolnechnogo-masla-infografika. Accessed 2 August 2021.

7 Halal in Contemporary Ukraine: Markets and Administration 153

At the same time, there are other factors that hinder the development of the halal industry in Ukraine. Specifically, Muslim communities—like individual Muslims—remain in the shadows of public space. Since 1989, government agencies began registering Islamic communities, and Muslims have been able to practice their rituals openly and without fear, including food-related practices. It is important to note that Muslims live under a pressure of anti-Islamic and anti-Muslim discourses both at the society level as well as at the level of state administration and politics. First of all, it should be noted that although several Muslim groups have lived on Ukrainian territory for centuries, the majority of the population is Christian, and all non-Christian confessions are perceived ambiguously by the majority of the population, as well as by the authorities. Official Muslim communities operated on the territory of Ukraine from the end of the nineteenth century, primarily in Kyiv, Kharkov, Odessa, and the Donetsk region (Brylov 2017a: 155), but in the decades after World War II, the ombudsmen for religious affairs in Soviet Ukraine saw it as their task to prevent the registration of Muslim communities, adhering to the rule—"there is no Islam in Ukraine" (Interview, September 2015, Kyiv). Though Muslims remained part of the population, they did not practice their faith openly and therefore often "passed" as Christian; indeed, with the absence of functioning Islamic institutions, most people assumed that there were no Muslims in Ukraine.

Much of the ambiguity toward Muslims is linked to collective memory of the complex historical relations between the Ukrainian lands and the Crimean (Tatar) Khanate. In many ways, this attitude was formed during the time of the Russian Empire, when after the Treaty of Jassy (1791) Russia annexed the Crimean Khanate and pursued a repressive policy toward the Crimean Tatars. During this period, a historical narrative was formed that described the Crimean Tatars as enemies who took the Slavs (Ukrainians and Russians) into slavery. In Soviet times, especially after the deportation of the Crimean Tatars in 1944, this narrative was supported by the authorities and has been existing until this day.

Until now, Ukraine has one of the highest levels of Islamophobia in Europe. According to a Pew Research Center report, only 25% of Ukrainians would agree to see a Muslim as a member of their family; in neighboring Russia, this percentage is 34 (Pew Research Center 2018).

154   D. Brylov

Under the heading, "Regional tolerance, xenophobia, and human rights in 2012," another report gives an index of interethnic distance in 2012 as 4.5 out of a maximum 7. This index characterizes interethnic, interracial, and international relations in Ukrainian society as "alienating." Yet antagonism toward Muslims seems most especially connected to 'foreigners' and visible or recently established communities. In Western Ukraine, xenophobia is primarily directed at Arabs, Africans, Crimean Tatars, and Jews, while in Eastern Ukraine it targets Asians, Arabs, and the representatives of Western European and Atlantic national and cultural groups (Germans, French, Americans, Canadians). Whether 'foreign' or 'indigenous,' Muslim ethnicities are at the top of the lists. In general, one can agree with opinion the head of the Group for Monitoring Minority Rights, Vyacheslav Likhachev, who thinks that Islamophobia is one of the most prominent forms of xenophobia in Ukraine (Brylov 2016: 268–69).

In such a national context, many Muslims prefer not to identify very publicly with their faith.[10] Explicit purchase, consumption, or use of halal products therefore has little appeal. Even the concept of 'halal' itself, as understood across the industry, may be unknown or—more recently—ignored. According to Idil Izmirli (2012), most Ukrainian Muslims who grew up during the Soviet era did not know the basic tenets of Islam, nor did they understand the differences between the various Islamic trends and ideologies. Even the majority of the traditional Crimean Tatars seem to profess what Izmirli calls 'cafeteria Islam,' picking and choosing Islamic teachings based on their own lifestyles and interpretations. For example, many Crimean Tatars drink alcohol even during Ramadan, and they eat pork; but they may refuse to touch a dog because it is considered haram. For many Ukrainian Muslims, and in general post-Soviet Muslims, everything that is not pork is halal. For example, in Central Asia (where Crimean Tatars, who make up the majority of Ukrainian Muslims, were deported for almost 50 years) vodka drinking became an integral part of 'Muslim' celebrations during the

---

[10] The situation began to change in 2014, when, in the Russian-Ukrainian conflict, Crimean Tatars and natives of the North Caucasus, hostile against Russia, took the side of Ukraine, which contributed to the improvement of attitudes toward Muslims in Ukraine.

7 Halal in Contemporary Ukraine: Markets and Administration   155

Soviet period and has since been assimilated to national tradition (Khalid 2014: 101).

Until the early 2000s, the halal industry in Ukraine was not developed even in the food products segment. Halal food could be found only in areas that were densely and exclusively populated by Muslims: in the houses of prayers (*musallas*) and a few mosques. Even in the early 2000s, the halal industry was weakly developed throughout most of Ukraine, and believers could hardly buy products that complied with sharia norms. Some 55% of Muslims interviewed some two decades after independence noted that they had problems buying halal goods (Havrilova et al. 2011). The same study produced a figure of 42% of interviewees who did not report such problems, but the researchers believed that these respondents were aware of the shops near mosques and Muslim centers. Nevertheless, these small shops could not satisfy the demands of all Muslims, if desire for halal were to grow (Havrilova et al. 2011).

Thus, although Ukraine long had the potential to develop a domestic market for halal goods, in the sense that it had small but statistically noticeable Muslim communities, such a market did not develop with any speed, even when free market conditions were opened in the early 1990s. The 1990s did enable the registration of Islamic organizations, and, by the early 2000s, there were some organizations capable of certifying products as halal. The major developments in the halal market have been rapid and distinctly international in origin and scope. Russian Islamic organizations have set the pace. In 2012, the delegation of the International 'Halal' Certification Centre of the Russian Mufti Board (Sovet muftiev Rossii—SMR), headed by CEO Aidar Gazizov, paid a working visit to Ukraine. This visit to Ukraine was part of the SMR program for the creation and control of a single 'halal' economic space in the territory of the CIS countries (Bagautdinova 2012). During the visit, the delegation reached an agreement with Kanafia Husnutdinov, the head of RUNMHU, to open the Center's office in Kyiv. At the same time, the main customer of the halal certification of the new center was the Roshen confectionery concern, owned by Petro Poroshenko who later became president of Ukraine. The certification procedure was passed by the enterprises of this company, which are located in Vinnitsa, Kyiv, Kremenchug, and

156   D. Brylov

Mariupol. Nevertheless, with the beginning of the Russian-Ukrainian conflict over Crimea, the cooperation was phased out.

"Battlefield Halal"

The development of the halal industry in Ukraine must be seen partly as a matter of "market growth" and partly from the perspective that non-market factors influence the very institutional structuring of market activities.

Above, I have described some of the economic, demographic, and historical factors that account for Ukraine's apparently "underdeveloped" domestic halal market. In this section, I turn to a description of institutional and ideological factors from within Islam that have affected the development of the institutions and procedures that underlie 'halal' production. In other words, I show how competition between two Islamic organizations, with two different religious discourses, have affected who certifies what as 'halal' and how as well as why.

DUMU and Alraid (along with the DUMU-Umma) form two different religious discourses that are in competition. Each takes part in a transnational Islamic structure that has a long history of confrontation with the other. According to Mustafa Kabha and Haggai Erlich, this a confrontation between those striving for the political victory of Islam, widely referred to as Wahhabis, and the adherents of Sufism who favor the kind of political coexistence between Muslims and Christians personified by al-Ahbash (Kabha and Erlich 2006: 519). Being irreconcilable ideological opponents, they project their conflict onto Ukrainian everyday life, including the domain of halal certification.

DUMU is the oldest religious association of Muslims of Ukraine. It includes communities that operated informally on the territory of Ukraine in the Soviet period, and it is part of the transnational Sufi

7 Halal in Contemporary Ukraine: Markets and Administration

network, widely known as al-Ahbash, or *habashiyya*.[11] It therefore tends to favor political coexistence between Muslims and Christians.

Important to note about al-Ahbash adherents in Ukraine is that they mostly follow the Shafiʿi madhhab (law school), whereas in matters of faith they tend to be mostly Asharite. One of the most important tenets of the al-Ahbash ideology is the recognition of the complete sharia legitimacy of Sufism, along with its main rituals and practices such as *dhikr* (mention of God) and *ziyarat* (visits to the graves of saints and prophets). The ideology of al-Ahbash can be described using the concept of 'traditional Islam' proposed by K. Mathiesen which is based on the *hadith Jibril* that divides the religion into Islam, Iman, and Ihsan.[12] Each of these represents an anthropological aspect—Islam (body/practice), Iman (mind), and Ihsan (spirit/soul)—as well as subfields of revealed knowledge, traditions, practices, and institutions. This tripartite structure further contextualizes traditional Islam's discourse of orthodoxy in three major discursive fields of contention: Islam/fiqh, Iman/ʿaqida, and Ihsan/tasawwuf (Sufism) (Mathiesen 2013: 217). An important feature of the 'traditional Islam' of al-Ahbash is strict adherence to the rules of *madhhab*s, including the issues of determining the criteria for halal. Therefore, the criteria of what can be considered a halal product are often stricter among the representatives of al-Ahbash than among those of other Islamic groups.

The mufti of DUMU, Sheikh Ahmed Tamim, is Lebanese by origin and was a student of Abdullah Al-Harari. It was Tamim who became one of the first Al-Harari supporters in Ukraine; later, he was actively engaged in disseminating his teacher's ideas. Having arrived in Kyiv in 1976 (then still the Ukrainian SSR), Ahmed Tamim turned out to be one of the leaders of the revival of Islam in Ukraine after independence in 1991, rallying around himself a group of Kyiv Muslims.

DUMU became the first Ukrainian organization to issue halal certificates. According to Sheikh Ahmed Tamim himself, the first certificates

---

[11] Both terms, al-Ahbash and *habashiyya*, refer to the *Jam'iyyat al-mashari' al-khayriyya al-Islamiyya* (Association of Islamic Charitable Projects—AICP). The term al-Ahbash (lit. the Ethiopians), used to describe the movement's members, is connected with the name (*nisba*) of the movement founder Abdullah Al-Harari al-Habashi, an Ethiopian native.

[12] For more information about the discourse of the 'traditional Islam' of DUMU, see Brylov (2018).

158   **D. Brylov**

were issued in 1994 to a sunflower oil producer who needed halal certification to enter the Indonesian market. Until 2011, DUMU itself carried out halal certification; however, due to the increase in the number of clients, it became necessary to establish a separate certification center.

Today the Certification Center 'Halal' by DUMU is an independent organization with the status of an international institution.[13] It certifies the compliance of production processes with sharia law. It also organizes and carries out the certification of goods and services, guaranteeing an independent and professional evaluation of compliance with the 'halal' standard. The Center sets its main goals as follows:

- To check and confirm that halal-marked products do not contain forbidden ingredients
- To check and confirm that halal-marked meat products are in fact made from the meat of the allowed animals that were slaughtered in compliance with sharia requirements
- To increase the quality of goods and services
- To protect customers from negligent producers and service providers
- To promote the competitiveness of 'made in Ukraine' products on the global market (primarily in Muslim countries) (Brylov 2017b: 112)

Representing a conservative group that zealously defends the Ashʿari doctrine from modern Salafism and the reformed *fiqh* of the Muslim Brotherhood and strictly following Shafiʿi law, Ukrainian Habashites consider halal norms primarily as a religious issue, not an economic one. As noted by the head of the Certification Center 'Halal' by DUMU, Ruslan Borichevskyi, very often they refuse halal certification to Ukrainian manufacturers because production conditions and raw materials do not meet all Shariʿah requirements. (As a rule, DUMU refers to the Shafiʿi tradition, less often—Hanafi). For example, the Certification Center 'Halal' by DUMU failed to agree on the certification of the largest chicken producer, 'Mironivsky Hliboproduct' (Myronivka Bread-Produce), due to its strict requirements for the slaughtering process, which demand the constant presence of a representative of the center in

---

[13] The official website is www.halal.ua.

7 Halal in Contemporary Ukraine: Markets and Administration

the slaughterhouse. As a result, the company received a certificate from the competitors of DUMU—the certification center of the Alraid Association, which agreed to certify chicken meat on the condition of regular visits of a representative of its certification center to the slaughterhouse.

Despite the fact that the conservative position and strict requirements for the products themselves and production conditions reduce the economic competitiveness of the DUMU certification center, their close ties with Sufi circles in the Islamic world save the situation. The halal certificate issued by DUMU is recognized in almost all countries where Sufism has a strong position (first of all, Egypt, the largest importer of Ukrainian products in the Islamic world, and the UAE, one of the main buyers of Ukrainian chicken and eggs). For example, the Certification Center 'Halal' at DUMU for a long time was the only one in Ukraine that had accreditation issued by EIAC (Emirates International Accreditation Center) and JAKIM (Department of Islamic Development Malaysia). This means that DUMU-certified products have stronger access to the markets of Muslim countries in the Middle East and Southeast Asia.[14]

The main competitor of DUMU in the halal industry is the Alraid Association and the DUMU-Umma connected with it. An unconditional authority for the Alraid and the DUMU-Umma is the leading ideologist of the Muslim Brotherhood, Yusuf al-Qaradawi, who has a critical attitude toward the classical Sunni madhhabs, considering their rules outdated. Following him, Ukrainian Muslim brothers likewise do not associate Islam with the religious tradition of any particular Muslim peoples. This was stressed by DUMU-Umma mufti Said (Serhei) Ismagilov in my interview with him. In the words of S. Ismagilov, religious views and practices that do not conform to the strict limits of orthodox Sunnism become a private matter for individual believers (Brylov 2014: 73). Such a light attitude to halal standards can be seen in the activities of the halal cafe 'Jerusalem' at the Islamic Cultural Center of Kyiv (in Alraid's headquarters), whose director indicated that even though the Qur'an categorically forbids alcohol, if a person were to enter with a

---

[14] Dostijenia [Achievements]. 2019. Certification Center 'Halal' website https://halal.ua/jakim. Accessed 3 August 2021.

160   D. Brylov

bottle of vodka, he would not be expelled from the cafe: "We understand that we do not live in the United Arab Emirates, and respect Ukrainian customs" (Siyak 2008).

In 2012, together with the DUMU-Umma, Alraid registered the Centre for Research and 'Halal' Certification Alraid (CRHC Alraid). This Centre defines its goals as follows:

- To provide the Ukrainian food market with halal goods, available for Muslim customers
- To promote the export of Ukrainian goods to the markets of Arab and Muslim countries, [and] build bridges between the Islamic world and Ukraine
- To promote sales of 'made in Ukraine' goods that comply with halal standards
- To create workplaces for Muslims[15]

Nevertheless, Alraid is accused of insufficiently strict standards that affect the whole Ukrainian halal market. In May 2016, for example, numerous reports appeared in Ukrainian media that the United Arab Emirates had forbidden the import of Ukrainian halal-certified food.[16] The story was fabricated but had its motivation in the fact that the Alraid Center had lost the right to issue halal certificates. However, the UAE had not forbidden the import of Ukrainian food products nor had they ever expressed concerns about quality. UAE authorities questioned only the halal certificate issued by Alraid.[17] Alraid was the target of unfounded fears that lax standards of certification could interrupt Ukrainian exports. Before this organization had gained certification rights in February 2014,

---

[15] Tsentr doslidzhen ta sertyfikatsii Khalyal [Halal Research and Certification Center]. 12 June 2016. *Tsentr doslidzhen ta sertyfikatsii Khalyal* website, http://halal.org.ua/]. Accessed 3 August 2021.

[16] Emiraty zaboronyly import produktsii z Ukrainy [The Emirates banned the import of products from Ukraine]. Korrespondent, 30 May 2016. Available online, https://ua.korrespondent.net/ukraine/3689963-emiraty-zaboronyly-import-produktsii-z-ukrainy. Accessed 3 August 2021.

[17] Emiratska storona sprostuvala informatsiiu pro pryzupynennia importu do OAE ukrainskoi produktsii. [The Emirati side has denied information about the suspension of imports into the uae of Ukrainian products]. *AgroPolit*, 10 June 2016. https://agropolit.com/news/1424-emiratska-storona-sprostuvala-informatsiyu-pro-prizupinennya-importu-do-oae-ukrayinskoyi--produktsiyi%2D%2Dofitsiyno. Accessed 3 August 2021.

7 Halal in Contemporary Ukraine: Markets and Administration   161

Ukrainian exporters had used other means to obtain such certificates, including alternative certification centers in Ukraine and abroad.

In order to compensate for serious image losses and fulfill its business obligations to Ukrainian enterprises that had already passed certification at the CRHC Alraid, the association registered several new halal certification centers in 2016. In addition, DUMU-Umma founded a separate certification center, Halal Global Ukraine. Its mission statement read: "to help Ukrainian producers to expand their markets and develop export connections with Muslim countries, to protect customers of the halal products and services made in Ukraine."[18] In December 2016, the Ukrainian Association of the Halal Industry 'Ukrhalal' was created on the base of CRHC Alraid. It united CRHC Alraid and Halal Global Ukraine. The importance and the promise of the halal industry in Ukraine is even noted in the "Social Conception of the Ukrainian Muslims," the program document of the Alraid Association and DUMU-Umma, which was cosigned by some Ukrainian Muslim organizations. The document reads: "Taking into account the practices of Islamic banking, this sector of the economy is one of the most promising; with the development of the halal industry, it is the priority for the activities of Islamic organizations."[19]

Certifying many large Ukrainian producers (primarily meat producers and confectionery corporations), Alraid and DUMU-Umma consider halal an instrument of influence in the public sphere. For example, in October 2017, the Ukrainian Association of the Halal Industry 'Ukrhalal' sent an open letter to representatives of the largest retailers in Ukraine with a proposal to help them create and maintain a 'single halal shelf' to display products that have the appropriate certificate.

Thus, against the background of the growing market for halal products in Ukraine (mainly export-oriented), there is a clash between the two largest operators of halal certification—the Certification Center 'Halal' by DUMU and the certification centers of the Alraid Association and DUMU-Umma (which are, in essence, a single network). For the

---

[18] O nas [About us]. http://www.halalglobal.in.ua/o-nas/. Accessed 30 January 2020.

[19] Sotsialna kontseptsiia musulman Ukrainy [Social concept of Muslims of Ukraine], 2017. *DUMU-Umma* website, https://umma.in.ua/ua/node/1890. Accessed 3 August 2021.

DUMU, the main aspect of halal certification is not economic profitability, but the religious aspect—the building of orthodoxy in accordance with strict criteria within the framework of classical Sunni madhhabs. At the same time, thanks to the Sufi background of the DUMU, the low economic competitiveness is to some extent compensated by the advantages of freer access to the markets of Muslim countries in which Sufism is widespread. The Alraid Association and DUMU-Umma offer more flexible conditions for certification and consider halal certification as an important part of their public image in the eyes of the Ukrainian society, especially in the eyes of Ukrainian business community and government.

Pandemic as a Halal Industry Growth Driver

In 2021, quarantine restrictions caused by the COVID-19 pandemic unexpectedly came in handy for Ukrainian Muslims and the development of the halal industry within the country. Strict measures by European countries to prevent the spread of COVID-19 resulted in a significant number of tourists from the Gulf countries starting to look for new tourist destinations without such restrictions.

Ukraine became one of these destinations, thanks to its unilateral abolition of visa requirements in 2020 for the United Arab Emirates, Saudi Arabia, Qatar, Bahrain, and Kuwait. In addition, Ukraine recognized international vaccination certificates and eliminated mandatory testing and quarantine upon arrival. Against such liberalization, Saudi low-cost carrier Flynas opened charter flights from Riyadh to Kyiv and Lviv. The Ukrainian carrier SkyUp added the same routes. Kuwaiti carrier Jazeera Airways[20] also announced direct flights to Ukraine. In addition to all of the above, in May 2021, Saudi Arabia lifted the travel ban for its vaccinated citizens and those who had contracted the disease.

What is the outcome? According to the State Border Service of Ukraine, 35,000 tourists from Bahrain, Qatar, Kuwait, UAE, Oman, and Saudi

---

[20] Jazeera Airways Announces Flight Schedule to Antalya and Kyiv. *AviationPros*, June 30, 2021. Available online, https://www.aviationpros.com/airlines/press-release/21228754/jazeera-airways-jazeera-airways-announces-flight-schedule-to-antalya-and-kyiv. Accessed 3 August 2021.

7 Halal in Contemporary Ukraine: Markets and Administration   163

Arabia visited Ukraine from May to July 2021. Almost 30,000 (i.e., more than 85%) were citizens of Saudi Arabia. That is eight times more than the number of Saudi Arabians who visited Ukraine in 2019! The United Arab Emirates are second by the number of travelers to Ukraine, with 2677 people in three months, and Oman with 1007 tourists is third.[21]

According to Maryana Oleskiv, Chairperson of the State Agency for Tourism Development, "It's really a tourist boom, and there are more guests from Arab countries in Ukraine now than from other countries. They occupy up to 50% of rooms in hotels."[22]

Many experts in the Ukrainian tourism industry point to three main factors among the attractions of Ukraine for Arab tourists. These are food, shopping, the green areas, and the climate that is significantly different from Gulf countries.

At the same time, as many experts in the tourism industry observe, the key problem for Arab tourists, mostly coming to Ukraine with their families, has been the lack of halal food. So far, halal meat deficiency on the market has been compensated by vegetarian menus, fish dishes, and chicken (with the halal certification).

Interestingly, Lviv has become one of the main destinations for Gulf tourists. Lviv is the historical center of the Galicia region in Western Ukraine. It is known for the high level of religiosity of the population (which for the most part belongs to the Greek Catholic Church in Ukraine), but it has an extremely low percentage of Muslims. Most of the Muslims who do live in the region migrated from Crimea and settled only after 2014. Even compared to other regions of Ukraine, Lviv had an underdeveloped halal market. With the influx of Arab tourists, this fact has become a serious challenge for the tourism industry. According to Halina Hrynyk, Head of the Lviv City Council Tourism Department, tourists from Saudi Arabia are used to high standards of service and demand halal food in hotel restaurants, while not all hotels are prepared

---

[21] Ukraina pryiniala 35 tysiach turystiv z Perskoi zatoky za try misiatsi [Ukraine received 35,000 tourists from the Persian Gulf in three months]. *Ekonomichna pravda*, 17 August 2021. Available online, https://www.epravda.com.ua/news/2021/08/17/676959. Accessed 18 August 2021.

[22] Kuryshko, Diana and Heorhii Erman. Yak i chomu arabski turysty poliubyly Ukrainu [How and why Arab tourists fell in love with Ukraine]. *BBC News Ukraine*, 7 August 2021. Available online, https://www.bbc.com/ukrainian/features-58120247. Accessed 8 August 2021.

164   **D. Brylov**

to offer it to their guests. As a manager of a Lviv hotel, popular among Arab tourists, noted, "We will find out who in the region produces halal food and order it for our guests from Saudi Arabia. It turns out that there is a big problem with this in Lviv."[23]

Sometimes tourists 'source' their own halal food, and the practice of Arab tourists buying live lambs and slaughtering them has become widespread. This practice is predominantly common among those vacationing in Western Ukraine, in the Carpathian Mountains, where many locals keep sheep. One of the villages near the popular Carpathian resort of Bukovel reports that it sells five sheep daily.[24] Locals say—whether it is true or not—that Arab tourists sometimes slaughter animals in their hotel rooms. Certainly, this 'unregulated' procurement of halal food underscores the overall lack of a sufficient halal industry and its recognition as a 'problem' in need of solution with respect to international relations.

Both representatives of the tourist business in Ukraine and representatives of the diplomatic department emphasize the need for further development of Arab tourism in the country. According to Ukrainian Foreign Minister Dmytro Kuleba, the ministry is actively cooperating with its foreign colleagues in the Persian Gulf countries to increase the number of tourists from this region in Ukraine:

> This week, I had a telephone conversation with the Foreign Minister of Saudi Arabia. He noted the warm welcome of his compatriots traveling to Ukraine this summer. We agreed that we would continue to work to

---

[23] Dorotych, Mariia. Khalialnoho miasa brakuie. Tomu yidiat pisnyi borshch... [Halal meat is in short supply. Therefore, they eat lean borscht...]. *Vysokyi Zamok*, 8 July 2021. Available online, https://wz.lviv.ua/article/438462-khalialnoho-miasa-brakuie-tomu-idiat-pisnyi-borshch. Accessed 18 August 2021.

[24] Miroshnichenko, Bogdan and Maryana Tsyimbalyuk. Arabskie turistyi zapolonili ukrainskie kurortyi: chem ih privlekaet Ukraina i kak eto ispolzovat [Arab tourists flooded the Ukrainian resorts: what attracts them to Ukraine and how to use it]. *Ekonomicheskaya pravda*, 22 July 2021. Available online, https://www.epravda.com.ua/rus/publications/2021/07/22/676156. Accessed 18 August 2021.

increase the number of Saudi tourists in our country. We will carry out the same work with other Gulf countries.[25]

We can expect that this position of the Foreign Ministry and the tourism industry of Ukraine will contribute to the active development of the domestic market of halal products, especially halal food. Truly a blessing in disguise or as the local proverb with the same meaning says, "There was no luck, but misfortune did help."

Conclusion

For now, the halal industry in Ukraine aims mainly at large producers. Meanwhile, ordinary Muslims face certain troubles due to the underdevelopment of the halal industry. Namely, Islamic banking and halal healthcare are absent; halal catering establishments and kindergartens and schools with a halal food option are underdeveloped. Nevertheless, lately, cafes and restaurants that position themselves as 'halal' have appeared. Mainly, these establishments represent Arab or Turkish cuisine and are controlled by such nationals. Large Islamic organizations such as DUMU and Alraid (together with DUMU-Umma) are opening private schools that serve halal food. Halal infrastructure is developing actively in places where Crimean Tatars who left Crimea after the annexation live compactly.

Unexpectedly, the development of the halal industry in Ukraine got a strong impetus by the sharply increased flow of tourists from the Persian Gulf who demanded halal food. Given the intention of the Ukrainian government and the tourism industry to increase the flow of tourists from the Gulf, we can expect an active development of the intra-Ukrainian segment of halal products.

Hence, one can state that the halal industry in Ukraine is present and promising. This is proved by the work of 28 organizations that issue halal

---

[25] Klochko, Nadezhda. Rabotaem nad uvelicheniem kolichestva arabskih turistov v Ukraine—Kuleba [We are working to increase the number of Arab tourists in Ukraine—Kuleba]. *Depo.ua*, 13 August 2021. Available online, https://news.depo.ua/rus/news/pratsyuemo-nad-zbilshennyam-kilkosti-arabskikh-turistiv-v-ukraini-kuleba-202108131356598. Accessed 18 August 2021.

166   D. Brylov

certificates. It should be noted, though, that most of them are not connected to the existing religious administrations, so they cannot guarantee that their certificates comply with sharia standards. Despite the growing popularity of halal certification, these products are mainly exported. This is why the internal market will not be satiated for a long time. At the same time, the competition between the certification centers could lead to the development of an efficient certificate-issue algorithm and the enhancement of the performance of such centers.

References

Bagautdinova, D. 2012. Halyal: pokorenie sng [Halal: the conquest of the CIS]. *Medina al-Islam*, 133. Accessed 30 January 2020. http://www.idmedina.ru/medina/?4868.

Bogomolov, Alexander, Serhei Danylov, Ihor Semivolos, and Halina Iavorskaia. 2006. *Islamskaia identichnost' v Ukraine* [Islamic identity in Ukraine]. Kyiv: ID Stilos.

Brylov, Denis. 2014. Ukrainian modernist groups in an international context. *Anthropology & Archeology of Eurasia* 53 (3): 72–80.

———. 2016. Transformed perceptions of Islam and Muslims in Ukraine in the wake of the social and political changes caused by Euromaidan. In *Islam, religions, and pluralism in Europe*, ed. Adnan Aslan, Ranja Ebrahim, and Marcia Hermansen, 267–284. Wiesbaden: Springer VS.

———. 2017a. 'Zapretnyi Islam' v sovetskoi Ukraine ['Forbidden Islam' in Soviet Ukraine]. *Islamology* 7 (2): 150–163.

———. 2017b. *Instytualizatsiia musulmanskoi spilnoty Ukrainy: Dukhovne upravlinnia musul'man Ukrainy (dumu)* [The institutionalization of the Muslim community of Ukraine: The Religious Administration of Muslims of Ukraine (DUMU)]. *Naukovyi chasopys Natsionalnoho pedahohichnoho universytetu imeni M.P. Drahomanova. Seriia 7: Relihiieznavstvo. Kulturolohiia. Filosofiia* 38 (51): 106–114.

———. 2018. Islam in Ukraine: The language strategies of Ukrainian Muslim communities. *Religion, State & Society* 46 (2): 156–173.

Havrilova, Natalia, Oleh Kyselov, and Tetiana Khazyr-Ohly. 2011. Svitohliadno-politychni pohliady musulman Ukrainy (za materialamy sotsiolohichnoho doslidzhennia) [Worldview and political views of Muslims of Ukraine (based

7 Halal in Contemporary Ukraine: Markets and Administration   167

on sociological research)]. Accessed 30 January 2020. https://www.religion.in.ua/main/analitica/12445-svitoglyadno-politichni-poglyadi-musulman-ukrayini-za-materialami-sociologichnogo-doslidzhennya.html.

Izmirli, Idil. 2012. *Competing narratives of Islam in post-Soviet Ukraine against the background of global Islamic movements.* IREX Research Brief. Accessed 30 August 2015. http://www.irex.org/resources/competing-narratives-islam-post-soviet-ukraine-against-background-global-islamic-movements.

Kabha, Mustafa, and Haggai Erlich. 2006. Al-Ahbash and Wahhabiyya: Interpretations of Islam. *International Journal of Middle East Studies* 38 (4): 519–538.

Khalid, Adib. 2014. *Islam after communism: Religion and politics in Central Asia.* Berkeley: University of California Press.

Mathiesen, Kasper. 2013. Anglo-American 'traditional Islam' and its discourse of Orthodoxy. *Journal of Arabic and Islamic Studies* 13: 191–219.

Pew Research Center. 2018. Eastern and Western Europeans differ on importance of religion, views of minorities, and key social issues. Accessed 30 January 2020. https://www.pewforum.org/2018/10/29/eastern-and-western-europeans-differ-on-importance-of-religion-views-of-minorities-and-key-social-issues/.

Siyak, Ivan. 2008. Halyalnyiy Kiev: eda dlya pravovernyih musulman [Halal Kiev: Food for faithful Muslims]. Accessed 30 January 2020. https://nash-kiev.ua/zhournal/vkousnaya-eda/halyal-nyy-kiev-eda-dlya-pravovernyh-mousoul-man.html.

Volovych, Olexii et al. (2011). *Stratehiia aktyvizatsii spivpratsi Ukrainy z derzhavamy Perskoi zatoky: analitychna dopovid* [Strategy of enhancing cooperation of Ukraine with the Gulf States: An analytical report]. Odesa: Feniks.

Yarosh, Oleh, and Denis Brylov. 2011. Muslim communities and Islamic network institutions in Ukraine: Contesting authorities in shaping of Islamic localities. In *Muslims in Poland and Eastern Europe: Widening the European discourse on Islam,* ed. Katarzyna Górak-Sosnowska, 252–265. Warsaw: University of Warsaw.

Part III

Moral Economy of Halal

8

Sufism and Islamic Market in Central Asia: From Kolkhoz to Halal Economy in Kazakhstan?

Yana Pak

Introduction

As the principles of Islamic economy have been put into practice and the Islamic market is growing at global and local levels, a wide array of actors, including Muslims and non-Muslims, appears and participates in the development of a halal market. These professional activities follow the conventional practices of the secular context, but at the same time, actors do their business in what they claim is a 'sharia-compliant' way, creating their Islamic way of life.

The Islamic economy is meant to cover all socio-economic actions. It is perceived as an application of precepts stated in divine law, and it is said to generate a strong connective bond among those who participate in it. Divine law regulates the sociability of men by addressing their reason (in Arabic *'aql* is the regulating principle of *nafs*, the carnal soul) (e.g., Mayeur-Jaouen 2019). Significantly, the Arabic equivalent of the word

---

Y. Pak (✉)
EHESS (School of Advanced Studies in Social Sciences), Paris, France
e-mail: yana.pak@gmail.com

© The Author(s), under exclusive license to Springer Nature Switzerland AG 2023
R. Turaeva, M. Brose (eds.), *Religious Economies in Secular Context*, New Directions in Islam, https://doi.org/10.1007/978-3-031-18603-5_8

'economy' is *iqtisad*, which designates aspiration, purpose, and goal, but also the golden middle way of moderation. What should be sought, ideally, is 'sufficiency' (*kifaya*), the right balance of wealth to satisfy basic needs and for alms to rehabilitate the least wealthy. This is how a believer can find his insertion and commitment to the world order of equity—'the profit and loss sharing method that [is] supposed to embody the 'spirit of Islam" (Coste 2017: 269). In this intimate union of the spiritual and the temporal, faith appears to be the foundation of economic life, where religious sets of values condition economic performance (Zelizer 1994; Boltanski and Chiapello 1999).

Beyond these engaging generalities, however, it may be necessary to ask whether a specificity of Islamic capitalism, as it unfolds nowadays, does not lie in the diversity—notably geographical—of its economic visions of the world. According to Timur Kuran (1995, 2011), Islamic legal institutions did not have an impact on the development of corporate structures and financial credit practices in the medieval age. Recent research shows that in the context of contemporary economic life, the relation between Islam and economy has changed. Globalization and neoliberal capitalism play a decisive role in the development of Islamic economy, which has become an essential area of analysis for researchers studying modern Islam (Rudnyckyj 2010; Warde 2010; Green 2015; Bergeaud-Blackler et al. 2016; Tobin 2016; Bergeaud-Blackler 2017; Sloane-White 2017).

Taking into account studies of the capitalist experience of Muslims (Tripp 2006; Rehman 2010; Nagaoka 2012; Njoto-Feillard 2012; Yankaya 2013; Coste 2017), the present sociological case study contemplates how globalized capitalism transforms and extends the socio-economic organization of Sufi brotherhoods that were impacted previously by kolkhoz engineering (i.e., collective economy) during the communist era. It also sheds light on how the halal market offers a new field of Islamic expression. The focus is on the present-day development of the Süleymancı branch of the Naqshbandiyya, as an economic actor on the Islamic market in Kazakhstan. How, I ask, does it combine both Soviet and Sufi legacies? In what respects should we think of the brotherhood's economic organization as global in form, and in what respects— local (i.e., regional)? Through Sufi sociability and economic solidarity, the community offers its members daily opportunities to become 'true Muslims' and successful businessmen: socialization, religious and business training, work, loans and other funding, commercial export/import partnerships, and philanthropic projects. All of these may lead an individual to religious achievement. I ask these questions in a context where the imagination of the global umma demonstrates nostalgia for the Golden Age's Caliphate (Mouline 2016). Expressed in the most diverse social circles, this nostalgia does not hide the current disputes of the various Islamic worlds and their varied readings of the Quran. More than ever, fine contextualization and regional and local case studies are important to comprehend many processes, in particular, those related to the transfer and transformation of Islam in specific places and over longer and shorter durations. The post-Soviet context, for example, has been affected and is characterized by a frantic competition between ethnic-religious teachings of various origins since 1989. This competition has continued even after the adoption in the 2010s of legislation banishing denominational proselytism.

Through a historical overview of Soviet Islam in Central Asia, the following chapter aims to assess whether the current model of Muslim network-based entrepreneurship among Sufis in Central Asia is a new social phenomenon or whether it was born from collectivization and has only been transformed and readapted to new economic realities. The paper is based on two years of intense fieldwork in Kazakhstan in 2014–2016, combining observation, discourse analysis, and semi-structured interviews with economic and religious actors. The following sections examine the ways in which they put into practice the Sufi Path's vision of Islamic economy and re-adapt their socio-economic organization based on spiritual sociability and community solidarity according to new economic realities and opportunities associated with the halal market.

Origins of the Süleymancı

Sufi movements played an important role in the pre-modern era in articulating 'Islam's capacity to weave dense long-distance ties and turn them into a versatile source of civility' (Salvatore 2016: 75). In Central Asia, following history and hagiography, Sufism appeared by the tenth century, with a significant expansion of Sufism's prominence in religious, social, and political life in the period of the Mongol conquest of the thirteenth century (DeWeese and Gross 2018). Later, one of the largest Sufi groups, the Naqshbandi group, was founded at Maverannahr, in the oasis of Bukhara, and named after Khwaja Bahâ ud-Dîn Muhammad Naqshband (718–91/1318–89). They relied on self-steered local, regional, and transnational networks to unfold their full potential charismatically and organizationally. Today, the Naqshbandiyya Mujaddidiyya Süleymancı Sufi Path is characterized (as in the past) by strict compliance with the precepts of the sharia and the permanent consolidation of the brotherhood's structure (Gaborieau et al. 1990; Trimingham 1998; Zarcone 2004). This path follows the teachings of its founder Abu'l-Faruq Süleyman Hilmi Tunahan Silistervî (1888–1959), who was originally from Silistra on the lower reaches of the Danube River (the present border of Romania and Bulgaria). It also follows, through him, the teachings of Ahmad Sirhindi, the creator of the Mujaddidiyya in the seventeenth century. Sirhindi developed the idea of Millennial Reform (Ar. *tajdid al-alf*) as an intellectual basis for the brotherhood. He asserted that on the Day of Judgment, people would be asked about their adherence to sharia (Buehler 2003, 2011; Weismann 2007). Despite their long history in Turkey (where they originated and where their headquarters are still located), as well as in Europe, Africa, and Central Asia, the Süleymancıs' activities were restricted by Atatürk and his immediate successor. From the 1970s onward, they gradually re-emerged, offering their religious teachings through preparatory classes and tutoring, and offering shelter in their dormitories to students and followers who were flocking to Turkey's metropolis from the campaigns of Anatolia and Thrace (Friedmann 2000; Aydın 2004).

Economic and political opportunities further shaped the evolution of the Suleymancı movement. Sufi brotherhoods do not reject the search for profit, especially if it serves religion and the well-being of members. Since 1985, with the support of the Naqshbandis and Nurcus, a new generation of businessmen has emerged. The legalization of charitable donations in 1983 in Turkey provided the grounds for developing social and cultural activities and funding opportunities within the framework of *waqfs*. Through the development of religious education and solidarity networks, the Süleymançı invest into the public space and extend their influence on the local and transnational levels (Gökalp 1990; Jonker 2006a, 2006b; Dressler et al. 2009; Landman and Sunier 2015).

Unlike other initiatory, transnational, or, more specifically, Central Asian forms of sociability, the Süleymancı movement practices a form of self-isolation from global society. As such, it publishes few doctrinal texts or commentaries. The anthropologist Altan Gökalp wrote in 1990, on the eve of the expansion of the movement toward Central Asia, 'it has no attributed written work of reflection, and it seems that most of its activity has manifested itself through the establishment of Quran courses and the careful organization of these teaching[s]' (Gökalp 1990: 423). The lack of a literary tradition makes it difficult to research the history of the movement and its gradual transplantation from the lower Danube to the foothills of the Tian Shan Mountains.

Between Sufi Sociability and Economic Solidarity: Combining the Soviet and Sufi Legacies?

A particularly close interaction between faith and law, and between religion and socio-economic life, has long been regarded as specific to the world of Islam. Nourished by orientalist tradition, this vision has become particularly significant over the past quarter of a century in the post-Soviet universe as newly independent Muslim-majority states have confronted the diverse political expressions of Islam. From the years of *perestroika* (i.e., from 1987), a new feeling of closeness to the worlds of Islam emerged among the economic and intellectual elites of Central Asia and the Caucasus. The organization of a first mass hajj from the former Soviet Union in 1990, however, marks a clear beginning to the region's mass exposure to the eruption of religious knowledge and ethical standards from the vast Middle East.

At the same time, many values cultivated and widely disseminated during the Soviet era, through school education in particular (Dudoignon

1994), have found a way to reinvest and re-legitimize themselves in the 'imported' Islamic value systems. Among these is the culture of social egalitarianism and redistribution. Muslims sought to rediscover Islamic legacies and vernacular religious customs that had been excluded from official culture and the public sphere in the Soviet period, they also hastened to locate the bases of a *halal* resourcing for an ethics of the relations between people and between groups. Among other aspects, post-Soviet Muslims in Central Asia rediscovered the possibility of belonging to different Muslim groups of various dimensions and contents: the global umma, traditional Sufi paths, and various *jama'at* or territorialized local communities. Some of these communities facilitate connections across state political boundaries and national sentiments.

Far from reconnecting with a pre-Soviet past, the Muslim enterprise as it is known today in Central Asia appears to be a religious and cultural legacy of the Soviet Union. Soviet policies sometimes supported local culture, indigenous elites, and local languages; this support, when it existed, facilitated the continuity of some religious practices, customs, and ideas. Specifically, a central element of Soviet social engineering was indigenization (Ru. *korenizatsiia*), a process which included in the setting up of loyal national elites to replace the previous political leadership. This meant that some Muslim clans and ethnic groups rose to prominence over others. World War II changed the political relations between the Soviet state and Islam. In the war years, public religious practice was banned—not least because some Muslim elites had favored alliances with Nazi Germany—and supranational Soviet patriotism was promoted to the detriment of local and national identities. In 1943, the ban on public religious practice was relaxed, but Islam became more regulated. Confessional administrations, the *muftiyat*, were established in 1944 along with the Council for the Affairs of Religious Cults to mobilize the Muslim populations of the Union (cf. Hiro 1994: 33; Tasar 2012).

The oscillations of the state on religious questions in the years 1940–1950 favored the reappearance and development of an unaccredited Islam, in particular in the rural areas of the Caucasus and Central Asia (Dudoignon and Noack 2014). Islam's ability to function without a hierarchical infrastructure enhanced its ability to survive and transform during the post-war decades. Islam inhabited Soviet space and

8 Sufism and Islamic Market in Central Asia: From Kolkhoz...

unregulated space. State-sanctioned institutions on the collective farms enabled some religious practices and beliefs to continue in daily life— from the 'rest areas' of cotton plantations to cultural clubs. The number of non-accredited mosques (Ru. *nezaregistrirovannye*) tended to fluctuate from year to year and across the regions, but there were up to 1800 non-accredited mosques for 230 official ones in Central Asia (Tasar 2017). There were also numerous sanctuaries that were allowed to exist; these were guarded by dynasties of wardens granted with sacred ascendance from Prophet Muhammad (for the *sadat*) or from the Arab conquerors of Central Asia (for the *khwajas*). This 'informal' religious staff (a term that, in the 1970s, referred to a whole group of communities and movements not sanctioned by the party-state) of mosque officials and sanctuary wardens was in charge of the main rites of passage in a Muslim life cycle.

With the partial destruction of mosques and religious centers, numerous imams, mullahs, and their followers went underground. According to Bobokhonov's research (2012), in the 1960s and 70s, small secret *khufiya* schools (Ar. clandestine, hidden) were organized at the teacher's house, where students in groups of 5 to 20 studied the Quran, the Sunna and Hadith, the basics of sharia, and the works of Sufi philosophers and poets. These students went to a regular public school during the day but to the *khufiya* in the evenings, several times a week, gathered in the house of their spiritual teacher. More intensive study could be undertaken during the summer vacations or upon graduation from high school in less regulated regions—for example, in Qurgan-Tyubinsk Province of Tajikistan. Many students learned the Quran by heart and became Qori (experts in the Quran) before they returned to their home village. (Bobokhonov 2012). As they grew up and became members of men's houses, these students gradually took their religious ideas to the masses. These private spaces, men's houses (Ru. *muzhskie doma*) appeared in a dynamic way as a response to anti-Islamic politics.

The men's houses in which Islam found increasingly open expression are among Central Asia's traditional forms of gendered sociability. Many of these forms are distinguished by a great capacity for resilience and adaptability, even under brutal socio-economic transformations. 'Men's houses' occupy an additionally special place because of the studies devoted to them by Soviet ethnography. As early as 1948, the archaeologist S. Tolstov described the presence of 'unions of men' (Ru. *muzhskie soiuzy*) as secret societies in his work on the Khwarezm (a vast agricultural region centered on the delta of the river Oxus / Amu-Darya) in ancient and medieval times (Tolstoi 1948). Long neglected by observers, this institution of pre-modern Central Asian society was the subject of numerous studies in the decades that followed (e.g., Snesarev 1963; Kisliakov 1973; Bushkov 2002; Bobokhonov 2012), including the reference work by ethnographer Rahmat Rahimov on 'men's houses' in Tajik society (Rahimov 1990). Soviet ethnography varied in whether it treated these societies as evidence of 'primitive communism' or as evidence of transhistorical cultural continuities. Nevertheless, they point to some intersection between Islam and these groups.

Most of the literature on men's houses focuses on regions with a sedentary agricultural tradition and where Tadjic Persian or Chaghatay Turkic language (which is deeply marked by Persian) is spoken. It records two local terms that designate the ritualized sociability of regular assemblies of men, which in some cases can bring together a neighborhood or an entire village (See Kisliakov 1973; Bushkov 2002; Ruffier et al. 2002; Bobokhonov 2012). One is *jura* (a Tajik word that is shared by Uzbek and refers to a friend or group of friends); the other is *gashtak* or *gap* (both meaning discussion or conversation) (Mills and Rahmoni 2015). One of the derivations of the second is the *juma gap* that used to take place on Fridays in the pre-Soviet period after the community prayer (Ar. *jumʿa*). In town, these weekly circles brought together prominent members of the community, representatives of the wealthy social stratum of the *bay* (landowners), a local elite able to pay a membership fee (*tuqma*) (Rahimov 1990; Dudoignon 1994; Bushkov 2002).

Belonging to a *gap* could bring then (as it does now) social prestige and protection. Then, prestige was especially derived from *gap*s that took the form of literary *majlis*es or *mahfil*s (lit. *get-together*), in which members' verses were debated in relation to works from the classical repertoire of Persian poetry (Dudoignon and Zevaco 2009). More generally, the *gap* remained an important instrument of socialization for the youngest adult males of the community in particular. It was there that the problems of the daily life of the neighborhood unit (*mahalla*) were discussed, and from which social and religious norms were disseminated. A network of mutual aid broadened on the basis of one or more *gaps*, the *jura* thrived thanks to the financial support and active cooperation of its members.

Some *jura*, developed to the point of taking on the dimension of a trust, have had a significant impact not only on the daily life of a local community but also on the economic and political life of a region as a whole (Ilkhamov 2006: 39–48; Turaeva 2016). In the 1980s, the *gashtak* or *jura* were under state control: the police went there to ensure that there were no violations (Bushkov 2002: 65).

Post-Soviet Islam: An Exception to Global Evolutions?

Even though the USSR has disappeared, its heritage in the domain of religion still stands in Central Asia. Islam never disappeared in the Soviet Union. To the contrary, anti-religious politics fostered dynamic practices and the sustainability of Islam in Kazakhstan and elsewhere (Dudoignon and Noack 2014; Turaeva 2016; Tasar 2017; Frank 2019). They also fostered the emergence of new forms of solidarity groups with a significant socio-economic impact on the Muslim population in the post-Soviet area.

In the post-Soviet area, the interrelations between religions and states remain framed by religious administrations (Alniyazov 2005). The DUMK (Spiritual Administration of the Muslims of Kazakhstan) is heir to the Central Asian *muftiyat* created during World War II to support the conscription of Muslim citizens for the USSR's war against Nazi Germany. Another Soviet legacy is found in the 'substitute religious communities' formed by collective farm brigades in the wake of the massive population resettlements in the years and decades after World War II. These resettlements were connected in many cases with the development of cotton monoculture. Collective farm brigades were formed, in many cases, from the inhabitants (already closely related) of a single village or valley. In turn, through the farms, groups and networks of solidarity of various dimensions and contours emerged (Ar., Pers., Turk., Kaz. *jama'at*; Ru. *obshchina*).

During the decades after World War II, oscillations and contradictions within the general anti-religious policy of the Soviet Union sometimes favored the emergence and development of non-accredited Islam in the countries of Central Asia and the Caucasus, if only for short periods of time (Khalid 2007; Sartori 2010; Dudoignon and Noack 2014; DeWeese and Gross 2018). As indicated above, private houses were used to host rich, variously ritualized forms of sociability (Babadjanov 1998, 2014; Dudoignon and Zevaco 2009; Ducloux et al. 2011; Vicini 2014), and local peer-to-peer networks expanded based on *gap*s and *jura*s prospered thanks to the active socio-economic cooperation of its members (Kisliakov 1952; Poliakov 1980; Kandiyoti 1998; Humphrey 2002; Schmoller 2014). Of course, even in the late 1980s, these ritualized sociabilities remained under police control.

Nevertheless, over time, some of these networks gained popularity and increased status and influence in socio-economic and political life. In the 1980s–90s, one *jura*, known as Akramiyya (Akramis), was inspired by an Islamized ideology of redistribution in the context of the late-Soviet chronic scarcity of consumer goods. The Akramiyya's membership came from a network of agriculture and bazaar workers that extended across the entire northeast of the Ferghana Valley. Akramiyya continued to be influential in the post-Soviet period, but after the May 2005 demonstrations and counterinsurgency in Andidjan (Ilkhamov 2006), it became internationally known as 'radical' and was officially eliminated. The Akramiyya has since been re-read, in a less exclusively security-minded manner, as an indigenous response to the domination of the post-Soviet economy by the ruling oligarchy in Tashkent (Ilkhamov 2006).

Despite its dismantling in 2005, Akramiyya continues to be seen in Central Asia as a possible model for economic organization and redistribution. It promotes a discourse of social justice that is largely inherited from the Soviet period, even though it appears in the trappings of Islam. It values private initiative but also solidarity and denounces the excess concentration of wealth and power induced by privatization. More than a decade after its elimination, Akramiyya has a recurrent popularity, fueled by the confiscatory policies of the oligarchies in power. Like other contemporary movements, as diverse as Turkey's AKP and Egypt's Muslim Brotherhood, the appeal and political fortune of Akramiyya are built on the network's economic initiatives and local-level redistribution. In this respect, the Akramiyya network could be seen as a prototype of modern socio-economic organization of Muslim entrepreneurs' networks.

Dynamic Development of a Halal Market

According to the 2009 national census, Kazakhstan has a 70% Sunni Hanafi Muslim population. In 1995, Kazakhstan was registered as a member of the Organization of Islamic Cooperation (OIC). A decade later, in 2006, in the light of growing economic interest in developing halal markets, the Kazakhstan Halal Industry Association (AHIK) was established, following the Malaysian model for developing and regulating the halal market. In 2006, the Ministry of Industry and Trade established a Halal Standards Committee to issue certificates and, within 'a short period, many dietary products produced in Kazakhstan started to carry halal labels to appeal to a wider population … this development help substantiate the extent of Islamic revival in Kazakhstan' (Achilov 2015: 87).

Regarding the dynamic development of the sharia-compliant market, Kazakhstan strives to become the international hub for the halal economy in the post-Soviet region (Botoeva 2017). According to Thomson Reuters and Dinar Standard (2018), Kazakhstan is a leader in the Islamic financial sector and was ranked at the second place within the Eurasian region in terms of its degree of development of Islamic economy. Halal media and recreation, as well as food, pharmaceuticals, and cosmetics, also contributed to Kazakhstan's second place in the region in the Islamic economic ecosystem ranking. The legislative environment and economic prerequisites have allowed the establishment of the Astana International Financial Centre (AIFC), which is now considered a modern financial hub for the countries of Central Asia, the Eurasian Economic Union, the Caucasus, and the western China region. Situated between Europe and Asia, the country has already built necessary international road and rail links for the transfer of goods, opening access to the vast market of the former USSR, especially to the free-trade market of the Eurasian Economic Union (Kazakhstan, Russia, Belarus, Armenia, and Kyrgyzstan), which has a population of some 86 million Muslims (Nurgalieva 2018).

The evident emergence of a halal market in the twenty-first century begs certain questions. In the context of the financial globalization of modern capitalism, which is, according to Keynes, 'absolutely irreligious' and 'without much civic spirit,' one might wonder if there really can be an Islamic economy that is compatible with the principle of the free market. Muslim merchants think it is possible: in Kazakhstan, as in other Muslim-dominant communities, is yes. Muslims are said to be merchants in their soul, like the Arabs of Hejaz in the first century of the Hegira, and the believer is invited to rely on a particular social and symbolic capital and on a recognizable associability to develop an economic praxis on a large scale that has been confined for a long time to a strictly framed cultural arena.

On the other hand, observers who are theoretically inclined have worked harder to outline the specificities of an Islamic economy. Many have turned to Max Weber and his explanatory model based on a causal relationship between religiously based ethics and a type of organization of the economic activity. Indeed, Islamic economy was theorized by thinkers close to the Egyptian Muslim Brotherhood and the Pakistani Jama'at-i Islami, who were deeply influenced by the holistic ideologies of the early twentieth century. These oppose Western capitalism by aiming to put an end to debt (Coste 2017). For Mawdudi (1903–1979), the most influential of these thinkers, Islam must permeate all of society, including economic activity—the latter through the prohibition of interest (Ar. *riba*) and the exercise of legal alms (*zakat*) as an instrument of redistribution. Prohibition of *riba* and practice of *zakat* are conceived as archetypal elements of Islamic activity against both capitalist and communist ideologies. The logic of debt was to be overcome by resorting to the opposite of interest—that is, it foregrounded equity as a method for sharing profits and losses as embodying the 'spirit of Islam.'

In post-Soviet Kazakhstan, the practical and theoretical sides of Islamic economy are largely fused. According to the Süleymancı brotherhood's tradition, Qur'anic guidelines for doing business as a good Muslim include 'the best man is he who is useful to mankind and one should give more to have more in the afterlife.' According to contemporary respondents of the Süleymancı brotherhood, their businesses represent about 20% of the halal market in Kazakhstan. They have this level of success

8 Sufism and Islamic Market in Central Asia: From Kolkhoz...

because Sufi sociability and shared normativities create and seal trust among businessmen as members of the *jama'at*. This enhances economic solidarity under the roof of the religious community, and members find a way to realize their business projects within the *jama'at*, following not only self-interested but also community-interested initiatives.

Süleymancıs and the Halal Economy

My first observations, combined with studies of social history and sociology conducted in other regions of the majority Muslim population of the former USSR, suggest that since the 1980s, 'entrepreneurs' in Kazakhstan have shown themselves generally oriented toward an Islamic economy. The Süleymancıs are therefore both unique and representative of a broader pattern.

For the Süleymancıs, communal solidarity is based on the concept of the initiatory pact (Ar. *tawajjuh*), coupled with attendance to the same teachings. The spiritual leaders of the *tariqa* willingly say, to justify the importance given to religious magisterium: 'The fruit of a tree, [should one] seek it in the branches or in the roots?' (Gökalp 1990: 428). What matters to them is the product obtained from action (i.e., the formation and multiplication of philanthropic structures). They are relatively uninterested in articulating the doctrinal aspects that link them to historical Naqshbandiyya and its reformed branch, the Mujaddidiyya, of an old settlement in Central Asia. Their priority is to supervise the young generation.

In Kazakhstan, there were 60 Süleymancı madrasas endowed with madrasa-college status as of 2017. They are dispersed in all regions of the country, which gives them a much broader reach than the 30 Turkish high schools managed by the Fethullacı movement that are, moreover, concentrated in a small number of urban centers. Initially designed to fill the ideological 'vacuum' of the end of the Soviet period, these centers for religious teaching also sought to ameliorate the socio-economic upheavals of the 1990s and 2000s by promoting the social mobility of Kazakhs from the periphery (Balci 2003). At the same time, the Süleymancı *jama'at* was part of a broader movement characterized by the concomitant emergence of small and medium-sized business interests and religious associations offering places of prayer, Qur'anic teaching, and socio-economic sociability.

For the youngest, madrasas and their dormitories are not only a place of religious education and sociability but also an institution for social redistribution. The entrepreneurs of the Süleymancı *jama'at* pay *zakat* and offer other help to families who face hardships. Senior members consider that *suhbat* (Ar. *suhba*, a mystical meeting) refers almost indifferently to Sufi sociability and to economic solidarity. A ritualized *suhbat* follows Friday's community prayer. It is held at private residences according to a rotating principle, as it was during the *gap* or *jura* of yesteryear.

Socialization into the brotherhood proceeds through a master-disciple relationship, which is of central importance in the Naqshbandi tradition, and through regular participation in Qur'anic commentary courses and workshops. As in the traditional Gnostic ways, the recipients also participate in intense pilgrimage activity to the holy places of Central Asia (e.g., the Mausoleum of Khwaja Ahmad Yasawi in Turkestan and ancient Yasï) and of Turkey and aspire to participate in the Hajj. These pilgrimages are organized through service companies owned by members of the *jama'at*.

Members of a local branch meet to discuss economic and philanthropic projects. It is not rare for the youngest specialists to find their first job or loans within a fellow Süleymancı's company. 'When I wanted to open my first halal restaurant, I did not have the means to pay the rent for a commercial space', a Süleymancı member told me in 2016, continuing: 'a brother (i.e., fellow member) of mine, he kindly offered a commercial location on the ground floor of his hotel. Thanks to this support, to his reliance, I could realize this project'. This co-location of a halal business within another commercial enterprise is not unique. There are many entrepreneurs among the Süleymancı offering services of the 'halal businesses'. These include initiatives in the food trade and catering, but also in travel agencies, fashion, security, and building construction. Religious scholars of the *jama'at* give monthly classes on economic ethics to these entrepreneurs at the madrasas. These courses are designed to answer questions about the legitimacy of a business, according to sharia, and the application of Islamic ethics to business management.

8 Sufism and Islamic Market in Central Asia: From Kolkhoz...   185

There is a strong sense of belonging within the *jama'at*. It is expressed primarily through socio-economic activism, which is at the forefront of the inclusion of young people in a defined world of work in ethno-confessional terms (as it already was in the bazaars of the Ferghana Valley at the time of the Akramiyya and, more generally, in 'Allah's kolkhozes'). 'The sharing of common values and standards facilitates commercial relations: Islam is the only religion that focuses on the interest-free economy, simplicity in life and the prevention of greed', I was told in Almaty. Süleymancı entrepreneurs tend to modernize their representation and organization with a spiritual connection to economic and political realities in Kazakhstan: they dress in elegant suits, with a preference for dark blue, and are always clean-shaven to project the image of a modern, prosperous, and reliable businessman.

On the political side, Sufism was the guardian of Islam under communism. Today it is an agent for compromise with the authorities, who are themselves descended from the old communist elites. The politicization of Islam following the dissolution of the USSR bases its legitimacy on ethnic nationalism and sees Sufi brotherhoods as guarantors of an authentic, national, and moderate Islam (Papas 2005; Olcott 2007; Roy 2010; DeWeese and Gross 2018; Muminov 2018). In this sense, Sufi brotherhoods are considered fundamentally hostile to the 'innovations' of Islamism.

Conclusion

Today in Kazakhstan, a growing number of businesses are creating economic halal opportunities. So-called halal markets offer not only food, but also cosmetics, Islamic fashion, tourism, healthcare, pharmaceutical products, Islamic education, banking, and insurance services. Various *jama'at* participate in the development of this market and occupy specific niches within it. In post-Soviet Central Asia, which we have tackled here in the particular case of Southern Kazakhstan, religious entrepreneurs from the 1990s to the present day are actors in globalization. They issue modern preaching at the heart of economic decision-making. Working to combine religious knowledge and economic management, they embody

186   Y. Pak

today what they perceive as a transhistorical tradition of Central Asian origin, updating the Persian formula *'dast be kar, del be yar'* (hands to work, heart to God) found in Naqshbandi Gnosticism.

Although widely documented in the world of Islam for the contemporary period, high variety of interpenetration between socio-economic norms and religious lawstill challenge sociological thinking. Here, I propose the need to conceptualize a certain re-enchantment of commercial relations in the context of globalization. Central Asia offers a particular substratum of the sometimes paradoxical legacies of Soviet collectivism, the kolkhoz in particular, or brigade, and their particular community consciousness. Yet more specifically, this case study of the Naqshbandi Mujadiddiya Suleymancı tradition emphasizes the socio-economic transformation and adaptation of cross-border Sufi orders to a regional local context and culture, shaped by an emerging global halal market. These orders serve as reciprocal references, through the relation between master-disciple, to evaluate their socio-economic actions in accord with discourses of religious legitimation. Also, the doctrine of Sufi masters offers a set of values (shared common interpretation of economic actions and coordination) passing through Sufi mystical sociability to economic solidarity as frameworks that allow overcoming uncertainty. Members of a *jama'at* have reasonable confidence that others will follow common guidelines and community-based norms.

Against supposedly secular capitalist societies that are dedicated to producing profits, Muslim entrepreneurs produce religious narratives that explain their activities as a site of Islamic expression, expansion, and modernization. Power, relationships, actors, and financial resources are mobilized in the name of Islam by structuring a new form of social organization, economic coordination, and the processes of production and redistribution.

References

Achilov, D. 2015. Islamic revival and civil society in Kazakhstan. In *Civil society and politics in Central Asia*, ed. C.E. Ziegler, 81–110. Lexington: University Press of Kentucky.

8 Sufism and Islamic Market in Central Asia: From Kolkhoz...   187

Alniyazov, N. 2005. La communauté musulmane du Kazakhstan, acteurs officiels et groupes officieux. In *Islam et politique en ex-URSS, Russie d'Europe et Asie Centrale: Actes enrichis du Colloque de Kazan, 1–2 avril 2004*, ed. M. Laruelle and S. Peyrouse, 287–299. Paris: L'Harmattan.

Aydın, M. 2004. Süleymancılık. In *Modern Türkiye'de Siyasi Düşünce: İslamcılık*, ed. T. Bora and M. Gültekingil, vol. 6, 308–322. Istanbul: İletisim Yayınları.

Babadjanov, B.M. 1998. Le renouveau des communautés soufies en Ouzbékistan. *Cahiers d'Asie centrale* 5 (6): 285–300.

Babadjanov, B. 2014. The economic and religious history of a kolkhoz village: Khojawot. From Soviet modernisation to the aftermath of the Islamic revival. In *The Kolkhozes of Allah: Migration, de-Stalinisation, privatisation and new Muslim congregations in the USSR and after (1950s–2000s)*, ed. S.A. Dudoignon and C. Noack, 202–264. Berlin: Klaus Schwarz.

Balci, B. 2003. *Missionnaires de l'islam en Asie centrale, les écoles turques de Fethullah Gülen*. Paris: Maisonneuve & Larose and Istanbul: IFEA.

Bergeaud-Blackler, F. 2017. *Le marché halal ou la réinvention d'une tradition*. Paris: Seuil.

Bergeaud-Blackler, F., J. Fischer, and J. Lever. 2016. *Halal matters: Islam, politics and markets in global perspective*. New York and London: Routledge.

Bobokhonov, R. 2012.'Muzhskie kluby' kak institut grazhdanskogo obschestva v Tadjikistane (xx vek), ['Men's clubs' as institutions of civil society in Tadjikistan (XX century)]. *Politika i Obschestvo* 5: 55–66.

Boltanski, L., and E. Chiapello. 1999. *Le nouvel esprit du capitalisme*. Paris: Editions Gallimard.

Botoeva, A. 2017. Transnational Islamic banks and local markets in Central Asia. In *Islam, society and politics in Central Asia*, ed. P. Jones, 245–262. Pittsburgh: University of Pittsburgh Press.

Buehler, A.F. 2003. Shari'at and Ulamâ in Ahmad Sirhindi's collected letters. *Die Welt des Islams* 43 (3): 309–320.

———. 2011. Ahmad Sirhindi: A 21st century update. *Der Islam* 86 (1): 122–141.

Bushkov, V. 2002. Muzhskie ob'edineniya v Ferganskoi doline v xx stoletii: printsipy organizatsii i transformatsionnye protsessy [Men's unions in the Ferghana Valley in the twentieth century: principles of organization and process of transformation]. *Etnograficheskoe obozrenie* 2: 58–68.

Coste, F. 2017. La strucuturation financiere comme enjeu de définition de l'islamité: Pakistan, Golfe et Malaisie. *Studia Islamica* 112: 264–293.

188   **Y. Pak**

DeWeese, D., and Jo-Ann Gross. 2018. *Sufism in Central Asia: New perspectives on Sufi traditions, 15th–21st centuries*. Leiden: Brill.

Dressler, M., R. Geaves, and G. Klinkhammer. 2009. *Sufis in Western society: Global networking and locality*. New York: Routledge.

Ducloux, A., et al. 2011. *Anthropologie des réseaux en Asie Centrale*. Paris: CNRS Éditions Alpha.

Dudoignon, S.A. 1994. Permanence des sociabilités traditionnelles: le gap. *France-Ouzbékistan* 2 (février): 14–16.

Dudoignon, S.A., and C. Noack. 2014. *Allah's kolkhozes: Migration, de-Stalinisation, privatization and the new Muslim congregations in the Soviet Realm (1950s–2000s)*. Berlin: Klaus Schwarz Verlag.

Dudoignon, S.A., and A. Zevaco. 2009. Sur le 'Mail des Rhapsodes': Ethnies minoritaires, groupes de statut et sociabilités traditionnelles en Asie Centrale soviétique. *Asiatische Studien /Études asiatiques* 63 (2): 273–322.

Frank, A.J. 2019. *Gulag miracles: Sufis and Stalinist repression in Kazakhstan*. Vienna: Academy of Sciences Press.

Friedmann, Y. 2000. *Shaykh Ahmad Sirhindi: An outline of his thought and a study of his image in the eyes of posterity*. New Delhi: Oxford University Press.

Gaborieau, M., A. Popovic, and T. Zarcone. 1990. *'Naqshbandis. Cheminements et situation actuelle d'un ordre mystique musulman*. Istanbul and Paris: IFEA & Editions Isis.

Gökalp, A. 1990. Les fruits de l'arbre plutôt que ses racines: le Suleymanisme. In *Naqshbandis. Cheminements et situation actuelle d'un ordre mystique musulman*, ed. M. Gaborieau, A. Popovic, and T. Zarcone, 421–435. Istanbul and Paris: Isis Publications.

Green, N. 2015. *Terrains of exchange: Religious economies of global Islam*. New York: Oxford University Press.

Hiro, D. (1994), *Between Marx and Muhammad*, London: Harper Collins Publishers.

Humphrey, C. 2002. *The unmaking of Soviet life: Everyday economies after socialism*. Ithaca and London: Cornell University Press.

Ilkhamov, A. 2006. The phenomenology of 'Akromiya': Separating facts from fiction. *The China and Eurasia Forum Quarterly. Central Asia-Caucasus Institute & Silk Road Studies Program* 4 (2): 39–48.

Jonker, G. 2006a. The evolution of the Naqshbandi-Mujaddidi: Sulaymançis in Germany. In *Sufism in the West*, ed. J. Malik and J. Hinnells, 71–85. New York: Routledge.

———. 2006b. The transformation of a Sufi order into a lay community: The Süleymanci movement in Germany and beyond. In *European Muslims and the secular state: The network of comparative research on Islam and Muslims in Europe*, ed. J. Cesari and S. McLoughlin, 265–287. Hampshire, UK: Ashgate.

Kandiyoti, D. 1998. Rural livelihoods and social networks in Uzbekistan: Perspectives from Andijan. *Central Asian Survey* 17 (4): 561–578.

Khalid, A. 2007. *Islam after communism: Religion and politics in Central Asia*. Berkeley, Los Angeles, London: University of California Press.

Kisliakov, N.A. 1952. K voprosu ob etnograficheskom izuchenii kolkhozov [About the ethnographic study of kolkhozes]. *Sovetskaia etnografiia* 1952 (1): 146–149.

———, N.A. 1973. *Alovkhona—'dom ognya' u tadzhikov* [Alaw-khana: The Tadjik 'House of Fire']. Moscow: Nauka.

Kuran, T. 1995. Islamic economics and the Islamic sub-economy. *Journal of Economic Perspectives* 9: 155–173.

———. 2011. *The long divergence: How Islamic law held back the Middle East*. Princeton: Princeton University Press.

Landman, N., and T. Sunier. 2015. *Transnational Turkish Islam: Shifting geographies of religious activism and community building in Turkey and Europe*. Hampshire and New York: Palgrave Macmillan.

Mayeur-Jaouen, C. 2019. *Voyage en Haute-Égypte. Prêtres, coptes et catholiques*. Paris: CNRS Éditions.

Mills, M.A., and R. Rahmoni. 2015. Gashtak: Oral performance and literary memory in Tajikistan. In *Orality and textuality in the Iranian world*, ed. J. Rubinovich and S. Shaked, 316–341. Leiden: Brill.

Mouline, M.N. 2016. *Le Califat: Histoire politique de l'islam*. Paris: Flammarion.

Muminov, A. 2018. Sufi groups in contemporary Kazakhstan: Competition and connections with Kazakh Islamic society. In *Sufism in Central Asia*, ed. D. DeWeese and Jo-Ann Gross, 284–298. Leiden: Brill.

Nagaoka, S. 2012. Critical overview of the history of Islamic economics: Formation, transformation, and new horizons. *Asian and African Area Studies* 11 (2): 114–136.

Njoto-Feillard, G. 2012. *L'islam et la réinvention du capitalisme en Indonésie*. Paris: Karthala.

Nurgalieva, G. 2018. *The Islamic economy—The fastest growing economy, Eurasian focus*. Moscow: IEMS.

Olcott, Martha Brill. 2007. Sufism in Central Asia: A force for moderation or a cause of politicalization? *Carnegie Papers, Carnegie Endowment for International Peace, Russian and Eurasian Program* 84: 2–40.

Papas, A. 2005. Soufisme, pouvoir et sainteté en Asie centrale: Le cas des Khwâjas de Kashgarie (xvie–xviiie siècles). *Studia Islamica* (100/101): 161–182.

Poliakov, S. 1980. *Istoricheskaia etnografiia Srednei Azii i Kazakhstana* [Historical ethnography of Central Asia and Kazakhstan]. Moscow: Moscow State University.

Rahimov, R. 1990. '*Muzhskie doma' v traditsionnoj kul'ture Tadzhikov Ferganskoi doline v XX stoletii: Printsipy organizatsii i transformatsionnye protsessy* ['Men's house' in Tadjik traditional culture of the Ferghana Valley in the 20th century]. Leningrad: Nauka.

Rehman, A. 2010. *Gulf capital & Islamic finance: The rise of new global players*. New York: McGraw-Hill.

Roy, O. 2010. *L'Asie centrale contemporaine*. Paris: PUF.

Rudnyckyj, D. 2010. *Spiritual economies: Islam, globalization, and the afterlife of development*. Ithaca: Cornell University Press.

Ruffier, A., M. Laruelle, J. Uhres, and G. Bertrand. 2002. Les gap et ziyâfat. Reconstitution du passé à partir du regard d'un ethnographe soviétique sur une société centre-asiatique traditionnelle. *Cahiers d'Etudes sur la Méditerranée Orientale et le monde Turco-Iranien* 34: 43–57.

Salvatore, A. 2016. *The sociology of Islam: Knowledge, power and civility*. Oxford: Wiley Blackwell.

Sartori, P. 2010. Towards a history of the Muslim's Soviet Union: A view from Central Asia. *Die Welt des Islams* 50: 315–334.

Schmoller, J. 2014. *Achieving a career, becoming a master: Aspirations in the lives of young Uzbek men*. Berlin: Klaus Schwarz.

Sloane-White, P. 2017. *Corporate Islam: Sharia and the modern workplace*. Cambridge: Cambridge University Press.

Snesarev, G. 1963. "Traditsiia muzhskih soyuzov v ee pozdneishem variante u narodov Srednei Azii". [*Tradition of male unions in its late variant among the peoples of Central Asia], Khorezmskaia arkheologo-etnograficheskaia ekspeditsiia* (pp. 155–205). Moscow: Akademiia nauk SSSR.

Tasar, E. 2012. Soviet policies toward Islam. Domestic and international consideration. In *Religion and the Cold War*, ed. Ph. Muehlenbeck, 158–181. Nashville: Vanderbilt University Press.

Tasar, E. 2017. *Soviet and Muslim: The institutionalization of Islam in Central Asia*. Oxford: Oxford University Press.

Thomson Reuters and Dinar Standard. 2018. *State of the global Islamic economy report 2018*. https://haladinar.io/hdn/doc/report2018.pdf.

Tobin, Sara. 2016. *Everyday piety: Islam and economy in Jordan*. Ithaca: Cornell University Press.

Tolstoi, S.P. 1948. *Drevnii Khorezm [Ancient Khorezm]*. Moscow: MGU.

8 Sufism and Islamic Market in Central Asia: From Kolkhoz... 191

Trimingham, Spencer J. 1998. *The Sufi orders in Islam*. New York and Oxford: Oxford University Press.

Tripp, Charles. 2006. *Islam and the moral economy: The challenge of capitalism*. Cambridge: Cambridge University Press.

Turaeva, R. 2016. *Migration and identity in Central Asia: The Uzbek experience*. London, New York: Routledge.

Vicini, F. 2014. 'Don't cross your legs': Islamic sociability, reciprocity and brotherhood in Turkey. *La Ricerca Folklorica* 69: 93–104.

Warde, I. 2010. *Islamic finance in the global economy*. Edinburgh: Edinburgh University Press.

Weismann, I. 2007. *The Naqshbandiyya: Orthodoxy and activism in a worldwide Sufi tradition*. London: Taylor & Francis.

Yankaya, D. 2013. *La nouvelle bourgeoisie islamique: le modèle turc*. Paris: PUF.

Zarcone, Th. 2004. *La Turquie moderne et l'islam*. Paris: Flammarion.

Zelizer, V. 1994. *The social meaning of money*. New York: Basic Books.

9

Sustainable Halal? The Intersection of Halal, Organic, and Genetically Engineered Food in Turkey

Nurcan Atalan-Helicke

Introduction

This chapter examines the convergence of halal and organic standards in female consumers' definitions of 'wholesome food' in Turkey. These two standards, while different, appear at least partially interchangeable for consumers who are concerned about genetically engineered food, environmental balance, and Islamic principles.

Changing ingredients and processes in agri-food systems create new questions for Muslims who would like to live according to Islamic principles since these complex issues and ingredients require better interpretation and application of those principles (Fischer 2011: 15–17; Armanios

---

N. Atalan-Helicke (✉)
Skidmore College Environmental Studies and Sciences Program,
Saratoga Springs, NY, USA
e-mail: natalanh@skidmore.edu

© The Author(s), under exclusive license to Springer Nature Switzerland AG 2023   **193**
R. Turaeva, M. Brose (eds.), *Religious Economies in Secular Context*, New Directions in Islam, https://doi.org/10.1007/978-3-031-18603-5_9

and Ergene 2018: 40). Genetically engineered food[1] is a controversial topic in many places. In Turkey, it is especially controversial for Muslim consumers. They have broader concerns about the agri-food system, such as the traceability of food, health risks, and ethics; they lack trust in the state and markets (Atalan-Helicke 2015: 672); and they seek to observe Islamic principles.

Consumer perceptions of halal food demonstrate that Muslim consumers associate halal—its nature, ingredients, and processing techniques—with cleanliness and food safety (Mutmainah 2018). The additional and more complicated principle of tayyib, which is also used in connection with halal food, refers to whether food is wholesome (Armanios and Ergene 2018: 191–92). This principle is particularly critical for consumers who are concerned about the industrial food system and its impacts on both the environment and animal welfare. For instance, industrially produced beef can be halal certified if slaughtered following Islamic principles and hygienic practices. However, because Islamic principles forbid cruelty to living beings and mandate that meat come from animals raised in sanitary and humane conditions, some Muslim consumers are concerned that halal-certified meat coming from concentrated animal factory operations (CAFOs) compromises the integrity of these values (Friedlander 2014). From this perspective, it is not only about just the end product or about how animals are slaughtered that is the main focus of many halal standards and certifiers; it is also about the quality of life of the animals (Armanios and Ergene 2018: 195).

Halal and organic production converges in consumer perception and choice for multiple reasons. As a foundation, it can be noted that Islamic concepts, such as halal and tayyib, are seen to predate the emergence of industrialized agriculture and factory farms. This means they are seen as compatible with environmental solutions (Iqbal 2015); this association is strengthened by the fact that Islamic teachings generally advocate for the preservation of the natural environment. This means showing respect for

---

[1] Genetic engineering and genetic modification are often used interchangeably to refer to biotechnology applications in agriculture. Following the United States' Food and Drug Administration's definition, this chapter refers to genetic engineering as the use of recombinant DNA and cell fusion techniques to introduce new characteristics or traits into an organism, which entails producing a piece of DNA and introducing it into the organism (FDA 2018).

9 Sustainable Halal? The Intersection of Halal, Organic...

the sources of food and respecting the environmental balance created by God (*mizan*) (Akhmetova 2016).

Correspondingly, both are seen as a response to the problematic aspects of genetically engineered foods. Genetically engineered foods are produced from organisms that have had specific changes introduced into their DNA using the genetically engineered methods and require an invasive level of human interference in the ecosystem. This raises concerns that genetically engineered food may bring on damage to environmental balance (Akhmetova 2016). Muslims advocating for more sustainable food practices argue that wholesome food that Muslims consume should not just 'be healthy, relatively unprocessed and processed without degrading the environment, but also promote healthy social and economic relationships among people' (Iqbal 2015: 55). Ethical considerations also shape the definition of healthy food and overall human well-being: Thus, genetically engineered food, despite its promise to provide food security in a changing climate and growing population, is not seen as compatible with the overall human good (Akhmetova 2016).

Tayyib requirements extend beyond organic certification. Nevertheless, for some Muslim consumers, organic certification, halal organic food, and halal organic farms seem to provide viable approaches to sustainability and action-based solutions to climate change and environmental degradation (Iqbal 2015: 56). While not all Muslims agree with these broader interpretations and seek out organic halal food, the tayyib-halal lens helps some Muslim consumers bridge their identity and faith in their quest for healthy, clean, and good food.

Genetically Engineered Food in Turkey

This chapter examines the convergence of halal and organic through genetically engineered food with recourse to women consumers' definitions of 'wholesome food' in Turkey. Two questions guided this research: What are the concerns of consumers about food in a Muslim-majority country that is fully integrated into globalized markets? Second, how do women consumers negotiate their food choices, particularly in relation to halal, organic, and genetically engineered food? While most of the chapters in this book focus on non-Muslim majority states, the introduction of genetically engineered food in Turkey provides an additional variable in our collective studies of halal. In treating the joint appeal of halal and organic food, vis-à-vis genetically engineered food, we learn more about how Muslim consumers navigate, and seek to transform, the food systems available to them.

In Turkey, both secular and devout Muslim mothers have growing concerns about feeding their families with clean and healthy food, and halal would seem to provide a safe option. However, halal certification does not address their concerns about genetically engineered food. Is it wholesome and safe? The use of genetic engineering and GE organisms, however, are prohibited in organic products (McEvoy 2017)—an additional point of appeal for organic products.

Despite consensus-building efforts by the international Muslim business community, such as the World Halal Forum and Muslim theologians, there are multiple perspectives about the halal status of genetically engineered food (Armanios and Ergene 2018: 199; Atalan-Helicke 2015: 671). Moreover, the scientific complexity of genetic engineering in agriculture and the uncertainty of the health impacts of genetically engineered food raise questions for Muslim consumers, businesses, and associations. Of the 57 members of the Organization of Islamic Cooperation (OIC) countries, only 4 countries currently cultivate genetically engineered crops (Pakistan and Sudan grow genetically engineered cotton since 2010, Bangladesh grows genetically engineered eggplant, and Indonesia grows genetically engineered sugarcane). Other OIC members, such as Malaysia, Egypt, and Turkey, however, have approved the import of genetically engineered crops for use as animal feed and/or food processing (ISAAA 2019a).[2] Genetically engineered crops, such as

---

[2] Among OIC members, Burkina Faso cultivated genetically engineered cotton from 2008 until 2016, and there is research and development in the form of confined field testing and contained research in several countries, including Egypt, Tunisia, Nigeria, Cameroon, and Mali, among others (ABNE 2017). While Indonesia has completed biosafety assessment of two genetically engineered corn and one genetically engineered potato variety, these are not yet commercially cultivated (USDA FAS 2020). The list of non-planting countries which granted approvals for import of genetically engineered crops for feed, food, and processing can be found in the annual reports of the International Service for the Acquisition of Agricultural Biotechnology (ISAAA). According to ISAAA (2018), Iran approved the import of genetically engineered rice, soybeans, and rapeseed from 1996 till 2016; Malaysia approved genetically engineered canola and potato for food, cotton for clothing, and maize and soybeans for animal feed.

corn and soybeans, are used as animal feed and become ingredients in hundreds of industrially processed foods (Atalan-Helicke 2015: 663–664).

Turkey,[3] the subject of this chapter, is one of the top ten ranking countries in terms of halal food markets (ninth), halal pharmaceuticals and cosmetics (ninth), modest fashion (second), and Muslim-friendly travel (third) (Dinar Standard 2019: 13). It has been importing genetically engineered corn and soy as animal feed since 2011. Turkey's Biosafety Law, which came into force in 2010, requires the monitoring of genetically engineered animal feed and their products and labeling them from a genetically engineered content threshold of 0.9% content and above. It does not, however, require labeling most food destined for human consumption with its genetically engineered content.[4] Thus, the concerned consumer is left to her own devices to assess the potential genetically engineered content in the food she buys and serves to her family.

The Female Burdens of Consumption

Household food-related labor (e.g., planning, preparation, and clean up) falls universally and unevenly on women (Cairns and Johnston 2015). Earlier involvement of women in food-related activities is further enhanced by the traditional roles of motherhood and caregiving, as well as culturally articulated contemporary standards of being a good mother,

---

[3] Turkey is a major exporter of agricultural products to other OIC countries (Dinar Standard 2019). Turkey has also played a central role in the development of Standards and Metrology Institute for Islamic Countries (SMIIC) standards, a subsidiary body of the OIC (Armanios and Ergene 2018: 135).

[4] The current Biosafety Law and Regulation 5977 on Genetically Modified Organisms and their Products, in force since 2010, prohibits the use of genetically engineered organisms for baby food specifically and specifies labeling requirements for the animal feed and monitoring of animal feed based on the import of the approved genetically engineered varieties in Turkey (Official Gazette 2010). The Ministry of Agriculture and Forestry of Turkey specifies that the monitoring and controlling requirements apply to three categories only (baby food, soybean and products, and maize and products) and there is no requirement for labeling of food designated for human consumption because 'there is no approved genetically engineered organism for direct human consumption' (Ministry 2019).

a responsible caregiver, and a healthy woman (Cairns and Johnston 2015: 4–6). In such a context, it would not be surprising to find that women's food preferences and perceptions matter greatly. Studies about food preferences among consumers in the West, for example, have found that a preference for food free from genetic engineering is highest among female consumers (Bellows et al. 2010). There are limited studies examining halal preferences among male and female consumers. A study with 255 Malaysian consumers (ages 16–35) found that there is 'a significant difference between male and female consumers in their intention to choose halal food', and women showed more concern about their food choices (Khalek et al. 2015: 94). Thus, globally, consumer research would predict that female consumers exhibit more pronounced concerns for and considerations of socially held views on the qualities and marks of clean, healthy, and safe food.

Therefore, this chapter follows out that prediction with data collected in Turkey using qualitative methods during the summers of 2015 and 2019. Thirteen focus groups were carried out with eighty three women: nine focus groups with a total of fifty six women in the cities of Ankara and Konya in the summer of 2015, and four focus groups with a total of twenty seven women in the cities of Ankara and Balikesir in the summer of 2019. The participants also completed a survey including 12 questions about their socio-economic status, education, shopping preferences for organic and halal food, knowledge of genetically engineered food, and sources of information about healthy food. The age range of participants in 2015 was 27–64 and 19–74 in 2019.[5] All of the participants lived in urban areas. All of the participants except two (one in 2015 and one in 2019) were married. In addition, 48 participants (84%) of the 2015 focus groups and 25 participants (92%) of the 2019 focus groups had a child (or grandchild) under the age of 18 living in the same household at

---

[5] The age of research participants correlated (inversely) with their levels of education and employment outside the house.

9 Sustainable Halal? The Intersection of Halal, Organic... 199

Table 9.1 Educational attainment of 2015 and 2019 focus group participants

	Participants % (number)2015 (Total n = 56)	Participants % (number) 2019 (Total n = 27)
Secondary or primary & secondary	10.5% (n = 6)	48% (n = 13)
High school	28.5% (n = 16)	29.6% (n = 8)
University and/or higher	61% (n = 34)	22.4% (n = 6)

the time of research. The educational attainment of participants was higher in 2015 compared to those in 2019 (Table 9.1). All focus groups were carried out in Turkish. The quotes were translated into English by the author. All names were anonymized.

Tayyib-Halal: Ethics, Environmental Sustainability, and Genetically Engineered Food

Genetically engineered crops have been available commercially in the world since the mid-1990s. Due to the complexity of the methods used and their impacts on human health, the approach to genetically engineered food shows great variance among countries and within countries and involves science, economics, and religion (Atalan-Helicke 2015; Kurth and Glasbergen 2017). Since the early 2000s, various bodies of Islamic scholars have declared that basic genetic engineering of food is acceptable as long as no haram substances have been used (IWISA 2012). In 2010, the Malaysian Biotechnology Information Center (MABIC) and the International Halal Integrity Alliance organized an international workshop for Islamic scholars and concluded that Islam supports beneficial scientific innovations for humans and that genetic engineering methods used in plant improvement are not different from other plant improvement techniques from the sharia point of view. Their decision was based on a wide consideration of the permissibility of genetically engineered food in terms of the methods of genetic alteration[6]; the purpose of sharia (*maqasid al-shariah*); necessity (*Dharurah*); chemical transformation (*Istihalah*); and the effects of combining permissible and non-permissible sources. They also considered the possibility and ethics of transgenic animals (Bouzenita and Mirghani 2014; Günay and Özdemir 2016; Al-Attar 2017; Bouzenita 2018).

Muslim scholars and consumers frame opposition to genetically engineered food using Islamic principles and ethics. They draw on such principles in terms of health, food safety, environmental stewardship, and questions of fair trade. Bouzenita (2010) examines the methods of genetic alteration and the implications of even the smallest change in genetic material from an Islamic perspective and raises at least two objections to the acceptability of genetically engineered food as halal. The first objection concerns mixing pure and impure substances (*istihlak*). Although this notion can be used to assess the permissibility of accidental mixing of impure substances into food, there is a recognized difference in the intentional combination and large-scale industrial production of such genetically altered food. Alteration at the genetic level may be small but the notion of 'a mixture of minimal substance' can be misleading due to the role that that gene, enzyme, or protein plays in the organism.

The second objection is related to the *al jallah* principle—the effect of a permissible animal feeding on impure food. Today, the global meat production is dependent on genetically engineered animal feed (van Eenennaam 2013: 2). Lacking adequate research on its impacts on the human body, there is a concern about the transferability of the genetically

---

[6] The most common commercially available genetically engineered traits of insect resistance and herbicide tolerance are produced through the method of transgenesis. Transgenesis allows genes and DNA sequences to be moved between any species (e.g., insertion of *Bacillus thuringiensis* (Bt)-toxin gene into corn for resistance to European corn borer) (Holme et al. 2013). Other genetic modification methods include cisgenesis, which involves using a gene pool identical to the gene pool available for conventional breeding or introduction of native genes from a crop's own gene pool (ISAAA 2014), and genome editing, which uses a series of technologies, such as CRISPr-Cas9, to silence or edit an organism's DNA. Current research and expansion efforts also focus on drought-tolerant varieties (ISAAA 2019a, b).

9 Sustainable Halal? The Intersection of Halal, Organic...   201

engineered animal feed to humans.[7] In Islam, there are different approaches to animals feeding on impure food: one approach takes the view that the animal does not become impure by consuming impure food. A second approach does not resolve the animal's status but discourages the consumption of impure food. A third approach assumes a reversible impurity and judges that the meat of an animal that has fed on impure food may be consumed after a certain period of confinement while it feeds on pure food.

Nevertheless, there are voices that find no solution to the *al jallah* principle. For example, Bouzenita (2010) presents the argument that even if there is no exchange of mutation in the genetic blueprint of either the genetically engineered food or the animal that feeds on it, genetically engineered food disturbs the balance that Allah has created by deliberation and may lead to unforeseeable and unchangeable consequences both for humans and ecosystems (p. 25). Such concerns about ecosystem effects also connect with recent scientific studies related to field-evolved resistance of pests[8] and resistant weeds.[9] These problems have broader

---

[7] So far, any impact on the human body is undetectable. Van Eenennaam (2013), who examined the costs and benefits of genetically engineered agriculture for livestock, argues that studies conducted to look for the presence of recombinant DNA (rDNA) or the protein encoded by the rDNA construct in the milk, meat, and eggs from animals fed genetically engineered crops found no expression of rDNA or protein products which came from food animals raised on genetically engineered feed. Another study by Vicini and colleagues reviewed multiple methods assessing glyphosate in feed residues and animal health and found that 'glyphosate use in crops fed to poultry and livestock has not affected animal health, rumen/gut microbes' (Vicini et al. 2019: 4509). However, the same study also points out the limitations of empirical models and the need to evaluate risks in the context of 'realistic exposures and conditions' (4515).

[8] Studies have demonstrated growing field-evolved resistance to genetically engineered crops expressing *Bacillus thuringiensis* (*Bt*). Bt is a species of bacteria that lives in the soil; it makes proteins that are toxic to some insects when eaten. Crops integrated with Bt toxins have been effective initially by controlling target pests while allowing a reduction in insecticide use in large-scale monoculture operations. However, field-evolved resistance indicates that insects have become resistant to Cry1 toxins in Bt corn and to Crt1Ac toxins in Bt cotton in places including South Africa, Puerto Rico, Brazil, and the continental United States (Tabashnik 2015).

[9] Also known as 'Roundup Ready' (RR), herbicide-tolerant crops incorporate glyphosate, a nonselective, systemic herbicide that controls more weed species than any other herbicide (Heap and Duke 2018: 1040). However, studies show that since 1996, 38 weed species distributed across 37 countries have evolved resistance to glyphosate. (Powles 2008; Heap and Duke 2018).

impacts on agriculture and food security and have been raised by the anti-genetically engineered food activists worldwide.[10]

The Turkish non-profit organization, Gıda Güvenliği Hareketi (Association of Health and Food Safety Movement), which has been a leading voice of the Islamic anti-genetically engineered food movement in Turkey since 2008, opposes agriculture involving genetic engineering due to health and food safety concerns. The president of the association, Kemal Özer (2010), argues that the quest for clean and halal food involves complex processes that should involve the genetic structure of the food. Quoting the verses of the Quran, Baqarah 29 (2:29) and Ibrahim 34 (14:34), Özer (2010: 196–97) argues that Allah has given all the sustenance (*Rizq*) for humans, but humans are destroying nature and balance (*mizan*) as well as their own values by altering God's creation and intervening into *fitrah*. Özer continues that chemicals used in agriculture involving genetically engineered seeds turn the human body and the environment into a waste dump (p. 196), while multinational companies keep reaping financial gains. Similarly, Büyüközer (2012) argues that genetically engineered food is anti-Islamic because of the multinational corporations responsible for its production. Islamic law requires that trade should be fair, but agriculture involving genetic engineering is not fair because it is driven by large biotechnology firms that control too much of the market share through mergers and acquisitions (Atalan-Helicke 2015: 667). From these perspectives, not only the Islamic principles about genetic alteration but also the socio-economic concerns about agriculture involving genetic engineering undermine its tayyib-halal status. Özer's concerns are shared by other Turkish scholars: In a retreat of religious scholars organized by the Turkish Directorate of Religious Affairs in 2011, one Turkish theologian argued that it would be wrong to define genetically engineered food as haram, but, he continued, 'one can tell that genetically engineered food is not *tayyib*' due to the difficulty of assessing 'where the alteration starts' (Beşer 2011: 78) and the broader impacts of that alteration.

---

[10] There is a significant body of literature on anti-genetically engineered food activism. See Bawa and Anilakumar (2013) for a review; Kinchy (2012) for the intersection of science and politics in anti-genetically engineered food activism; and Kurzer and Cooper (2007) for European Union countries.

Despite standardization initiatives among states, businesses, and non-profit agencies, the understanding and practice of halal requirements vary at a global level. This fragmentation of halal certification is particularly significant in terms of genetically engineered food. Often, there is not even a national consensus. For example, although they do not explain why, two of the halal standards used by five certification bodies in the Netherlands prohibit the use of genetically engineered organisms in food (Kurth and Glasbergen 2017). In Turkey, the prevailing consensus has been, as suggested above, to exclude genetically engineered food from halal certification. Yet, as suggested by the national laws governing Turkey's overall food and supply, different interpretations exist about indirectly consumed genetically engineered products.

For example, GIMDES (Association for the Inspection and Certification of Food and Supplies), a halal certification agency and a non-profit engaged in consumer education and advocacy, implements confinement periods for animals fed genetically engineered animal feed before slaughtering them (Atalan-Helicke 2015: 669). And the state-led halal certification agency, Turkish Standards Institute (TSI), also an important actor for regional and global halal meat markets, declares 'halal certification will not be issued for GE food destined for human consumption'.[11] But TSI still exempts genetically engineered animal feed from the category of 'direct' human consumption (Yeni Soluk 2019). While current halal standards and national law agree on the general permissibility of genetically engineered animal feed as 'safe' for animals and humans alike, they do not address a wider range of consumer concerns.

As Muslim consumers seek quality, they juxtapose more natural and local foods against those associated with industrialization and globalization. Embedded in these juxtapositions are assumptions that the higher the natural content of food and the more local it is, the less susceptible it will be to malign human interference. Elsewhere, consumer movements and producers have responded to such concerns. For example, 'green halal', an organic and halal food movement in Belgium, encourages 'ethical, responsible, mindful consumption' and supports animal

---

[11] Turkish Standards Institute Halal Standards. https://tse.org.tr/IcerikDetay?ID=41&ParentID=34 (Accessed 20 December 2019).

204 N. Atalan-Helicke

welfare-approved meat. Other 'eco-halal' initiatives (such as the Norwich Meadows Farm in upstate New York) integrate organic and halal farming respecting labor justice and non-genetically engineered agriculture. Highlighting these examples from Belgium and the United States, Iqbal (2015) argues that these initiatives show the desire of Muslim consumers, producers, and businesses for environmental sustainability. Moreover, genetically engineered-free, organic, and halal statuses represent additional messages about health and safety and cater to a specific group of health-conscious consumers who seek to buy 'what is best for themselves and their families' (Armanios and Ergene 2018: 209). These narratives can also be seen through the case study of women consumers in Turkey.

Case Study: Female Consumers and Access to Clean and Healthy Food in Turkey

The research participants came from diverse socio-economic backgrounds. In 2015, 61% of research participants had a university degree or higher, while 22% of participants in 2019 had a university degree or higher. In 2019, almost half of the participants (48%) had a secondary degree as their highest educational level. Educational attainment is correlated to income as education provides employment and higher-paying job opportunities: In 2015, 60% of the participants (n = 33) were employed full-time, whereas in 2019, only 29% of the participants (n = 8) were full-time or part-time employed. In 2015, 42.8% of participants earned more than 1500 USD monthly (Table 9.2), whereas in 2019, only 18.2% of participants earned a monthly income of more than 1000 USD (Table 9.3). The participants in 2015 were recruited via online mothering groups and word-of-mouth through key informants. Regarding the representation bias of relatively high-income participants in 2015, the participants in 2019 were recruited only through word-of-mouth and key informants, with a shift to low- and middle-income

9 Sustainable Halal? The Intersection of Halal, Organic... 205

Table 9.2 Economic status of 2015 focus group participants (n = 56)

2015 focus group participants		
Monthly income(Turkish lira)	Monthly income(USD)[a]	Research participants(Percent)
1000–2500	418–950	35.7 % (n = 20)
2501–4000	950.1–1520	21.4 % (n = 12)
4000+	1520.1 +	42.8 % (n = 24)

[a]The USD income was calculated based on the Turkish National Bank currency exchange rates of 15 July 2015
The minimum wage at the time of calculations was 1000 Turkish lira/month (418 USD)

Table 9.3 Economic status of 2019 focus group participants (n = 27)

2019 focus group participants		
Monthly income(Turkish lira)	Monthly income(USD)[a]	Research participants(Percent)
1500–2500	250–417	48.5 % (n = 13)
2501–4000	418–667	14.8% (n = 4)
4001–6000	668–1001	18.5 % (n = 5)
6000+	1002+	18.5 % (n = 5)

[a]The USD income was calculated based on the Turkish National Bank currency exchange rates of 16 May 2019
The minimum wage at the time of calculations was 2020 Turkish lira/month (net) (427 USD)

neighborhoods.[12] The second round of data collection was intended to gauge whether the concerns I first documented were income-, class-, or education dependent. Generally speaking, they were not.

Due to a growing emphasis on health and food in recent years, more consumers have learned about genetically engineered food through the media. Exposed to both facts and myths (Atalan-Helicke 2020), and often ill-prepared to distinguish reliable sources of information, female consumers are anxious. It is women who are mainly in charge of planning

---

[12] However, the income differences between 2015 and 2019 participants were also exacerbated by the loss of Turkish currency against the USD in this period (2015–2019) and by the absence of inflation-based income adjustments following the economic crisis of 2018. This crisis entails a prolonged recession with persistent low (negative) rates of growth, dwindling investment performance, debt repayment problems, rising unemployment, a spiraling currency depreciation, and high inflation (Orhangazi and Yeldan 2020).

and preparing the food that their family eats; they bear the responsibility for the quality of the food. Their views reflect anxieties about the changing agri-food system in general and genetically engineered food in particular. Participants mentioned that they pay attention to the ingredients of the food (e.g., gelatin) as well as how the food was produced. While they were worried about the effects on health of agricultural chemicals, hormones, and food additives (e.g., cancer, chronic disease, obesity, early menarche), they were also concerned about the 'mixed messages' concerning genetically engineered crops that they received from officials, business, media, and celebrity doctors.

While paying attention to taste, freshness, seasonality for fresh fruits and vegetables, and ingredients in processed items, one issue expressed was the amount of time it takes to be 'vigilant'. Because Turkey is a Muslim-majority but secular country, it is presumed that food production and processing follow Islamic rules. However, due to the import-export relationship of Turkey with non-Islamic countries and the laxity or negligence in controlling these imported products as well as its secular governance structure, questions are raised as to whether the available food is generally permissible as halal. For example, Aysin (Konya, 2015) who spends a lot of time reading labels, mentioned her concerns about the 'gelatin' used widely in processed food, including clear fruit juices. There are no additional labels, she said, but 'I need to know that the gelatin comes from halal beef'. She knows that Turkey imports live cattle and is unsure if the gelatin from these animals meets all halal standards.[13]

Another major concern, repeated in 2015 and 2019, was about the widespread use of chemicals to produce fruit and vegetables, and the narratives used by officials, farmers, and businesses about the 'impossibility' of agricultural production without chemicals. Some reflect that seeds themselves have been altered to require chemicals. Fatma (Ankara, 2019) mentioned the challenges she faced with the garden she rented to grow vegetables for her family: 'Nothing grows without chemicals. It is not like

---

[13] Turkey has been importing live cattle to address the shortage of red meat in the domestic market, particularly from Brazil, Uruguay, and European Union countries. In 2018, Turkey imported a total of 1.4 million head of cattle, which was 63% higher than in 2017. Turkey also imported live cattle to address the needs during Eid Al-Adha for sacrifice ritual in 2010, 2011, 2017, and 2018 (USDA FAS 2019).

how it was when I was growing up.' Other participants in the group mentioned the impacts on health, such as 'chronic diseases' and 'increasing rates of cancer' related to these chemicals. A similar concern raised was about the use of hormones: Huner (Balikesir, 2019) worked in a greenhouse and was amazed by 'how much the cucumbers grew between collecting times in the morning and the evening'. While she was not sure what kind of 'hormone' the greenhouse owners used, she was concerned about how 'unhealthy' it could be.

Several participants mentioned the difficulty of knowing about all chemicals and learning to get rid of them in their own kitchens when there is a growing number of chemicals with increased potency and toxicity in the food supply. Deniz (Ankara, 2015) shared that she felt stressed even after reading every food label. Because her husband had cancer, she said, 'I buy only organic food. ... I feel that food is the only thing I can control when everything around us is carcinogenic.' Yet even the purchase of organic food does not alleviate all concerns about the food system. As Deniz points out, her child consumes conventional food and candy served at his daycare, and she has little to no control over what her child is exposed to outside the home.

Referring to the inconclusive scientific studies about the health impacts of genetically engineered food, Irem (Ankara, 2015) mentioned her precautionary approach. Because her daughter has several allergies and the underlying cause, soy lecithin, was not identified for years, she is cautious regarding sources of the secondary consumption of soy. She noticed that genetically engineered soy affects her daughter's reaction to milk: 'We buy only one brand of milk because if the cows eat genetically engineered feed, then [my daughter] definitely has flare ups.' Others also had their lists of GE food to avoid: Hulya (Ankara, 2015) said she avoids chicken due to her daughter's pediatrician's suggestion because her daughter has egg and milk allergies. While she 'did not know chicken could contain so many allergens', other participants mentioned how chickens 'now eat GE feed'.[14]

---

[14] After the 2006–2007 outbreak of avian flu, small producers left the poultry market in Turkey and it became dominated by large-scale confined operations depending on GE animal feed.

208   N. Atalan-Helicke

The diversity of participants in terms of age, educational attainment, income, and religious values in relation to halal[15] provides a broader perspective in terms of anxieties about the agri-food system and the complexity of negotiating values in food choices. While food is an emotional topic (Cairns and Johnston 2015: 16–17), the polarization among secular and Muslim citizens in Turkey initially brought another complexity to the focus groups (Tugal, 2012). However, as they shared their individual anxieties around food, and particularly access to wholesome food, participants realized the collective nature of these anxieties transcended an easy secular/devout division.

Although domestic consumption of organic food is increasing in Turkey, particularly due to aspirations to lead a healthy life and anxiety about the health of children, it is still limited to environmentally conscious, urban middle- to high-income consumers (Akgüngör et al. 2010). Fulya (Ankara, 2015) mentioned that 'everything in the organic market looks fresher and is tastier', and she used to shop in organic farmers' markets before moving to her new neighborhood. However, Esme (Ankara, 2019) complained about the cost of organic food: 'I want to eat and feed my family healthy food. I have Multiple Sclerosis so it is especially important. But organic certified rice at store [M] is three times the cost of regular rice. I cannot afford it as a household with two incomes. How can other families afford it?'

Other concerns were about the intersection of organic and halal products. Melda (Konya, 2015) mentioned that she trusts and consumes organic food for health. Yet, she said she 'trusts halal certified food more' because she was not sure whether organic certifiers and agencies follow all of the halal principles. Her choice is then to purchase food products that are both organic and halal certified, such as poultry. However, as ten other participants mentioned, items that have both halal and organic certification labels 'are more expensive than organic alone' (Fig. 9.1).

---

[15] Participants were not directly asked whether they were secular or devout Muslims. While some participants had headscarves to represent their religious identity, there were religiously devout participants without headscarves and secular participants with traditional headscarves. See Gökarıksel and Secor (2010) and Aygül and Gürbüz (2019) for a discussion of different clothing style and connections to class. I marked participants' preference for halal in different categories such as food, cosmetics, and tourism.

9 Sustainable Halal? The Intersection of Halal, Organic...

Fig. 9.1 Comparison of conventional, organic, natural, and halal chicken sold in markets based on 2016 prices in Carrefour national supermarket chain in Turkey. Here, 'conventional' refers to meat products from industrial feeding operations without any sustainability or health labels. Certified 'organic' fulfils organic production standards. There is no standard or regulation for 'natural' (*doğal*) in Turkey, but companies use the label generously

Some participants wished for a single label that could combine the ingredients and qualities that were important to them, as halal only covered some aspects. Rusen (Konya, 2015) wished for products that were 'natural'. Naile (Konya, 2015) shared her wish for a 'healthy' label that would combine halal and organic principles. These findings resonate with some of the tensions in the tayyib-halal movement and scholarly work. Against the contentions above that genetically engineered food disrupts environmental balance and promotes unfair trade, others argue that because of the cost, a greener lifestyle would be burdensome for ordinary people. Thus, it would undermine Islam's core egalitarian spirit (Armanios and Ergene 2018).

Assurances that Consumers Demand

Melda's quest for clean and healthy food raises new questions about the challenges and possibilities of converging organic and halal certification in Turkey and other Muslim-majority markets. While consumers' definitions of healthy food suggest an overlap between organic and halal food, the frameworks used by certification agencies continue to distinguish the categories. In Turkey, organic certification can be issued by private and state agencies following the 2004 State Organic Agriculture Law (Number 5262) and Directorate of Organic Agriculture issued in 2010. The organic legislation has extensive rules on animal welfare and plant production (Official Newspaper 2010). Halal certification in Turkey can also be issued by a state agency (TSI) or by multiple private agencies (e.g., GIMDES). Halal certification standards, however, are not uniform: TSI follows OIC Standards and Metrology Institute for the Islamic Countries Criteria (OIC/SMIIC 1). GIMDES has been accredited by multiple global halal certification agencies (e.g., Department of Islamic Development Malaysia, JAKIM, standards) and uses its own guidelines. Like TSI, GIMDES has also been working to create common standards for global markets (Atalan-Helicke 2015: 671).

Halal is often associated with stricter hygiene and food safety standards, particularly regarding meat. In 2015, almost all participants in Konya and one-fifth of the participants in Ankara said they preferred to shop for halal meat. In 2019, one-third of the participants in Ankara said they preferred halal meat. Concerns about meat, however, still surfaced. Turkey is connected to export markets through pork production, and in recent years, there were concerns about the introduction of pork into the national food supply chain. Sibel (Konya, 2015) said her family is particularly suspicious of meat while *vacationing* (in Turkey) because of what might be offered to foreign tourists. There was also concern that halal meat might not follow the broader tayyib principles.

Participants did not specifically use the word '*tayyib*' to express their concerns but talked of 'terms' and 'conditions' that defined food as halal but might not be incorporated into certification standards. Anka (Balikesir, 2019) complained about 'the fast pace of production' and said

9 Sustainable Halal? The Intersection of Halal, Organic... 211

'I want meat to come from animals raised without hormones and drugs. Then it would be halal.' Atiye (Ankara, 2019) was not sure about the halal status of meat from mechanized slaughterhouses: 'Would meat be halal if you pray once but slaughter 10,000 animals with the same machine?' For Esme (Ankara, 2019), the inhumane conditions of imported live animals were a concern: 'Those animals lived miserably in that ship.[16] They will not become halal if you kill them after prayer and let their blood [according to Islamic principles].' In her focus group, these comments led to a wider discussion of red meat consumption and live meat imports in Turkey, both of which were deemed as a 'problem' and raised questions about the morality of red meat consumption.

Participants generally thought that halal certification implied the absence of GE ingredients, but many shared that they had questioned their own assumptions and the companies from which they purchase. Some women received further guidance in terms of animal feed: Esra (Konya, 2015) said that she had started shopping for free-range and halal chicken due to concerns about genetically engineered feed. Later, due to her *hodja*'s suggestion that chicken can be *najs* (not clean), she stopped preparing chicken for her family altogether. Esra's choices resonated with others: Peri (Konya, 2015) was concerned because she was not sure whether the halal-certified companies where she shops have a mechanism to prevent the inclusion of genetically engineered food: 'It is ... not clear what [these companies] think about genetic engineering ... I know corn has genetically engineered ingredients. But I did not hear anything about its halal status.'

The lack of a clear stance on genetically engineered food by companies engaged in halal certification has created controversies for consumers in their food choices. Hatice (Konya, 2015) mentioned that she used to consume the products of a particular halal-certified company. However, after reading in the newspaper about tests conducted by state officials

---

[16] She refers to the shipment of 27,000 live cattle imported from Brazil in February 2018. There was a scandal when news stories showed animals that had not been provided water for the last two days of their journey and were living in cramped and unsanitary conditions. See, for example, Brezilya'dan canlı hayvan getiren Nada gemisi Mersin'e yanaştı [Nada, the ship bringing livestock from Brazil came to Mersin port], 25 February 2018. https://www.cnnturk.com/turkiye/brezilyada-canli-hayvan-getiren-nada-gemisi-mersine-yanasti (Accessed 31 August 2020).

212   N. Atalan-Helicke

that confirmed the presence of genetically engineered ingredients in the company's food items, she stopped consuming their products. In another focus group, the same company came up: Semiha (Konya, 2015) said she had visited the company's slaughterhouse: 'It was very hygienic and they follow halal slaughtering practices. Even though they were accused of using genetically engineered ingredients, I trust them.' She trusted the halal meat production process and did not care about GE.

From any number of directions, female consumers in Turkey are anxious about the food available to them. While they shared factors such as their knowledge of genetically engineered food or organic food affecting their food choices, they also raised concerns about the price premiums of organic and halal food. The lack of a clear stance on genetically engineered food by halal-certified businesses in Turkey often frustrated participants in terms of who and what to trust. As women consumers discussed their food choices, several also expressed their wish for an intersection of different certifications, particularly organic and halal, to cater to their expectations of healthy, clean, and religiously proper food. These expectations can be viewed as consumers' desire for a broader definition of morally permissible and wholesome food that goes beyond labels and leads to a faith-based, sustainable food system.

Discussion

The complexity of the agri-food system transitions changes consumer anxieties and urges consumers' to reflect on their values and their food choices: while some of these concerns can be directly related to increased use of chemicals in agricultural production and the fast pace of production in livestock operations, others are related to lack of knowledge about long-term impacts on health and the environment. While the expansion of halal certification and its institutionalization provide some assurances to Muslim consumers, broader dimensions of the agri-food system create new questions. Genetically engineered food is a particularly poignant and complex issue in the food system because it raises questions that can only be answered from an intersection of religious, scientific, business, environmental, and social perspectives. Despite declarations by religious authorities in different Muslim countries, including those that have institutionalized halal certification, that genetically engineered food is halal, Muslim consumers seek a broader definition of halal that encompasses well-being for humans, animals, and the earth. This might be described as a quest for wholesome or tayyib food.

Consumer concerns about genetically engineered food stem from multiple sources. Moreover, how the halal certification business, the markets, and the state deal with genetically engineered food raises more questions for consumers and does not alleviate their concerns about whether GE food is clean and healthy. It may be beyond the scientific knowledge of religious scholars and halal certification agencies to address the complexities of the genetically engineered process and its ramifications (Atalan-Helicke 2015). These new questions may include the following: What kind of environmental impacts do the alterations that take place at the genetic level of the plant have on nature? Does genetic alteration in agriculture mean that humans are intervening with the *fitrah* and the *mizan?* What happens to an animal that is fed on GE animal feed? What kind of secondary changes can we talk about in the human body after consuming milk or meat coming from genetically engineered animal feed? Is it possible to trace these changes in the human body with scientific studies designed for short-term intervals?

From the consumer perspective, sometimes the regulations fall short of providing assurances: what happens when genetically engineered animal feed and genetically engineered food are subject to different regulations and the consumers' right to know is not answered? In other instances, the fragmentation of the halal certification and the diversity of opinions among halal certification agencies about genetically engineered food and animal feed frustrate consumers (Atalan-Helicke 2015). What happens when one halal certification agency says meat from animals fed genetically engineered animal feed is halal and another, in the same country, applies confinement periods for animals fed similar diets? For Muslim consumers who seek a more deliberately ethical halal lifestyle in globalized markets, the pace of production and lack of monitoring for animal welfare also becomes a problem: Can the meat be halal if thousands of livestock are imported in unsanitary conditions and face miserable

214 N. Atalan-Helicke

conditions on a ship sailing thousands of kilometers before they are sent to facilities for halal slaughter and processing?

These and similar questions were raised by participants in focus groups in Turkey in 2015 and 2019. Rather than conclusive answers, as participants shared their concerns, their questions led to deeper conversations about the ethics of meat consumption and of the agri-food system transformations in Turkey (through both environmental and religious lenses). As the participants shared their visions for structural changes that could provide more assurances, the collective nature of their anxieties drew women closer regardless of their consumption patterns, class, or levels of religious devotion. Together, they imagined alternatives to a system that had not incorporated their inputs.

As participants voiced their concerns, it became clear that the price premiums associated with organic and halal-certified products also frustrate consumers and create a burden on food choices. Rather than separate certifications that cater to different issues in the food system, consumers' desire for a 'wholesome', clean, and healthy label highlights the need to draw alliances within the alternative food network. Such alliances can also be critical to bring about structural changes in the agri-food system and to help capture Islam's true egalitarian and ethical spirit while balancing economic, social, ecological, and religious values in the quest for clean and healthy food.

References

ABNE. 2017. African biosafety network of expertise: Status of crop biotechnology in Africa. Accessed 31 August 2020. http://nepad-abne.net/biotechnology/status-of-crop-biotechnology-inafrica/.

Akgüngör, Sedef, Bülent Miran, and Canan Abay. 2010. Consumer willingness to pay for organic food in urban Turkey. *Journal of International Food & Agribusiness Marketing* 22 (3–4): 299–313.

Akhmetova, Elmira. 2016. Genetically modified food and humanity's well-being: An Islamic perspective. In *Islamic perspectives on science and technology: Selected conference papers*, ed. Mohammad Hashim, Kamali Osman Bakar, Daud Abdul-Fattah Batchelor, and Rugayah Hashim, 275–287. Singapore: Springer.

9 Sustainable Halal? The Intersection of Halal, Organic... 215

Al-Attar, Mariam. 2017. Food ethics: A critique of some Islamic perspectives on genetically modified food. *Zygon®* 52 (1): 53–75.

Armanios, Febe, and Bogac Ergene. 2018. *Halal food: A history*. New York: Oxford University Press.

Atalan-Helicke, Nurcan. 2015. The halal paradox: Negotiating identity, religious values, and genetically engineered food in Turkey. *Agriculture and Human Values* 32 (4): 663–674.

———. 2020. Access to clean and healthy food in Turkey: Food activism and mothers' concerns about shopping for change. In *Environmental activism and the maternal: Mothers and Mother Earth in activism and discourse*, ed. Rebecca Bromwich, Noemie Richard, Olivia Ungar, Melanie Younger, and Maryellen Symmons, 99–132. Bradford, ON: Demeter Press.

Aygül, Hasan Hüseyin, and Gamze Gürbüz. 2019. Tüketim, moda ve islami giyim açısından tesettürlü/türbanlı öğrenciler: Akdeniz Universitesi örneği [Consumption, fashion and Islamic clothing, Women with a veil, case study of Akdeniz University]. *Muhafazakar Dusunce/ Conservative Thought* 15 (56): 161–209.

Bawa, A.S., and K.R. Anilakumar. 2013. Genetically modified foods: Safety, risks and public concerns—A review. *Journal of Food Science and Technology* 50 (6): 1035–1046.

Bellows, Anne C., Gabriela Alcaraz, and William K. Hallman. 2010. Gender and food, a study of attitudes in the USA towards organic, local, US grown, and GM-free foods. *Appetite* 55 (3): 540–550.

Beşer, Faruk. 2011. *Güncel dini meseleler istişare toplantısı* [Proceedings of the debates on current Islamic issues (26–28 November 2011)]. Directorate of Religious Affairs, Prime Ministry of Turkey. Ankara: Diyanet İşleri Başkanlığı Yayınları.

Bouzenita, Anke Iman. 2010. Islamic legal perspectives on genetically modified food. *American Journal of Islamic Social Sciences* 27 (1): 1–30.

———. 2018. The most dangerous idea? *Islamic deliberations on transhumanism. Darulfunun Ilahiyat* 29 (2): 201–228.

Bouzenita, Anke Iman, and Mohammed E.S. Mirghani. 2014. Transgenic organisms (chimeras) and their Islamic evaluation. *Science International* 26 (4): 1639–1641.

Büyüközer, Huseyin. 2012. *Yeniden gıda raporu: Yediklerimiz, içtiklerimiz helal mi haram mı ve sağlığımıza ne kadar uygun? [New food report: Are the food and drinks we consume halal or haram and how healthy are they?]*. Istanbul: Cevik Matbaacılık.

Cairns, Kate, and Josée Johnston. 2015. *Food and femininity*. New York: Bloomsbury Publishing.

Dinar Standard. 2019. *State of the global Islamic economy 2019/2020: Driving the Islamic economy revolution 4.0*. (The 7th Annual report, in partnership with Salaam Gateway). Accessed 20 December 2019. https://cdn.salaamgateway.com/special-coverage/sgie19-20/full-report.pdf.

FDA. 2018. How FDA regulates food from genetically engineered plants? Accessed 20 December 2019. https://www.fda.gov/food/food-new-plant-varieties/how-fda-regulates-food-genetically-engineered-plants.

Fischer, Johan. 2011. *The Halal frontier: Muslim consumers in a globalized market*. New York: Palgrave Macmillan.

Friedlander, Krystina. 2014. Talking chop: An interview with Imam Khalid Latif. Accessed 28 February 2019. https://beyondhalal.org/talking-chop-interview-imam-khalid-latif/.

Gökarıksel, Banu, and Anna Secor. 2010. Islamic-ness in the life of a commodity: Veiling-fashion in Turkey. *Transactions of the Institute of British Geographers* 35 (3): 313–333.

Günay, H. Mehmet, and Merve Özdemir. 2016. İslami açıdan genetiği değiştirilmiş ürünler [Genetically modified organisms from the perspective of Islam]. *Journal of International Social Research* 9 (45): 1004–1022.

Heap, Ian, and Stephen O. Duke. 2018. Overview of glyphosate-resistant weeds worldwide. *Pest Management Science* 74 (5): 1040–1049.

Holme, Inger Bæksted, Toni Wendt, and Preben Bach Holm. 2013. Intragenesis and cisgenesis as alternatives to transgenic crop development. *Plant Biotechnology Journal* 11 (4): 395–407.

Iqbal, Noor Fatima Kareema. 2015. From permissible to wholesome: Situating halal organic farms within the sustainability discourse. *Islamic Sciences* 13 (1): 49–56.

ISAAA. 2014. Late blight resistant potato developed using cisgenesis approach. Accessed 28 February 2019. http://www.isaaa.org/kc/cropbiotechupdate/article/default.asp?ID=12390.

———. 2018. *ISAAA in 2018: Accomplishment Report*. Accessed 17 November 2020. https://www.isaaa.org/resources/publications/annualreport/2018/pdf/ISAAA-Accomplishment_Report-2018.pdf.

———. 2019a. Biotech crops continue to help meet the challenges of increased population and climate change. Accessed 31 August 2020. https://www.isaaa.org/resources/publications/%20briefs/54/executivesummary/default.asp.

9 Sustainable Halal? The Intersection of Halal, Organic... 217

———. 2019b. Pocket K No. 54: Plant breeding innovation: CRISPR-Cas9. Accessed 20 December 2019. http://www.isaaa.org/resources/publications/pocketk/54/default.asp.

IWISA. 2012. Workshop resolution. In *International workshop for Islamic scholars on agribiotechnology (IWISA): Shariah compliance* (Georgetown, Penang, Malaysia 2010), ed. S.M.S.S. Mohd Salleh, 53–54. Selangor, Malaysia: MABIC; Los Banos, Laguna, Philippines: ISAAA.

Khalek, Aiedah Abdul, Sharifah Hayaati Syed Ismail, and Hairunnisa Mohamad Ibrahim. 2015. A study on the factors influencing young Muslims' behavior intention in consuming halal food in Malaysia. *Jurnal Syariah* 23 (1): 79–102.

Kinchy, Abby. 2012. *Seeds, science, and struggle: The global politics of transgenic crops.* Cambridge, MA: MIT Press.

Kurth, Laura, and Pieter Glasbergen. 2017. Serving a heterogeneous Muslim identity? Private governance arrangements of halal food in the Netherlands. *Agriculture and Human Values* 34 (1): 103–118.

Kurzer, Paulette, and Alice Cooper. 2007. Consumer activism, EU institutions and global markets: The struggle over biotech foods. *Journal of Public Policy* 27 (2): 103–128.

McEvoy, Miles. 2017. Organic 101: Can GMOs be used in organic products? Accessed 20 April 2022. https://www.usda.gov/media/blog/2013/05/17/organic-101-can-gmos-be-used-organic-products.

Ministry of Agriculture and Forestry. 2019. GDOya yönelik resmi control çalışmaları (Official monitoring of genetically modified food). Accessed 20 December 2019. https://www.tarimorman.gov.tr/Konu/1437/GDO-Resmi-Kontrol.

Mutmainah, Lu'liyatul. 2018. The role of religiosity, halal awareness, halal certification, and food ingredients in the purchase intention of halal food. *Journal of Islamic Economics, Finance and Banking* 1 (1&2): 33–50.

Official Gazette. 2010. *Tarim ve Köyişleri Bakanlığı. Genetik yapısı değiştirilmiş organizmalar ve ürünlerine dair yönetmelik.* Ministry of Agriculture and Rural Affairs: Regulation on genetically engineered organisms and products. Accessed 20 December 2019. https://www.resmigazete.gov.tr/eskiler/2010/08/20100813-4.htm.

Orhangazi, Özgür and Erinç Yeldan. 2020. *Re-making of the Turkish crisis.* University of Massachusetts Amherst Political Economy Research Institute, Working Paper Series 504. Accessed 30 October 2020. https://peri.umass.edu/publication/item/1254-re-making-of-theturkish-.

Özer, Kemal. 2010. *Deccal tabakta: Siyasi, dini ve vicdani acidan GDO* [The devil on the plate: GMOs from a political, religious, and conscience perspective]. Istanbul: HayyKitap.

Powles, Stephen B. 2008. Evolved glyphosate-resistant weeds around the world: Lessons to be learnt. *Pest Management Science* 64 (4): 360–365.

Tabashnik, Bruce E. 2015. ABCs of insect resistance to Bt. *PLoS Genetics*. https://doi.org/10.1371/journal.pgen.1005646.

USDA FAS. 2019. Agricultural Biotechnology Annual 2018: Egypt needs a biosafety framework for agricultural biotechnology. Accessed 28 February 2019. https://gain.fas.usda.gov/Recent%20GAIN%20Publications/Agricultural%20Biotechnology%20Annual_Cairo_Egypt_10-11-2018.pdf.

———. 2020. Agricultural Biotechnology Annual Indonesia: Biotechnology and Other New Production Technologies. Accessed 30 October 2020. https://apps.fas.usda.gov/newgainapi/api/Report/DownloadReportByFileName?fileName=Agricultural%20Biotechnology%20Annual_Jakarta_Indonesia_10-20-2020.

Van Eenennaam, Alison L. 2013. GMOs in animal agriculture: Time to consider both costs and benefits in regulatory evaluations. *Journal of Animal Science and Biotechnology*. https://doi.org/10.1186/2049-1891-4-37.

Vicini, John L., William R. Reeves, John T. Swarthout, and Katherine A. Karberg. 2019. Glyphosate in livestock: Feed residues and animal health. *Journal of Animal Science* 97 (11): 4509–4518.

Yeni Soluk 2019. 217 işletme helal belgesi alırken 495 ürün için belge verilmiş (217 institutions and 495 products received halal certificate) Accessed 13 December 2022. https://yenisoluk.com/217-isletme-helal-belgesi-alirken-495-urun-icinbelge-verilmis.

10

Sustainability and Halal? Global Trade, Molecular Halal, and Exclusionary Politics

Shaheed Tayob

Introduction

Halal certification is a technological and technocratic transformation of halal designed to facilitate increasingly complex food production and global supply chain management. Yet the very discourse and materiality of global trade and consumer growth that halal certification satisfies have been subject to an ethical critique that foregrounds the precarity of human, non-human, and environmental relations. Given a historical discursive tradition of halal rooted in intra-Muslim networks of labor, trade, and exchange, it is imperative to consider the ethical stakes of halal certification for marginalized and precarious Muslim populations around the world. Drawing on ethnographic insights obtained during fieldwork in South Africa, I highlight the material and ethical stakes of a new halal materiality on Muslim subjectivity. Turning to ethnographic insights in a meat market in Mumbai, and thus taking India as a case study of

---

S. Tayob (✉)
Stellenbosch University, Stellenbosch, South Africa
e-mail: shaheedt@sun.ac.za

© The Author(s), under exclusive license to Springer Nature Switzerland AG 2023   **219**
R. Turaeva, M. Brose (eds.), *Religious Economies in Secular Context*, New Directions in Islam, https://doi.org/10.1007/978-3-031-18603-5_10

sustainability and its relationship to halal, I then argue that the intimacy of exclusionary politics and economic growth means that halal certification potentially partakes in the marginalization of Muslim labor and trade in the city. Questions of sustainability and halal, in general, must therefore consider the ethical entailments of new formations of halal in order to bridge between an ethics of intra-Muslim trade and exchange, and the conditions of global trade.

Around the globe, the halal certification industry increasingly finds itself confronting questions of food security, quality, and sustainability. Muslim activists and consumers challenge the technical focus of halal certification and its intimacy with capitalist industrial production. They call for a return to the 'essence' of halal, which they argue is related to the notion of *tayyib* (goodness). Tayyib situates halal as not merely a question of permissibility, but it turns attention to processes of procurement, production, and care for both animal and human consumers (Yasin 2017). At the same time, the halal certification industry finds itself in the midst of a global critique of capitalism that foregrounds harm to humans, animals, and the environment that has been the outcome of a political and economic dispensation to achieve profit, production, and growth at all and any cost (Yusoff 2018). In this conjuncture, the very premise of the halal-certification industry to ensure and stimulate Muslim consumption runs up against a discourse that posits industrial production and consumption as the core issue of environmental and ethical sustainability. The certification industry is thus challenged to navigate between its role as a facilitator of Muslim public consumption and mediator of the always debated and contested question of halal quality. What does it mean to certify and assure the quality of halal on a global scale? Considering Muslim precarity in the contemporary world, what then is the ethics and politics of halal certification as a technocratic and bureaucratic formation of halal?

I argue that halal certification radically transforms and refigures a discursive tradition of halal in practice. The turn to what I have called 'molecular halal' situates expert scientific intervention, large-scale capital investment, and audit procedures as central to halal quality assurance (Tayob 2019b). The aim of certification is to devise procedures through which to abstract halal as a quality distinct from Muslim networks of trade and exchange. Once isolated, measured, and materialized 'halal' is then made amenable to globally circulated, standardized, and branded food production. Yet the development of audit process and procedure is not simply a translation of past practice into a new form, as if practice is left untouched by new forms of relation, new demands of evidence, and new spaces of production and consumption. Rather, the shift in evidence and forms of relation from Muslim networks of trade and exchange to industrial production both affords Muslim consumers an entry into a global market of industrially produced food and simultaneously alters the very material and ethical basis upon which halal is determined and practiced. To speak of sustainability without recognizing this crucial transformation and its contemporary critiques is to misapprehend the nature and problem of halal quality, ethical relations, and industrial production in the contemporary world. This paper attempts to illustrate these issues of the ethics of halal in practice, halal certification, and Muslim networks of trade and exchange in the following discussion. Given the close connection of neoliberal capitalist development to exclusionary politics, it is crucial that questions of halal quality and sustainability confront discussions on precarity, labor, and small business practice.

A Discursive Tradition of Halal in Practice: Trade and Exchange

A common thread in the sociological, anthropological, and industrial analyses of halal is that halal certification and halal practices are assumed to be interchangeable. Sociologists and anthropologists write about the commercialization, standardization, and bureaucratization of halal as a contemporary post-modern and neoliberal capitalist phenomenon whereby consumer concerns about food quality, purity, and health have translated into a desire for labeling, transparency of production, and ethical supply chain management (Bergeaud-Blackler et al. 2016; Bonne and Verbeke 2008). The novelty of halal practice in contemporary life is seen as a form of post-modern reflexive consumption (Lever 2018), a meeting of technoscience and ritual purity (Fischer 2016), or as an insidious

222   **S. Tayob**

practice 'invented' by Islamic fundamentalism (Bergeaud-Blackler 2017). But arguments concerning novelty and invention fail to consider the long history of halal in practice, in which it has also encompassed ritual concerns, human-animal considerations, and ethics of interpersonal and communal trade and exchange. Even the brilliant historical study by Armanios and Ergene treats the introduction of scientific reason into halal practice as a matter of direct translation, whereby historical forms of reasoning are quantified, measured, and observed (Armanios and Ergene 2018). There is little consideration of the phenomenon of halal in practice as both technical and ethical, nor of the way that a new materiality of substances and the scientific gaze may radically transform the kinds of ethical relations of consumption, sharing, and trade (Tayob 2020a).

Historically, halal entails a set of technical and ethical questions regarding what to eat, how to kill, and with whom to consume and trade. Divine instruction on the avoidance of pork and carrion is accompanied by prophetic guidelines regarding the method of slaughter and animal treatment. And an embodied discursive tradition of intention (*niyyat*), identity, doubt, and salvation sets up an entanglement between everyday culinary practice, social relations, and ultimate salvation. It is important to consider both the materiality and ethics of halal in order to gain a clear understanding of the stakes of halal certification in an increasingly unequal and precarious world.

The Prophet Muhammad advised his early followers on the basic ritual guidelines for halal slaughter. Widely practiced by Muslims across the world, the basic requirements are that *tasmiya* (*Bismillah-Allahu-Akbar*) is recited upon slaughter and that at least two of the three main arteries are severed. The spinal cord must remain intact so that the heart is not paralyzed and the blood drains from the carcass before preparation and consumption. Given the prevalence of debate between different Muslim schools and sects and the absence of Quranic reference, there are differences of opinion on the necessity of even these basic requirements, and there are different readings of the meaning of these practices. Nevertheless, it is widely accepted that prayer and non-paralyzing slaughter constitute the basic requirements of halal slaughter.

In addition, there are also a set of recommended practices (*sunnat*) that are usually not followed during industrial and commercial slaughter,

10 Sustainability and Halal? Global Trade, Molecular Halal...   223

which are crucial for understanding the ethics of halal. These include the recommendation that before slaughter, the animal should be offered a sip of water and the knife must be sharp. The animal should not see the knife before slaughter, nor witness the blood or the slaughter of other animals. Upon slaughter, the animal must be placed on a clean area facing the direction of Mecca. The prayer is then recited and slaughter proceeds. It is often explained in Muslim gatherings and sacrifice events in both South Africa and Mumbai where I conducted my ethnographic research that these practices ensure that the animal remains calm before slaughter. I argue that these requirements are not simply ritual repetitions, meaningful only within an Islamic cosmological order. Rather, taking an embodied and practical approach, these stipulations entail a recognition of the subjectivity of animal life, that while clearly hierarchical, recognizes the responsibility of human care and consideration for animals (Tayob 2019a).

The concern for the well-being of the animal before slaughter is not equivalent to modern debates about employee safety in slaughterhouses, which originally mobilized the debate on stunning (Bonne and Verbeke 2008). Nor is it parallel to post-Enlightenment doubts over animal sentience (Singer 2009). The provisions for halal slaughter are straightforward: they recognize animal sentience and subjectivity and demand that humans navigate their sacrifice for human consumption with an ethics of care.

In practice, however, the Muslim consumer of meat is usually not the person who slaughters. The profession of butchering and meat trade is not new. Outside of ritual occasions and rural communities, consuming meat is a market practice. The butcher (store owner) is very often not the person who actually performs the slaughter (slaughterer). Trust is therefore central to halal practice. The consumer trusts the butcher, who in turn trusts the slaughterer, that the procedures of halal slaughter have been observed. Stabilizing these relations of trust is an ethical discourse that articulates a link between intention or orientation (*niyyat*), intra-Muslim trade and exchange, doubt, and salvation. According to an embodied discursive tradition of halal, it is considered detestable (*makrooh*) or even sinful (*gunah*) to doubt the food of a fellow Muslim. The intention to consume halal within intra-Muslim networks of trade and exchange ensures compliance. On the other hand, if a supplier has deviously provided non-halal food to a fellow Muslim, then the sin for that transgression accrues to the supplier and not to the consumer. Within Muslim networks of trade and exchange, signs of identity and community are the media through which trust in halal is established. Doubt is frowned upon as an offense to the moral integrity of the supplier. In the absence of clear evidence of transgression, consumption within Muslim networks of trade exchange is the basis for halal practice. Material integrity is of secondary concern. The desire for evidence is normally considered an anathema to a community of shared belief.

This is to say that analyses of halal cannot simply infer the meeting point of religion, ritual, and economy. Clearly, it is imperative that assessments of the novelty, transformation, or sustainability of halal reckon with the ethics and materiality of an embodied halal archive now disrupted and challenged by new ideas of science, technology, production, and trade.

Halal Certification in Practice: Consumption, Evidence, and Community

Halal certification is a recent global development. Some scholars attribute its emergence to the Iranian Revolution and the demand for halal meat imports, while others situate it as central to the 1970s Islamization efforts of the Malaysian government (Fischer 2011). Regardless of origin, it is clear that halal certification today is inseparable from global trade, capitalist market formation, increasingly complex food production technology, and the growing Muslim diaspora in Europe and America. In the 1990s, as the pace of neoliberal reforms took effect around the world, municipal and state regulation of meat production turned toward privatization, regulation through standards rather than direct intervention, and reduction of import tariffs for meat and non-meat products.

Technological developments in industrial food production and the new scale and scope of trade shifted halal concerns in two significant ways. First, evolving food processing technologies introduced a new level of opacity to food production since even non-meat items could potentially contain products of animal origin, rendering them subject to halal concern. Second, global trade complicated the mostly local-based trajectories of food and meat production, rendering intra-Muslim trade and exchange almost impossible given the complexity of global supply chains. In response, halal certification introduced audit procedures and scientific testing in an attempt to assure the material substance of halal on a global scale. Yet, halal certification does not merely respond to new material conditions but seeks to actively demystify the complexity of industrial food production and global supply chains in an attempt to assure and promote Muslim public consumption (Tayob 2016).

Halal certification as a kind of 'supply chain capitalism' (Tsing 2009) does not consider abstinence from meat a viable option in the face of halal uncertainty. Rather, the industry mobilizes expert knowledge, molecular testing, and technocratic concerns for data and traceability to assure Muslim consumers of halal consumption even beyond Muslim networks. In doing so, it shifts the basis of halal practice from intra-Muslim networks of trade and exchange to the material integrity of the substance consumed. This is not only a translation of halal reason into a technical language of enzymes, proteins, DNA, and measurement, but a transformation of halal: new technologies and knowledges are always also implicated in subject formation and ethical relations (Foucault 2007). This is most apparent when we consider the question of metamorphosis (*al-istihaalah*) for how a new scientific gaze changes the very base upon which halal can be known and consumed. Here, I detail, specifically, a South African debate on the permissibility of gelatin between two prominent halal certification organizations over a period of two decades.

In 1983, the Muslim Judicial Council (MJC), the first official halal organization in South Africa, obtained an enquiry about the halal status of a corporate gelatin manufacturing plant. The MJC is a predominantly Shafii organization based in Cape Town; its ulama are comprised mostly of what is known as the Cape Malay community, decedents of slaves imported to the Cape from the Indonesian archipelago (Tayob 1999). Upon investigating the manufacturing facility and supply chain, the MJC was faced with the quandary that the largest and most prominent gelatin manufacturer in South Africa regularly uses bones and hides from non-halal slaughtered cows and sheep in its production process. Yet the

226   S. Tayob

gelatin could not necessarily be deemed haram. Islamic legal discussions on purity and permissibility also recognize the principle of *al-istihaalah*; this refers to the total and irreversible transformation of a haram substance into halal. For example, the use of manure from non-halal animals in farming is permitted, as is the oxidation of wine. Fruit yields carry no taint from the manure; vinegar is fully distinct from wine. Upon inspection of the manufacturing process, the MJC determined that since gelatin crystals are physically distinguishable in terms of taste, color, and smell from raw bones and hides, and because the process is irreversible, *al-istihaalah* occurs in the manufacture of gelatin. According to the MJC fatwa, gelatin produced from the bones and hides of non-halal slaughtered animals is halal.

SANHA is a competing organization founded in 1996 by Deobandi-aligned ulama who follow the Hanafi school. Given that *al-istihaalah* is a Hanafi legal principle, SANHA originally accepted the MJC fatwa. Meanwhile, developments in the genetic modification of food and new medical technologies have introduced new questions about the ontology of substances into Muslim legal discussions (Padela et al. 2014). In the early 2000s, therefore, SANHA revised its position and disagreed with MJC. SANHA argued that on a molecular level, collagen is a dominant protein found in bones, muscles, skins, and tendons and that gelatin is still a form of collagen, albeit hydrolyzed. Since collagen is the main substance before and after manufacture, SANHA ruled that gelatin manufacture is in fact a process of extraction rather than one of *al-istihaalah*. SANHA's new ruling disregards evidence of observable transformation in visible particulate form, taste, color, and smell in favor of molecular-level continuity. It advises clients to use imported Pakistani-produced gelatin.

On one level, this shift, which is happening around the world and continuously debated, is simply a kind of scientific consideration of a discursive tradition. For proponents of the scientific gaze, *al-istihaalah* does occur when wine becomes vinegar through a chemical process of oxidation. The medieval test of transformation of taste, color, and smell is, from this view, an outdated scientific method applied to a valid and sacred prophetic injunction (Moosa 2021). This kind of technocratic reason, however, fails to appreciate the kinds of sensory observation that establishes *al-istihaala*. Such observations also ensure that Muslim signs of identity, especially clothing, names, and greetings, are the basis for trust, trade, and consumption in many arenas of daily life. Emphasizing a scientific gaze necessarily disrupts the communal and interpersonal assertion of halal quality, since expert mediation and intervention are the only means of assuring halal.

Situating halal as a question of material integrity rather than a community of intention (*niyyat*), trade, and trust means that even Muslim suppliers, friends, and family may now be a source of impermissible consumption. For example, in South Africa, an early SANHA publication called on housewives to inspect the ingredients of their own kitchens since ignorance of complex food production could surreptitiously permit the entry of non-halal substances into the home (SANHA 2008). *Niyyat*, a subjective assertion of will central to Islamic ritual practice (Powers 2004), is here sidelined in favor of scientifically 'objective' material information. Halal is thus reduced to a question of what to eat, rather than with whom.

Practically, householders must consume food that has been halal certified, and consumers should visit establishments that have been subject to a halal audit. But what of the networks of Muslim traders, butchers, and entrepreneurs who have historically serviced Muslim consumption? What is the impact of a system of audit inspection and standardization on small businesses, home manufacturers, and traders who do not have the financial means, stable premises, or complex organizational structure that are so central to audit practice? What are the ethical stakes of halal certification sustainability given the intimacy between neoliberal policy and exclusionary politics that have particularly affected Muslim minorities around the world?

Sustainable Capitalism, Precarity, and the Anthropocene

Halal markets are not insulated from other aspects of global trade, and therefore it is necessary to raise a question about how halal intersects with 'sustainability.' The sustainability of halal or the development of a sustainable halal industry must consider debates and critiques of sustainable capitalism that foreground the increasing precarity of labor and the natural environment over the past two hundred years. According to the critique, the technocratic refusal to include environmental and human externalities as part of the cost of industry has wrought immeasurable damage to both natural environments and precarious human populations (Yusoff 2018). Where halal certification entails a shift of ethical consideration from human and animal relations to technical rules, the critique of capitalism argues for a consideration of forms of relation in what has been conceived and practiced as a technocratic, functionalist process.

Sustainable capitalism introduces measures, metrics, and standards to report on the environmental footprint of products. For example, with Life Cycle Analysis (LCA) corporations now employ LCA consultants to trace, measure, and evaluate the environmental impact of a product over its life cycle. But LCA analysis, although presenting a discourse of sustainability and environmental concern, remains profit-driven. For example, Walmart famously installed methane digesters at a supply facility that reduced greenhouse emissions and yielded cost savings of $250 million (Freidberg 2013: 579). According to Freidberg, for Walmart 'eco-efficiency does not challenge their business model; it does not require consumers to buy less' and 'does not necessarily challenge yield-maximising practices' (2013: 582). Comparable to halal certification, LCA reports on certain measures regarding the quality of the supply chain (environmental impact quality or halal quality). But thus far, both fail to challenge the ethical presumptions of growth and profit. LCA practitioners, in particular, have promoted environmental solutions that are in the long term as equally destructive as established practices (Freidberg 2013: 587). The establishment of measures and metrics is, on closer inspection, subject to the 'green-washing' critique that argues that companies mobilize environmental concern as a marketing technique to promote the very consumption that environmentalists recognize as the cause of environmental decay.

Sustainability practitioners often subdue ethical concerns in favor of technical and technological solutions. For example, in Masdar City in Abu Dhabi, an eco-city built for zero-carbon living, consultants are clear that the aim of zero-carbon living is not to rethink lifestyles and

10 Sustainability and Halal? Global Trade, Molecular Halal... 229

consumption patterns, but rather to secure a future where consumer lifestyles can continue carbon-neutrally. Gunel's term 'technical adjustment' captures the way that sustainable capitalism focuses on responses that sustain the status quo by sidelining 'ethical, moral and political entailments' (2019: 11). The aim is a future 'where humans will continue to enjoy technological complexity without interrogating existing social, political and economic relations' (Gunel 2019: 10). The problem for consultants is not how to limit growth, but rather how to achieve a utopian ideal of carbon-free living for a select and elite few. At Masdar, technical adjustments and reporting technologies that market and represent sustainability for a consuming public ignore critical analyses that situate the ideology of capital and consumption as central to environmental destruction, human inequality, and precarity.

Halal certification, as I presented it, is a technical, technological, and market-friendly translation and transformation of halal practice. Aiming to facilitate and assure the halal quality of global trade, it is predominantly focused on the certification of industrially produced packaged food and mass-produced meat. Its dependence on intensive manufacturing plants, the excessive use of packaging, and large transportation distances prompt questions about the sustainability of the halal industry. Moreover, the halal industry provides certification contracts to large meat producers who are responsible for the ecological entailments of mass farming, the unethical treatment and rearing of animals, and terrible working conditions and low pay for slaughterhouse labor (Pachirat 2011). Surely these practices demand ethical discussion, but they have not been central ones in halal certification as a technical and technological project. Moreover, in following consumer-centric neoliberal policies, halal certification obtains both its legitimacy and demand, but it should also thus shoulder responsibility for the increasing precarity of disadvantaged populations across the world as land, bodies, and labor become subject to the demands of global trade and the relentless search for profit. Given the discursive tradition of halal and intra-Muslim networks of trade and exchange, it is important to consider how halal certification is impacting small traders and laborers in precarious conditions, whose bodies and profession of faith have been so central to their livelihoods for a long time and who are now threatened by the demands of a neoliberal aesthetics and ethics of trade.

Notes from the Field: Muslim Trade and Exclusionary Politics in Mumbai

In India, neoliberal economic policy is associated closely with the rise of a virulent form of right-wing Hindu nationalism, Hindutva. For Hindutva ideologues, Muslim bodies, labor, food, and ritual practice evoke disgust and are inimical to their idea of a Hindu majoritarian nation. Hindutva discourse imagines the Muslim-as-butcher, who through Islam and livelihood is always intimate with violence and death, and therefore worthy of expiatory sacrifice (Ghassem-Fachandi 2012). The Hindutva idea of a modern, financially and militarily powerful, and globally competitive India is one in which Muslim bodies and labor do not figure in public life. In Mumbai, in particular, the Hindu middle-class imagination of neoliberalism is a shiny new cityscape devoid of Muslim presence (Appadurai 2000). Materially, this means that Muslim neighborhoods and infrastructural facilities have been subject to a process of state neglect and decay that further authorizes the stigma of Muslim neighborhoods as crowded, dirty, and dangerous (Anand 2012).

But Mumbai is a diverse, meat-consuming city. While Muslims comprise only 20% of the total population, Muslim butchers, laborers, and traders are responsible for almost all of the meat supply to both small and large hotels, restaurants, fast-food outlets, and other related businesses. Inner-city meat markets, both large and small, as well as the Municipal Deonar Abbatoir, are dominated by Muslims. Here, halal certification intersects with economic practice, everyday livelihoods, and nationalist politics.

The intersection of politics and halal turns on the aesthetics of slaughter. Inner-city markets and butcher shops prepare meat on customer request. At many locations, live chickens in cages await customer orders. The birds are weighed, slaughtered, skinned, and prepared according to customer specification, all within a period of two to three minutes. The process of meat production is not hidden from view, and the halal quality of the Muslim-slaughtered and supplied meat is rarely in doubt.

In contrast, a new form of packaged chicken, known in Mumbai as 'frozen chicken,' is produced in large corporate production facilities on the outskirts of the city. Chickens are slaughtered, cleaned, hygienically packaged, and refrigerated before being delivered to retail outlets and butchers across the city. Partaking in an ethics and aesthetics of concealment, the process of slaughter is hidden from view. Such industrially produced chicken has two significant impacts on the economy of meat in the city. First, these products threaten the place and profits of small Muslim butchers; they have more to gain from continuing to work in small stores than from transferring to large corporate abbatoirs (Ahmad 2013, 2014). Second, the very presence of these products in hygienic packaging, where slaughter and its by-products are concealed, threatens to further intensify the place and body of the Muslim butcher as a site of disgust, reinforcing the rhetoric of the Hindu-right.

Regarding halal, both forms of chicken are slaughtered by Muslim labor and therefore considered halal. Yet only 'frozen chicken' complies with the supply chain management practices of halal certification. To be certified 'halal' in India, meat must have been slaughtered in a fixed premise, under a set of consistent operating procedures, packaged under tight seals, and labeled consistently. Small-scale butchers have difficulty meeting the requirements of packaging and labeling, if not the others. Thus for some of the consuming public, their products become 'not-halal,' and it can be seen that halal certification itself partakes in the very same exclusion of Muslim bodies as does the ideology of Hindu-nationalist economic development. This fact is not lost on Muslim butchers and meat traders in Mumbai, who actively negotiate and evade the demands of halal certification that is increasingly encroaching on their livelihood. Certainly, the butchers with whom I conducted research always promoted the many virtues of live-slaughtered chicken over frozen chicken.

In practice, butchers at markets and small shops can still achieve certification of their products and entry into the new halal market. But to do so often requires partial subventions of the certification system through networks of trust. These practices became most apparent during my

232 S. Tayob

research conducted in Mumbai between 2012 and 2014 when I spent time at the Crawford Mutton Market, a prominent wholesale market at the entrance to the Muhammad Ali Road area. This Muslim-majority neighborhood is famous for its long history, which contributes to Mumbai's own reputation as a 'travel hub of the west Indian Ocean' and a 'primary city of Islam' that rivaled Istanbul, Alexandria, and Beirut in terms of 'demographic and cosmopolitan expansion' (Green 2011: 3). Muslims contribute to a dense and diverse urban topography of mosques, madrasas, and shrines, mostly in the vicinity of this very market location (Green 2011: 17).

The Crawford Mutton Market is housed in an old and now derelict structure in need of basic maintenance and repair. It stands as an example of the way the state neglects Muslim infrastructures in the city. Inside the market are stalls where licensed butchers display and prepare meat. Sheep and goats are slaughtered at the Deonar Municipal Abattoir in the early hours of the morning and the carcasses are transported for 18 kilometers in non-refrigerated vans to the vendors for preparation and wholesale supply. Just outside is an area where live chickens are slaughtered, processed, and delivered to restaurants and hotels across South Mumbai.

Siraj, the nephew of the owner of one of the largest chicken wholesalers in the market, introduced me to his uncle's operation. The staff of Siraj's uncle slaughter, clean, feather, and cut 5000–6000 chickens per day. Un-skinned chicken is in high demand by 4- and 5-star hotels and restaurant chains in the city. The elite hotel chains have, during the past decade, begun demanding that all meat supplied is halal-certified in order to cater to the certification demands of foreign Muslim visitors. Siraj's uncle's operation is not certified, so he supplies the hotels via an intermediary. Agents send him their orders daily. His staff slaughters the chickens, which are then transported to a separate premises, washed, packaged, labeled, and then sent to the hotels. Siraj sees the contravention of procedure as an ethical practice through which his uncle remains competitive and profitable. The halal certificate is just a documentary supplement to the necessary activity of halal slaughter. As a butcher, his duty to ensure the provision of halal meat to the Muslim community does not necessitate compliance with the documentary demands of the halal certification industry. Evading certification is thus ethical because it allows him to

10 Sustainability and Halal? Global Trade, Molecular Halal...   233

partake in a competitive industry that is increasingly closed off to small businesses, due to both discriminatory anti-Muslim politics and the bureaucratic demands of halal certification.

Sustainable Capitalism or Sustainable Consumption?

Sustainability is a buzzword of the contemporary moment that is as ambiguous as it is popular. The Oxford English Dictionary defines 'sustainable' at both general and specific levels; the specific definition of sustainable is 'environmentally sustainable; the degree to which a process or enterprise is able to be maintained or continued while avoiding the long-term depletion of natural resources'. Sustainability is thus directly related and opposed to the ideology and practice of capital growth and profit at all costs, which has been a dominant feature of industrial capitalism and is responsible for widespread ecological damage. Against a capitalist ideology of unlimited resources, sustainability posits the finiteness of the world and its fragility in sustaining human and non-human life.

But the dictionary's more general definition of this term refers to 'the quality of being sustainable at a certain rate or level'. In this general meaning, sustainability is the ability to maintain a certain level of speed, growth, or profit. Not necessarily relating to economics, the general definition nevertheless illuminates how sustainability has been appropriated as a language of marketing and consulting, where the aim is sustainable growth, profit, and market development (Hirsch 2020). These two articulations of sustainability are potentially antagonistic as the desire for sustainable growth or profit may compromise environmental and human sustainability.

Halal certification is closely linked to neoliberalism, industrial practices of food production, livestock handling and slaughter, and global trade. Focusing on the materiality and forms of relation that halal certification promotes illustrates the ethical stakes of halal auditing in potentially disrupting and marginalizing Muslim networks of labor and trade. Of course, halal certification does not disrupt Muslim networks per se

234 S. Tayob

since the very relations of halal certification have given rise to new halal specialists and auditors whose Muslim identity remains central to their industry practice (Tayob 2020b). But marginalized populations, small traders, and labor are cut-off from the organizational, technological, and financial demands of halal certification. This is particularly significant given a discursive tradition of halal that establishes trust in halal quality through intra-Muslim networks of trade and exchange. Shifting the evidence of halal from persons to substances necessarily alters the kinds of relations and ethics of exchange. To think of sustainability and halal together is a productive move that needs to be cognizant of the ethical stakes of halal certification and attentive to alternative kinds of ethical relations of trade, production, and exchange.

Conclusion

Certification, as I have argued, radically transforms the ethical and relational practice of halal. Once rooted in intra-Muslim trade and exchange, halal is now abstracted as a quality that can be isolated, measured, tested, and known. It is thus made amenable to industrial food production and global supply chains. This process is both an outcome of changes in the global economy as well as active attempts by halal certification actors to publicize halal risk and thereby promote halal certification expertise as indispensable for Muslim public consumption. In the process, halal becomes available for global public consumption in non-Muslim spaces, while potentially excluding established local networks of halal production from partaking in the halal economy. Halal certification, while situating itself in industrial and corporate food production processes, thus potentially partakes in the very same forms of exclusion that scholars argue is endemic to contemporary forms of capital-intensive global production and trade.

In this chapter, I draw on fieldwork conducted in Mumbai to illustrate the ethical stakes of halal certification and industrial production in an exclusionary context. I argue that the desire for environmental sustainability and halal must reckon with the exclusionary ethics and politics of capital-intensive production. Industry goals of expanding the reach of halal certification into new markets, and of increasing the efficiency and technological aspects of halal research, need to also consider the ethics of technocratic forms of production and trade.

One way of linking sustainability and the ethics of halal is to strengthen Muslim networks of labor, trade, and exchange. This can be done, not by submitting existing networks to the technocratic demands of a new materiality and economy, but by facilitating interactions and translations between local intra-Muslim practices of halal and global networks of trade. Doing so may mean rethinking the presumed necessity of global trade, whose diverse production networks reduce prices in exchange for high human and environmental costs. It also means reconsidering the imperative to consume with convenience which has become the taken-for-granted goal of a comfortable and successful consumer life. The very basis and premises of halal certification must be rethought in order to consider the ethical stakes of trade, exchange, and food production on human, non-human, and environmental life.

References

Ahmad, Z. 2013. Marginal occupations and modernising cities: Muslim butchers in urban India. *Economic & Political Weekly* XLVIII (32): 121–131.

———. 2014. Delhi's meatscapes: Cultural politics of meat in a globalizing city. *IIM Kozhikode Society & Management Review* 1: 21–31.

Anand, N. 2012. Municipal disconnect: On abject water and its urban infrastructures. *Ethnography* 4: 487–509.

Appadurai, A. 2000. Spectral housing and urban cleansing: Notes on millennial Mumbai. *Public Culture* 3: 627–651.

Armanios, F., and B.E. Ergene. 2018. *Halal food: A history*. Oxford: Oxford University Press.

Bergeaud-Blackler, F. 2017. *Le Marché halal ou l'invention d'une tradition*. Paris: Le Seuil.

Bergeaud-Blackler, F., J. Fischer, and J. Lever, eds. 2016. *Halal matters: Islam, politics and markets in global perspective*. London and New York: Routledge.

Bonne, K., and W. Verbeke. 2008. Religious values informing halal meat production and the control and delivery of halal credence quality. *Agriculture and Human Values* 25: 35–47.

Fischer, J. 2011. *The halal frontier: Muslim consumers in a globalized market.* New York: Palgrave Macmillan.

———. 2016. *Islam, standards, and technoscience: In global halal zones.* New York and London: Routledge.

Foucault, M. 2007. *Security, territory, population: Lectures at the College De France.* New York: Palgrave Macmillan.

Freidberg, S. 2013. Calculating sustainability in supply chain capitalism. *Economy and Society* 4: 571–596.

Ghassem-Fachandi, P. 2012. *Pogrom in Gujarat: Hindu nationalism and anti-Muslim violence in India.* Princeton and Oxford: Princeton University Press.

Green, Nile. 2011. *Bombay Islam: The religious economy of the West Indian Ocean, 1840–1915.* Cambridge: Cambridge University Press.

Gunel, G. 2019. *Spaceship in the desert: Energy, climate change, and urban design in Abu Dhabi.* Durham: Duke University Press.

Hirsch, E. 2020. Sustainable development. In *Anthropology*, Oxford Research Encyclopedia. https://doi.org/10.1093/acrefore/9780190854584.013.155.

Lever, J. 2018. *Consuming halal in the age of globalised mass production: Compound practice—Knowing what to eat?* Proceedings from 'Rethinking halal: Genealogy, current trends, and new interpretations,' Louvain-la-Neuve.

Moosa, E. 2021. Considering being and knowing in an age of techno-science. In *Medicine and shariah: A dialogue in Islamic bioethics*, ed. I.A. Padela, 87–119. University of Notre Dame Press.

Pachirat, T. 2011. *Every twelve seconds: Industrialized slaughter and the politics of sight.* New Haven and London: Yale University Press.

Padela, A.I., S.W. Furber, M.A. Kholwadia, and E. Moosa. 2014. Dire necessity and transformation: Entry-Points for modern science in Islamic bioethical assessment of porcine products in vaccines. *Bioethics* 2: 59–66.

Powers, P.R. 2004. Interiors, intentions, and the 'spirituality' of Islamic ritual practice. *Journal of the American Academy of Religion* 2: 425–459.

SANHA. 2008. Brush with haraam: Don't sweep it under the carpet. *Halaal Gazette* 10: 4.

Singer, P. 2009. *Animal liberation: The definitive classic of the animal movement (4).* New York: Harper Collins Publishers.

Tayob, A. 1999. *Islam in South Africa: Mosques, imams, and sermons.* Gainesville: University Press of Florida.

Tayob, S. 2016. 'O you who believe, eat of the *ṭayyibāt* (pure and wholesome food) which we have provided you'—The role of risk and expertise in producing certified halal consumption in South Africa. *Journal of Religion in Africa* 1: 67–91.

———. 2019a. Disgust as embodied critique: Being middle class and Muslim in Mumbai. *South Asia: Journal of South Asian Studies* 6: 1192–1209.

———. 2019b. Molecular halal: Producing, debating and evading halal certification in South Africa. In *Insatiable appetite: Food as cultural signifier in the Middle East and beyond*, ed. K. Dmitriev, J. Hauser, and B. Orfali, 100–118. Leiden and Boston: Brill.

———. 2020a. The material semiotics of halal: Neoliberal Islam in practice. *Anthropological Theory Commons*. http://www.at-commons.com/2020/04/12/the-material-semiotics-of-halal-neoliberal-islam-in-practice/.

———. 2020b. Trading halal: Halal certification and intra-Muslim trade in South Africa. *Sociology of Islam* XX: 1–21.

Tsing, A. 2009. Supply chains and the human condition. *Rethinking Marxism: A Journal of Economics, Culture & Society* 2: 148–176.

Yasin, D. 2017. Tayyib: The foundation of ethical eating & conscious consumption. Accessed 10 July 2019. https://medium.com/@zaytunacollege/tayyib-the-foundation-of-ethical-eating-conscious-consumption-b397f728617f.

Yusoff, K. 2018. *A billion black Anthropocenes or none*. Minneapolis: University of Minnesota Press.

Index

A
Al-Ahbash, 156, 157
Al-istihaalah, 225, 226
Al jallah, 200, 201
Alraid Association, 149, 151,
    159, 161–162
American Halal Company, 34
American Halal Institute, 25, 30, 45
Association of Islamic Charitable
    Projects (AICP), 157

B
Bacillus thuringiensis, 200n6, 201n8
Bashkortostan, 72, 74

C
Centro Islamico d'Italia, 62
Chechen Republic, 78–79
Chechnya, 72–73, 79–80, 125

Coreis, 57–59, 61–65
Crescent Halal, 46

D
Dagestan, 72–73, 77–78, 80, 124–125
Department of Islamic Development
    Malaysia (JAKIM), 39, 105, 159
Dukhovnyi tsentr musul'man
    Ukraïny (DTsMU), 150

E
Emirates International Accreditation
    Center (EIAC), 159

F
Fair trade, 3, 14, 22, 200
Federal Meat Inspection Act
    (FMIA), 35

© The Author(s), under exclusive license to Springer Nature Switzerland AG 2023
R. Turaeva, M. Brose (eds.), *Religious Economies in Secular Context*, New Directions in
Islam, https://doi.org/10.1007/978-3-031-18603-5

240 Index

Fitrah, 202, 213
Food Safety and Inspection Service
    (FSIS), 34–35

G

Gıda Güvenliği Hareketi, 202
GIMDES, 203, 210
Genetically modified organisms
    (GMOs), 66–67
Green halal, 203
Gunah, 223

H

Halal Bavaria, 10
Halal Food Council USA, 26, 38
Halal Transactions of Omaha,
    26–27, 29, 39
Haribo halal, 10
Hazard Analysis and Critical Control
    Point (HACCP), 36, 61
Hindutva, 230
HMSA, *see* Humane Methods of
    Slaughter Act
Humane Methods of Slaughter Act
    (HMSA), 36–37

I

IHeartHalal, 30
Ijaza, 62
Indonesia Ulema Council
    (MUI), 38–39
Ingushetia, 72–73
International Halal Integrity
    Alliance, 45, 199
Iqtisad, 172

Islamic Association of China
    (IAC), 108
Islamic Cultural Centre of Italy, 63
Islamic Food and Nutrition Council
    of America (IFANCA), 22,
    25–26, 29–30, 37–39, 45, 67
Islamic Services of America (ISA),
    22, 26–27, 29–30, 32, 34
Istihlak, 200
Italian Islamic Association (CII), 63

J

Jura, 178–180, 184

K

Kabardino-Balkaria, 73
Kazakhstan Halal Industry
    Association (AHIK), 181
KERNEL, 152
Korenizatsiia, 176
Kifaya, 172
Kosher, 7, 22–23, 25, 41, 44, 48,
    66–67, 77

L

Life Cycle Analysis (LCA), 228
Lviv, 162–164

M

Mahalla, 178
Makrooh, 223
Midamar, 23, 46
Minzu, 97
Mironivsky Hliboproduct, 158

Index 241

Mizan, 195, 202, 213
Muftiat, 77–80, 126, 135, 149–151
Muftiyat, 149–150, 176, 179
Muslim Judicial Council
    (MJC), 225–226

N

Nestle, 9, 45
Ningxia Hui Autonomous
    Region, 86, 90

Q

Qingzhen, 10, 86, 90–92, 95–102,
    105–106, 108–117

R

Religious Administration of
    Independent Islamic
    Communities (RUNMHU),
    150, 155
Religious Administration of
    Muslims of Crimea
    (DUMK), 149–150
Religious Administration of Muslims
    of Ukraine (DUMU), 148, 150
Religious Center of Muslims of
    Ukraine (DTsMU), 150
Risq/rizq, 6, 202
Rospotrebnadzor, 75, 130,
    134, 136–137
Rosstandart, 128

S

Saffron Road, 24, 29, 34, 46–47
SANHA, 226–227
Second Vatican Council, 62

Süleymancı, 172–175, 182–186
Sunnat, 222

T

Ṭaʿām al-muslimīn, 101, 106
Tajdid al-alf, 174
Tariqa, 61, 183
Tasmiya, 222
Tatarstan, 72, 74, 80, 121–123, 125,
    128, 130–135
Tayib/tayyib, 13, 26, 47, 194, 195,
    199, 202, 209–210,
    213, 220
Tsaritsyno, 121, 123, 129–133,
    138, 140
Turkish Standards Institute
    (TSI), 203

U

Ukrainian Association of the Halal
    Industry (Ukrhalal), 161

W

Wertrational, 6
World Halal Council (WHC), 39,
    131, 205, 227
World Halal Forum, 45, 196

Y

Yisilanjiao, 94, 106, 115

Z

Zhengzhou, 87, 99
Ziyarat, 157
Zweckrational, 6

Printed in the United States
by Baker & Taylor Publisher Services